Anonymous

Collection of Psalms, Hymns and Spiritual Songs

suited to the various occasions of public worship and private devotion of the church of Christ

Anonymous

Collection of Psalms, Hymns and Spiritual Songs
suited to the various occasions of public worship and private devotion of the church of Christ

ISBN/EAN: 9783337089375

Printed in Europe, USA, Canada, Australia, Japan

Cover: Foto ©Lupo / pixelio.de

More available books at **www.hansebooks.com**

A COLLECTION

OF

PSALMS, HYMNS,

AND

SPIRITUAL SONGS,

SUITED TO THE VARIOUS OCCASIONS OF

PUBLIC WORSHIP AND PRIVATE DEVOTION

OF THE

CHURCH OF CHRIST.

WITH AN

APPENDIX OF GERMAN HYMNS.

BY A COMMITTEE OF MENNONITES.

LANCASTER, PA:
PRINTED AND PUBLISHED BY JOHN BAER'S SONS.
1869.

PREFACE.

Singing is an ordinance of divine worship; and when Christians unite with their hearts and voices, and "sing with the spirit and with the understanding also" the high praises of GOD, and thus express to HIM in psalms and hymns of adoration and praise, their gratitude for the manifold mercies bestowed upon them in Christ Jesus our Lord, or in penitent supplication, with melting strains, implore mercy for past offences, is one of the most delightful, edifying, and heart-soothing parts of His worship. Those heavenly strains heighten the believers' holy longing after God and heaven—animate them to press forward in their Christian course toward the mark for the prize of the high calling of God in Christ Jesus. It makes them feel more closely, that in God we live, and move and have our being; that all our blessings are bestowed by his paternal kindness, and that our everlasting welfare results from his redeeming love toward us in Christ Jesus our Lord.

Thus they are animated and strengthened to march on in their heavenly way, through this barren wilderness, to the wished-for Canaan—the heavenly Jerusalem—there to join the company of those who were redeemed from the earth, and are harping upon their harps, and singing a new song before the throne.

And, as the Church of Christ which is known by the name of the Mennonites, have, heretofore, performed their religious exercises in the worship of God almost altogether in the German language, it is thought expedient, as the English language has become so prevalent, to have the word of God preached in the church and the religious exercises in the worship of God performed in that language also.—Hence a committee was appointed by the Church, to make a selection of Psalms, Hymns, and Spiritual Songs, for the use of the Church, suited to the different occasions, to be sung in the time of her public worship, and in her private devotional exercises.

Accordingly the selection was made, and the hymns arranged under their different heads, and thus are presented to the friends of Zion, in the execution of which, however, there were difficulties found,—and the arrangement of the hymns under their proper heads was not one of the smallest, and may be found very much wanting in accuracy.

That believers may find this little work a pleasant and edifying companion on their way to the heavenly Zion, is the ardent wish of

THE COMMITTEE.

N. B.—The names of the tunes at the beginning of each hymn correspond with the Music book entitled "Genuine Church Music;" and the Peculiar Metres are numbered as they are in the Metrical Index of said Music book.

A COLLECTION OF HYMNS.

PUBLIC WORSHIP.

1   C. M.   *Divinity.*

1 AWAKE, awake the sacred song,
    To our incarnate Lord;
Let ev'ry heart and ev'ry tongue
    Adore th' Eternal Word.

2 That awful Word, that Sov'reign Power,
    By whom the worlds were made,
(O happy morn! illustrious hour!)
    Was once in flesh array'd.

3 Then shone Almighty power and love,
    In all their glorious forms,
When Jesus left his throne above,
    To dwell with sinful worms.

4 To dwell with misery below,
    The Savior left the skies,
And sunk to wretchedness and woe,
    That worthless man might rise.

PUBLIC WORSHIP.

5 Adoring angels tuned their songs,
  To hail the joyful day;
With rapture, then, let mortal tongues,
  Their grateful worship pay.

2   C. M.   *St. Martins.*

1 HOW shall we praise th' eternal God,
    That infinite Unknown?
  Who can ascend his high abode,
    Or venture near his throne?

2 The great Invisible? He dwells
    Conceal'd in dazzling light;
  But his all-searching eye reveals
    The secrets of the night.

3 Those watchful eyes that never sleep,
    Survey the world around;
  His wisdom is a boundless deep,
    Where all our thoughts are drown'd.

4 Speak we of strength? his arm is strong
    To save or to destroy:
  Infinite years his life prolong,
    And endless is his joy.

5 He knows no shadow of a change,
    Nor alters his decrees;
  Firm as a rock his truth remains
    To guard his promises.

6 Justice upon a dreadful throne
    Maintains the rights of God;

PUBLIC WORSHIP.

While mercy sends her pardons down,
  Bought with a Savior's blood.

7 Bought with that blood which freely flow'd
  From our Immanuel's veins;
Which his free love on us bestow'd
  To wash away our stains.

8 Now may that love, Immortal King,
  Speak some forgiving word,
To animate our hearts to sing
  The glories of the Lord.

---

3   S. M.   *Watchman—Oldford.*

1 COME, sound his praise abroad,
  And hymns of glory sing;
Jehovah is the sovereign God,
  The universal King.

2 He formed the deeps unknown;
  He gave the seas their bound;
The watery worlds are all his own,
  And all the solid ground.

3 Come, worship at his throne;
  Come, bow before the Lord;
We are his works, and not our own,
  He form'd us by his word.

4 To-day attend his voice,
  Nor dare provoke his rod;
Come, like the people of his choice,
  And own your gracious God.

PUBLIC WORSHIP.

5 But if your ears refuse
    The language of his grace,
And hearts grow hard, like stubborn Jews.
    That unbelieving race—

6 The Lord in vengeance dress'd,
    Will lift his hand, and swear—
"You that despise my promised rest,
    Shall have no portion there."

4   C. M.   *Primrose.*

1 COME, let us all unite to praise
    The Savior of mankind!
Our thankful hearts in solemn lays
    Be with our voices join'd.

2 But how shall dust his worth declare,
    When angels try in vain;
Their faces veil when they appear
    Before the Son of Man.

3 O Lord, we cannot silent be,
    By love we are constrain'd
To offer our best thanks to thee,
    Our Savior, and our Friend.

4 Though feeble are our best essays,
    Thy love will not despise
Our grateful song of humble praise,
    Our well meant sacrifice.

5 Let ev'ry tongue thy goodness show,
    And spread abroad thy fame:
Let ev'ry heart with praise o'erflow
    And bless thy sacred name!

6 Worship and honor, thanks and love
    Be to our Jesus giv'n!
By men below, by hosts above,
    By all in earth and heav'n!

---

5   C. M.   *Cambridge.*

1 HOW did my heart rejoice to hear
    My friends devoutly say
"In Zion let us all appear,
    And keep the solemn day!"

2 I love her gates, I love the road;
    The church, adorn'd with grace,
Stands like a palace built for God
    To show his milder face.

3 Up to her courts, with joys unknown,
    The holy tribes repair;
The Son of David holds his throne,
    And sits in judgment there.

4 He hears our praises and complaints;
    And, while his awful voice
Divides the sinners from the saints,
    We tremble and rejoice.

5 Peace be within this sacred place,
    And joy a constant guest;
With holy gifts and heavenly grace
    Be her attendants bless'd!

6 My soul shall pray for Zion still,
    While life or breath remains;
There my best friends, my kindred, dwell,
    There God, my Savior, reigns.

PUBLIC WORSHIP.

6   C. M.   *Rochester.*

1 COME, happy souls, approach your God
    With new melodious songs,
Come, tender to Almighty grace
    The tribute of your tongues.

2 So strange, so boundless was the love
    That pitied dying men,
The Father sent his equal Son
    To give them life again.

3 Thy hands, dear Jesus, were not arm'd
    With a revenging rod,
No hard commission to perform
    The vengeance of a God!

4 But all was mercy, all was mild,
    And wrath forsook the throne,
When Christ on the kind errand came,
    And brought salvation down.

5 Here sinners, you may heal your wounds,
    And wipe your sorrows dry;
Trust in the mighty Savior's name,
    And you shall never die.

6 See, dearest Lord, our willing souls,
    Accept thine offered grace;
We bless the great Redeemer's love,
    And give the Father praise.

7   S. M.   *Ninety-Third.*

1 MY Savior and my King,
    Thy beauties are divine;

PUBLIC WORSHIP.

Thy lips with blessings overflow,
  And every grace is thine.

2 Now make thy glory known,
  Gird on thy dreadful sword,
And rise in majesty to spread,
  The conquest of thy word.

3 Strike through thy stubborn foes,
  Or make their hearts obey,
While justice, meekness, grace, and truth
  Attend thy glorious way.

4 Thy laws, O God, are right,
  Thy throne shall ever stand;
And thy victorious gospel prove
  A sceptre in thy hand.

5 [Thy Father and thy God,
  Hath without measure shed
His Spirit, like a grateful oil!
  T' anoint thy sacred head.]

6 [Behold at thy right hand
  The Gentile Church is seen,
A beauteous bride, in rich attire,
  And princes guard the queen.]

7 Fair bride, receive his love,
  Forget thy father's house,
Forsake thy gods, thy idol gods,
  And pay the Lord thy vows.

8 O let thy God and King
  Thy sweetest thoughts employ:
Thy children shall his honor sing,
  And taste the heavenly joy.

PUBLIC WORSHIP.

8 C. M. *Fairfield—Dublin.*

1 WITH rev'rence let the saints appear,
  And bow before the Lord;
His high commands with rev'rence hear
  And tremble at his word.

2 How terrible thy glories rise!
  How bright thine armies shine!
Where is the pow'r with thee that vies,
  Or truth compared with thine?

3 The northern pole and southern rest
  On thy supporting hand;
Darkness and day, from east to west
  Move round at thy command.

4 Thy words the raging winds control
  And rule the boist'rous deep;
Thou mak'st the sleeping billows roll,
  The rolling billows sleep.

5 Heaven, earth and air, and seas are thine,
  And the dark world of hell;
They saw thine arm in vengeance shine
  When Egypt durst rebel.

6 Justice and judgment are thy throne,
  Yet wondrous is thy grace;
While truth and mercy, joined in one,
  Invite us near thy face.

9 C. M. *Mear.*

1 ONCE more we come before our Lord,
  Once more his blessing ask;

PUBLIC WORSHIP.

Oh! may not duty seem a load;
  Nor worship prove a task.

2 Father, thy quick'ning Spirit send
   From heaven, in Jesus' name,
 To make our waiting minds attend,
   And put our souls in frame.

3 May we receive the word we hear,
   Each in an honest heart;
 Hoard up the precious treasure there,
   And never with it part.

4 To seek thee all our hearts dispose,
   To each thy blessings suit,
 And let the seed thy servant sows,
   Produce a copious fruit.

5 Bid the refreshing north wind wake,
   Say to the south wind, blow;
 Let ev'ry plant the pow'r partake,
   And all the garden grow.

6 Revive the parch'd with heav'nly showers,
   The cold with warmth divine;
 And as the benefit is ours,
   Be all the glory thine.

10   L. M.   *Old Hundred.*

1 TO God, the great, the ever bless'd,
   Let songs of honor be address'd;
 His mercy firm for ever stands;
 Give him the thanks his love demands.

2 Who knows the wonders of thy ways?
 Who shall fulfil thy boundless praise?

Bless'd are the souls that fear thee still,
And pay their duty to thy will.

3 Remember what thy mercy did
For Jacob's race, thy chosen seed,
And with the same salvation bless
The meanest suppliant of thy grace.

4 O may I see thy tribes rejoice,
And aid their triumphs with my voice;
This is my glory, Lord, to be
Join'd to thy saints and near to thee.

11   METRE 5.   *Pleyel's Hymn.*

1 SINNERS, turn, why will ye die?
God, your Maker, asks you why?
God, who did your being give,
Made you with himself to live;
He the fatal cause demands,
Asks the work of his own hands,
Why, ye thankless creatures, why
Will you cross his love and die?

2 Sinners, turn, why will ye die?
God, your Savior, asks you why?
God, who did your souls retrieve,
Died himself that ye might live.
Will you let him die in vain?
Crucify your Lord again?
Why, ye ransom'd sinners, why
Will ye slight his grace, and die?

3 Sinners, turn, why will ye die?
God, the Spirit, asks you why?
He who all your lives hath strove,
Woo'd you to embrace his love:

Will ye not his grace receive?
Will ye still refuse to live?
Why, you long-sought sinners, why
Will you grieve your God, and die?

4 Dead already, dead within,
Spiritually dead in sin:
Dead to God, while hear you breathe;
Pant you after second death?
Will you still in sin remain,
Greedy of eternal pain?
O, ye dying sinners, why,
Why will ye for ever die?

12   C. M.   *Rochester.*

1 COME, children, learn to fear the Lord;
   And, that your days be long,
Let not a false or spiteful word
   Be found upon your tongue.

2 Depart from mischief, practice love,
   Pursue the works of peace;
So shall the Lord your ways approve,
   And set your souls at ease.

3 His eyes awake to guard the just,
   His ears attend their cry;
When broken spirits dwell in dust,
   The God of grace is nigh.

4 What tho' the sorrows here they taste
   Are sharp and tedious too,
The Lord who saves them all at last,
   Is their supporter now.

5 Evil shall smite the wicked dead;
  But God secures his own,
 Prevents the mischief when they slide,
  Or heals the broken bone.

6 When desolation, like a flood,
  O'er the proud sinner rolls,
 Saints find a refuge in their God,
  For he redeemed their souls.

13 L. M. *Loving Kindness.*

1 AWAKE my soul, in joyful lays,
  And sing thy great Redeemer's praise:
 He justly claims a song from thee,
 His loving kindness, oh how free!

2 He saw me ruined in the fall,
 Yet lov'd me notwithstanding all;
 He saved me from my lost estate,
 His loving kindness, oh how great!

3 Though numerous hosts of mighty foes,
 Though earth and hell my way oppose,
 He safely leads my soul along,
 His loving kindness, oh how strong!

4 When trouble, like a gloomy cloud,
 Hath gathered thick and thundered loud,
 He near my soul has always stood,
 His loving kindness, oh how good!

5 Often I feel my sinful heart,
 Prone from my Savior to depart;
 But though I oft have him forgot,
 His loving kindness changes not.

PUBLIC WORSHIP. 17

6 Soon shall I pass this gloomy vale,
Soon all my mortal pow'rs must fail;—
O! may my last expiring breath
His loving kindness sing in death.

7 Then let me mount and soar away,
To the bright world of endless day,
And sing with rapture and surprise,
His loving kindness in the skies.

14 L. M. *Magdeburg.*

1 BLESS, O my soul, the living God,
Call home thy thoughts that rove abroad,
Let all the powers within me join
In work and worship so divine.

2 Bless, O my soul, the God of grace,
His favors claim thy highest praise:
Why should the wonders he has wrought,
Be lost in silence and forgot?

3 'Tis he, my soul, that sent his Son
To die for crimes which thou hast done,
He owns the ransom and forgives
The hourly follies of our lives.

4 The vices of the mind he heals,
And cures the pains that nature feels;
Redeems the souls from hell, and saves
Our wasting lives from threatning graves.

5 Our youth decay'd his power repairs,
His mercy crowns our growing years:
He fills our store with every good,
And feeds our souls with heavenly food.

PUBLIC WORSHIP.

6 He sees th' oppressor and th' oppress'd.
And often gives the sufferers rest;
But will his justice more display
In the last great rewarding day.

7 [His power he show'd by Moses' hands,
And gave to Israel his commands;
But sent his truth and mercy down
To all the nations, by his Son.]

8 Let the whole earth his power confess,
Let the whole earth adore his grace;
The Gentile with the Jew shall join
In work and worship so divine.

15.   C. M.   *Tisbury—Augusta.*

1 LET every mortal ear attend,
    And every heart rejoice,
  The trumpet of the gospel sounds,
    With an inviting voice.

2 Ho! all ye hungry, starving souls,
    That feed upon the wind,
  And vainly strive, with earthly toys,
    To fill an empty mind:

3 Eternal wisdom has prepared
    A soul-reviving feast,
  And bids your longing appetites
    The rich provision taste.

4 Ho! ye that pant for living streams,
    And pine away and die;
  Here you may quench your raging thirst
    With springs that never dry.

5 Rivers of love and mercy here
   In a rich ocean join:
Salvation in abundance flows,
   Like floods of milk and wine.

6 [Ye perishing and naked poor,
   Who work with mighty pain,
To weave a garment of your own
   That will not hide your sin;

7 Come naked, and adorn your souls
   In robes prepar'd by God;
Wrought by the labors of his Son,
   And dyed in his own blood.]

8 Dear God! the treasures of thy love
   Are everlasting mines,
Deep as our helpless miseries are,
   And boundless as our sins!

9 The happy gates of gospel grace
   Stand open night and day;
Lord, we are come to seek supplies,
   And drive our wants away.

6   METRE 5.   *Divine Inquiry.*

1 HARK, my soul, it is the Lord;
   'Tis thy Savior, hear his word;
Jesus speaks, he speaks to thee:
"Say, poor sinner, lov'st thou me?

2 "I delivered thee when bound,
And when bleeding heal'd thy wound;
Sought thee wand'ring, set thee right,
Turn'd thy darkness into light.

3 "Can a mother's tender care
　Cease toward the child she bare?
　Yes, she may foregetful be,
　Yet will I remember thee.

4 "Mine is an unchanging love,
　Higher than the heights above;
　Deeper than the depths beneath,
　Free and faithful, strong as death.

5 "Thou shalt see my glory soon,
　When the work of grace is done;
　Partner of my throne shalt be,
　Say, poor sinner, lov'st thou me?"

6 Lord, it is my chief complaint,
　That my love is weak and faint;
　Yet I love thee and adore,
　Oh for grace to love thee more!

17　　　　S. M.　　　　*Ninety-Third.*

1 BEHOLD the lofty sky
　　Declares its Maker, God;
　And all the starry works on high
　　Proclaim his power abroad.

2 The darkness and the light
　　Still keep their course the same;
　While night to day, and day to night,
　　Divinely teach his name.

3 In every different land
　　Their general voice is known;
　They show the wonders of his hand,
　　And orders of his throne.

PUBLIC WORSHIP.

4 Ye Christian lands, rejoice;
   Here he reveals his word:
We are not left to nature's voice,
   To bid us know the Lord.

5 His statutes and commands
   Are set before our eyes;
He puts his gospel in our hands,
   Where our salvation lies.

6 His laws are just and pure,
   His truth without deceit,
His promises forever sure,
   And his rewards are great.

7 [Not honey to the taste
   Affords so much delight;
Nor gold that has the furnace pass'd
   So much allures the sight.]

8 While of thy works I sing,
   Thy glory to proclaim,
Accept the praise, my God, my King,
   In my Redeemer's name.

---

8   L. M.   *Old Hundred.*

1 WHERE two or three with sweet accord,
   Obedient to their sovereign Lord,
Meet to recount his acts of grace,
And offer solemn pray'r and praise;

2 "There," says the Savior, "will I be,
Amid this little company;
To them unveil my smiling face,
And shed my glories round the place."

3 We meet at thy command, dear Lord,
　Relying on thy faithful word;
　Now send thy Spirit from above,
　Now fill our hearts with heavenly love.

19   S. M.   *New Hope.*

1 How beauteous are their feet,
　　Who stand on Zion's hill!
　Who bring salvation on their tongues,
　　And words of peace reveal.

2 How charming is their voice,
　　How sweet there tidings are!
　"Zion, behold thy Savior King,
　　"He reigns and triumphs here."

3 How happy are our ears,
　　That hear this joyful sound,
　Which kings and prophets waited for
　　And sought, but never found!

4 How blessed are our eyes
　　That see this heavenly light:
　Prophets and kings, desired it long,
　　But died without the sight.

5 The watchmen join their voice,
　　And tuneful notes employ;
　Jerusalem breaks forth in songs
　　And deserts learn the joy.

6 The Lord makes bare his arm
　　Through all the earth abroad;
　Let every nation now behold
　　Their Savior and their God.

20   C. M.   *Miles' Lane.*

1 ALL hail, the pow'r of Jesus' name!
    Let angels prostrate fall;
Bring forth the royal diadem,
    And crown him Lord of all.

2 Crown him, ye martyrs of our God,
    Who from his altar call;
Extol the stem of Jesse's rod,
    And crown him Lord of all.

3 Ye chosen seed of Israel's race,
    A remnant weak and small!
Hail him who saves you by his grace,
    And crown him Lord of all.

4 Ye Gentile sinners, ne'er forget
    The wormwood and the gall;
Go—spread your trophies at his feet,
    And crown him Lord of all.

5 Babes, men, and sires, who know his love,
    Who feel your sin and thrall,
Now join with all the hosts above,
    And crown him Lord of all.

6 Let ev'ry kindred, ev'ry tribe,
    On this terrestrial ball,
To him all majesty ascribe,
    And crown him Lord of all.

7 O, that with yonder sacred throng,
    We at his feet may fall;
We'll join the everlasting song,
    And crown him Lord of all.

21 C. M. *Balerma—Solon.*

1 AWAKE, my heart, arise, my tongue,
  Prepare a tuneful voice,
In God, the life of all my joys,
  Aloud will I rejoice.

2 'Tis he adorn'd my naked soul,
  And made salvation mine;
Upon a poor polluted worm
  He makes his graces shine.

3 And lest the shadow of a spot
  Should on my soul be found,
He took the robe the Savior wrought,
  And cast it all around.

4 How far the heavenly robe exceeds
  What earthly princes wear!
These ornaments, how bright they shine?
  How white the garments are!

5 The Spirit wrought my faith and love
  And hope and every grace;
But Jesus spent his life to work
  The robe of righteousness.

6 Strangely, my soul, art thou array'd
  By the great sacred THREE!
In sweetest harmony of praise
  Let all thy powers agree.

22 L. M. *Hebron—Devotion.*

1 BEFORE Jehovah's awful throne,
  Ye nations, bow with sacred joy;

PUBLIC WORSHIP.

Know that the Lord is God alone;
He can create and he destroy.

2 His sovereign power without our aid,
Made us of clay and form'd us men;
And when, like wand'ring sheep we stray'd,
He brought us to his fold again.

3 We are his people, we his care,
Our souls, and all our mortal frame,
What lasting honors shall we rear,
Almighty Maker, to thy name?

4 We'll crowd thy gates with thankful songs,
High as the heavens our voices raise;
And earth, with her ten thousand tongues,
Shall fill thy courts with sounding praise.

5 Wide as the world is thy command,
Vast as eternity thy love;
Firm as a rock thy truth must stand,
When rolling years shall cease to move.

23   S. M.   *Ninety-Third.*
1 NOW is th' accepted time,
    Now is the day of grace:
Now, sinners, come, without delay,
    And seek the Savior's face.

2 Now is th' accepted time,
    The Savior calls to-day!
To-morrow it may be too late,
    Then why should you delay?

3 Now is th' accepted time,
    The gospel bids you come;

And every promise in his word
  Declares there yet is room.

4 Now is th' accepted time,
  O sinner! why delay?
Come while the gospel trumpet sounds,
  Come in th' accepted day.

5 All yesterday is gone!
  To-morrow's not our own;
O sinner, come, without delay
  To bow before the throne!

6 Oh, hear his voice to-day,
  And harden not your heart:
To-morrow with a frown, he may
  Pronounce the word—depart.

7 Lord, draw reluctant souls,
  And feast them with thy love:
Then will the angels swiftly fly
  To bear the news above.

24   C. M.   *Salvation.*

1 YOUNG people all, attention give
  And hear what I shall say;
I wish your souls with Christ to live
  In everlasting day.
Remember you are hast'ning on
  To death's dark gloomy shade;
Your joys on earth will soon be gone,
  Your flesh in dust be laid.

Death's iron gate you must pass through,
  Ere long, my dear young friends;
With whom then do you think to go,
  With saints or fiery fiends?

PUBLIC WORSHIP.

Pray mediate before too late,
  While in a gospel land,
Behold King Jesus at the gate,
  Most lovingly doth stand.

3 Young men, how can you turn your face,
  From such a glorious Friend?
Will you pursue your dang'rous ways?
  O don't you fear the end?
Will you pursue that dang'rous road
  Which leads to death and hell?
Will you refuse all peace with God,
  With devils there to dwell?

4 Young woman, too, what will you do,
  If out of Christ you die?
From all God's people you must go,
  To weep, lament and cry:
Where you the least relief can't find,
  To mitigate your pain:
Your good things all be left behind,
  Your souls in death remain.

5 Young people all, I pray then, view,
  The fountain opened wide;
The spring of life opened for sin,
  Which flow'd from Jesus' side,
There you may drink in endless joy,
  And reign with Christ your King,
In his glad notes your souls employ,
  And hallelujahs sing.

25   C. M.   *Arlington—Primrose.*

1 AM I a soldier of the cross,
  A follower of the Lamb?

PUBLIC WORSHIP.

And shall I fear to own his cause?—
Or blush to speak his name?

2 Are there no foes for me to face?
Must I not stem the flood?
Is this vile world a friend to grace,
To help me on to God?

3 Sure I must fight—if I would reign;
Increase my courage, Lord!
I'll bear the toil—endure the pain,
Supported by thy word.

4 Thy saints, in all this glorious war,
Shall conquer, though they die:
They see the triumph from afar,
And seize it with their eye.

5 When that illustrious day shall rise,
And all thine armies shine
In robes of victory through the skies,
The glory shall be thine.

26   C. M.   *St. Olaves.*
1 LORD, at thy temple we appear,
As happy Simeon came,
And hope to meet our Savior here;
O make our joys the same.

2 With what divine and vast delight
The good old man was fill'd,
When fondly, in his wither'd arms,
He clasp'd the Holy Child!

3 "Now I can leave this world," he cried,
"Behold thy servant dies;

"I've seen thy great salvation, Lord,
  "And close my peaceful eyes.

4 "This is the Light prepar'd to shine
  "Upon the Gentile lands,
  "Thine Israel's glory, and their hopes,
  "To break their slavish bands."

5 [Jesus! the vision of thy face
    Hath overpowering charms!
  Scarce shall I feel death's cold embrace,
    If Christ be in my arms.

6 Then while ye hear my heart-strings break,
    How sweet my minutes roll!
  A mortal paleness on my cheek,
    And glory in my soul.]

27   Metre 11.   *Wesley.*

1 COME Children of Zion, and help us to sing
  Loud anthems of praise to our Savior and King
  Whose life was once given our souls to redeem,
  And bring us to heaven to reign there with him.

2 In regions of darkness and sorrow and pains,
  We all lay in ruin, in prison, and chains;
  But Jesus has bought us with his precious blood,
  The ransom provided to bring us to God.

3 O come to the Savior, and take up the cross—
  Seek treasure in heaven, count all else but loss:
  His mercy invites us, then let us comply—
  O why should we linger when he is so nigh?

4 We'll fear not the dangers that lie in our way—
  His arm will protect us by night and by day;

And this we must suffer, and patiently bear,
Till Jesus shall take us where suff'rings are o'er.

28 L. M. *Retirement.*

1 JESUS! and shall it ever be
A mortal man ashamed of thee!
Ashamed of thee, whom angels praise,
Whose glories shine through endless days!

2 Ashamed of Jesus! sooner far
Let evening blush to own a star;
He sheds the beams of light divine
O'er this benighted soul of mine.

3 Ashamed of Jesus! just as soon
Let midnight be ashamed of noon,
'Tis midnight with my soul, till he,
Bright Morning Star! bid darkness flee.

4 Ashamed of Jesus! that dear friend
On whom my hopes of heav'n depend!
No, when I blush, be this my shame,
That I no more revere his name.

5 Ashamed of Jesus! yes I may,
When I've not guilt to wash away,
No tear to wipe, no good to crave,
No fears to quell, no soul to save.

6 Till then—nor is my boasting vain—
Till then I boast a Savior slain!
And O, may this my glory be,
That Christ is not ashamed of me!

7 His institutions would I prize,
Take up my cross—the shame despise!

Dare to defend his noble cause,
And yield obedience to his laws.

29   L. M.   *Salem.*

1 MY hope, my all, my Savior thou,
    To thee, lo! now my soul I bow;
I feel the bliss thy wounds impart,
I find thee, Savior, in my heart.

2 Be thou my strength, be thou my way,
Protect me through my life's short day;
In all my acts may wisdom guide,
And keep me, Savior, near thy side.

3 Correct, reprove, and comfort me;
As I have need, my Savior be:
And if I would from thee depart,
Then clasp me, Savior, to thy heart.

4 In fierce temptation's darkest hour,
Save me from sin and Satan's power;
Tear every idol from thy throne,
And reign, my Savior, reign alone.

5 My suff'ring time shall soon be o'er,
Then shall I sigh and weep no more;
My ransom'd soul shall soar away,
To sing thy praise in endless day.

30   L. M.   *Old Hundred.*

1 FROM all that dwell below the skies,
    Let the Creator's praise arise;
Let the Redeemer's name be sung,
Through ev'ry land, by ev'ry tongue.

2 Eternal are thy mercies, Lord,
  Eternal truth attends thy word:
  Thy praise shall sound from shore to shore,
  Till sun shall rise and set no more.

3 Your lofty themes, ye mortals, bring,
  In songs of praise divinely sing;
  The great salvation loud proclaim,
  And shout for joy the Savior's name.

4 In ev'ry land begin the song.
  To ev'ry land the strains belong;
  In cheerful sounds all voices raise.
  And fill the world with loudest praise.

31 C. M. *Primrose.*

1 COME, thou desire of all thy saints,
    Our humble strains attend;
  While with our praises and complaints,
    Low at thy feet we bend.

2 When we thy wondrous glories hear,
    And all thy sufferings trace,
  What sweetly awful scenes appear!
    What rich unbounded grace!

3 How should our songs, like those above,
    With warm devotion rise!
  How should our souls, on wings of love,
    Mount upward to the skies!

4 Come, Lord, thy love alone can raise
    In us the heavenly flame;
  Then shall our lips resound thy praise,
    Our hearts adore thy name.

PUBLIC WORSHIP.

5 Dear Savior, let thy glory shine,
  And fill thy dwellings here,
 Till life, and love, and joy divine,
  And heaven on earth, appear.

32   C. M.   *Divinity.*

1 AGAIN our earthly cares we leave,
   And to the courts repair;
  Again with joyful feet we come,
   To meet our Savior here.

2 Within these walls let holy peace,
   And love, and concord dwell;
  Her give the troubled conscience ease,
   The wounded spirit heal.

3 The feeling heart—the melting eye,
   The humble mind bestow;
  And shine upon us from on high,
   To make our graces grow.

4 May we in faith receive thy word,
   In faith present our prayers;
  And in the presence of our Lord
   Unbosom all our cares.

5 Show us some token of thy love,
   Our fainting hope to raise;
  And pour thy blessing from above,
   That we may render praise.

33   C. M.   *Balerma—Augusta.*

1 WITH sacred joy we lift our eyes
    To those bright realms above,

That glorious temple in the skies.
    Where dwells eternal love.

2 Before the awful throne we bow
    Of heaven's Almighty King;
  Here we present the solemn vow,
    And hymns of praise we sing.

3 While in thy house of prayer we kneel
    With trust and holy fear,
  Thy mercy, and thy truth reveal,
    And lend a gracious ear.

4 With fervor teach our hearts to pray.
    And tune our lips to sing;
  Nor from thy presence cast away
    The sacrifice we bring.

34   S. M.   *Little Marlborough.*

1 WELCOME, sweet day of rest,
    That saw the Lord arise;
  Welcome to this reviving breast,
    And these rejoicing eyes.

2 The King himself comes near,
    And feasts his saints to-day;
  Here we may sit and see him here,
    And love, and praise, and pray.

3 One day amidst the place
    Where my dear God hath been,
  Is sweeter than ten thousand days
    Of pleasurable sin.

4 My willing soul would stay
    In such a frame as this,

And sit and sing herself away,
  To everlasting bliss.

35   S. M.   *Ninety-Third.*

1 ASSIST thy servant Lord,
    The gospel to proclaim;
  Let power and love attend thy word,
    And every breast inflame.

2 Bid unbelief depart;
    With love his soul inflame;
  Take full possession of his heart,
    And glorify thy name.

3 May stubborn sinners bend
    To thy divine control;
  Constrain the wandering to attend,
    And make the wounded whole.

4 Extend thy conquering arm,
    With banner wide unfurl'd,
  Until thy glorious grace shall charm,
    And harmonize the world.

36   L. M.   *Portugal.*

1 THY presence, gracious God, afford,
    Prepare us to receive thy word;
  Now let thy voice engage our ear,
  And faith be mixed with what we hear.

2 Distracting thoughts and cares remove,
  And fix our hearts and hopes above;
  With food divine may we be fed,
  And satisfied with living bread.

3 To us thy sacred word apply,
With sov'reign power and energy;
And may we in true faith and fear,
Reduce to practice what we hear.

37 C. M. *Augusta.*

1 O HAPPY is the man who hears
Religion's warning voice,
And who celestial wisdom makes
His early, only choice.

2 For she has treasures greater far
Than east or west unfold;
More precious are her bright rewards,
Than gems, or stores of gold.

3 Her right hand offers to the just
Immortal happy days;
Her left, imperishable wealth,
And heav'nly crowns displays.

4 And as her holy labors rise,
So her rewards increase;
Her ways are ways of pleasantness,
And all her paths are peace.

38 L. M. *Old Hundred.*

1 LET me but hear my Savior say,
"Strength shall be equal to thy day,"
Then I'll rejoice in deep distress,
Leaning on all-sufficient grace.

2 I glory in infirmity,
That Christ's own power may rest on me;

When I am weak then am I strong,
Grace is my shield and Christ my song.

3 I can do all things, or can bear
All suff'rings if my Lord be there;
Sweet pleasures mingle with the pains,
While grace divine my heart sustains.

39   C. M.   *Solon.*

1 JESUS, thy blessings are not few,
    Nor is thy gospel weak;
  Thy grace can melt the stubborn Jew,
    And bow the haughty Greek.

2 Wide as the reach of Satan's rage,
    Does thy salvation flow;
  'Tis not confined to sex or age,
    The lofty or the low.

3 While grace is offered to the prince,
    The poor may take their share;
  No mortal has a just pretence
    To perish in despair.

4 Come, all ye wretched sinners, come,
    He'll form your souls anew;
  His gospel and his heart have room
    For rebels such as you.

40   C. M.   *Divinity.*

1 I'M not ashamed to own my Lord,
    Or to defend his cause,
  Maintain the honor of his word,
    The glory of his cross.

2 Jesus, my God! I know his name;
   His name is all my trust:
  Nor will he put my soul to shame,
   Nor let my soul be lost.

3 Firm as his throne his promise stands,
   And he can well secure
  What I've committed to his hands,
   Till the decisive hour.

4 Then will he own my worthless name
   Before his Father's face,
  And in the new Jerusalem
   Appoint my soul a place.

41   METRE 7.   *Dresden.*

1 COME ye sinners, come to Jesus;
   Think upon your gracious Lord;
  He has pitied your condition;
   He has sent his Gospel Word:
    Mercy calls you;
   Mercy flows in Jesus' blood.

2 Dearest Savior, help thy servant
   To proclaim thy wondrous love;
  Pour thy grace upon this people,
   That thy truth they may approve:
    Bless, O bless them,
   From thy shining courts above.

3 Now thy gracious word invites them,
   To partake the gospel feast;
  Let thy Spirit sweetly draw them,
   Every soul be Jesus' guest:
    O receive us!
   Let us find thy promised rest.

42   Metre 13. *Warning Voice.*

1 HELP thy servant, gracious Lord,
 Who comes in Jesus' name;
Only thou canst strength afford,
 Thy gospel to proclaim:
Grant his soul a heavenly ray,
 Fill his heart with holy fire;
Help thy servant, Lord, we pray,—
 Regard our souls' desire.

CHORUS.

O, for sanctifying grace!
 O, for love's inspiring power!
Lord, we beg for Jesus' sake,
 A sweet refreshing shower.

2 Give us to receive the word,
 With love, and joy, and fear;
Grant thy quick'ning grace, O Lord,
 On all assembled here:
Seal the truth on all to-day;
 All our hearts with heav'n inspire;
Help thy servant, Lord, we pray—
 Regard our souls' desire.

 O, for sanctifying grace,

43   C. M. *Primrose.*

1 NOW is the time, th' accepted hour,
 O sinner, come away:
The Savior's knocking at your door,
 Arise without delay.

Oh! don't refuse to give him room,
 Lest mercy should withdraw;

He will in robes of vengeance come
  To execute his law.

3 Then where, poor mortals, will you be,
    If destitute of grace,
  When you your injured Judge shall see,
    And stand before his face?

4 Oh! could you shun that dreadful sight,
    How would you wish to fly
  To the dark shades of endless night,
    From that All-searching eye?

5 The dead awaked must all appear,
    And you among them stand
  Before the great impartial bar,
    Arraigned at Christ's left hand.

6 Let not these warnings be in vain,
    But lend a listening ear;
  Lest you should meet them all again,
    When wrapped in keen despair.

44   S. M.   *St. Thomas—Aylesbury.*

1 LORD, at thy sacred feet,
    Joyful would we appear;
  Within thy earthly temple meet,
    To see thy glory here.

2 We come to worship thee,
    For thou art God alone;
  In humble prayer to bend the knee,
    Before thy holy throne.

3 Thy word is our delight,
    Thy truth will make us free;

'Tis from thyself a heav'nly light,
  It leads our souls to thee.

4 Thy goodness we behold,
  While in thy presence, Lord;
Thy wondrous truth and love unfold—
  The treasures of thy word.

5 In all our meetings here,
  Our souls are blessed with good;
Thou wilt to waiting minds be near,
  And give thy children food.

6 So will we render praise
  To thee, the God of love;
With pleasure walk in all thy ways,
  Till we shall meet above.

45   L. M.   *Portugal.*

1 "WE'VE no abiding city here"—
    This may distress the worldly mind:
  But should not cost the saint a tear,
    Who hopes a better rest to find.

2 "We've no abiding city here"—
    Sad truth, were this to be our home:
  But let this thought our spirits cheer.
    "We seek a city yet to come."

3 We've no abiding city here"—
    Then let us live as pilgrims do;
  Let not the world our rest appear,
    But let us haste from all below.

4 "We've no abiding city here"—
    We seek a city out of sight:

Zion its name—the Lord is there,
  It shines with everlasting light.

46   METRE 7.   *Sacred Herald.*

1 ON the mountain's top appearing,
    Lo! the sacred herald stands;
  Welcome news to Zion bearing,
    Zion long in hostile lands:
      Mourning captive,
  God himself will loose thy bands.

2 Has thy night been long and mournful,
    All thy friends unfaithful proved?
  Have thy foes been proud and scornful,
    By thy sighs and tears unmoved?
      Cease thy mourning,
  Zion's still is well beloved.

3 God, thy God, will now restore thee!
    He himself appears thy friend;
  All thy foes shall flee before thee,
    Here their boasts and triumphs end:
      Great deliv'rance,
  Zion's King vouchsafes to send.

4 Peace and joy shall now attend thee,
    All thy warfare now is past:
  God, thy Savior, shall defend thee,
    Peace and joy are come at last;
      All thy conflicts
  End in everlasting rest.

47   C. M.   *Awful Majesty.*

1 WE sing the glories of thy love,
    We sound thy dreadful name;

The Christian church unites the songs
   Of Moses and the Lamb.

2 Great God, how wondrous are thy works
   Of vengeance and of grace!
Thou King of saints, Almighty Lord,
   How just and true thy ways.

3 Who dares refuse to fear thy name,
   Or worship at thy throne!
Thy judgments speak thy holiness
   Through all the nations known.

4 Great Babylon that rules the earth,
   Drunk with the martyrs' blood,
Her crimes shall speedily awake
   The fury of our God.

5 The cup of wrath is ready mix'd,
   And she must drink the dregs:
Strong is the Lord her Sov'reign Judge,
   And shall fulfill the plagues.

48   L. M.   *Devotion.*

1 COMFORT, ye ministers of grace
   Comfort the people of your Lord,
O lift ye up the fallen race,
   And cheer them by the Gospel word.

2 Go into every nation, go,
   Speak to their trembling hearts, and cry,
Glad tidings unto all we show:
   Jerusalem, thy God is nigh.

3 Hark! in the wilderness a cry,
   A voice that loudly calls, Prepare;

PUBLIC WORSHIP.

Prepare your hearts, for God is nigh,
 And means to make his entrance there!

4 The Lord your God shall quickly come:
 Sinners, repent, the call obey:
Open your hearts to make him room;
 Ye desert souls, prepare his way.

5 The Lord shall clear his way through all;
 Whate'er obstructs, obstructs in vain:
The vale shall rise, the mountain fall,
 Crooked be straight and rugged plain.

6 The glory of the Lord displayed,
 Shall all mankind together view,
And what his mouth in truth has said,
 His own Almighty hand shall do.

49   L. M.   *Rockbridge.*

1 COME, let our voices join to raise
 A sacred song of solemn praise;
God is a sov'reign King: rehearse
His honor in exalted verse.

2 Come, let our souls address the Lord,
Who framed our natures with his word:
He is our Shepherd; we the sheep
His mercy choose, his pastures keep.

3 Come, let us hear his voice to-day,
The counsels of his love obey,
Nor let our harden'd hearts renew
The sins and plagues that Israel knew.

4 Israel that saw his works of grace,
 Yet tempt their Maker to his face;

PUBLIC WORSHIP. 45

A faithless unbelieving brood,
That tired the patience of their God.

5 Thus saith the Lord, "How false they prove.
"Forget my power, abuse my love;
"Since they despise my rest, I swear,
"Their feet shall never enter there."

6 [Look back, my soul, with holy dread,
And view those ancient rebels dead;
Attend the offer'd grace to-day,
Nor lose the blessings by delay.

7 Seize the kind promise while it waits.
And march to Zion's heavenly gates;
Believe, and take the promised rest;
Obey, and be forever bless'd."]

50   L. M.   *Conformity.*

1 HIGH on his everlasting throne,
   The King of saints his works surveys.
Marks the dear souls he calls his own,
   And smiles on the peculiar race.

2 He rests well pleased their toils to see;
   Beneath his easy yoke they move:
With all their heart and strength agree
   In the sweet labor of his love.

3 See where the servants of the Lord,
   A busy multitude, appear:
For Jesus day and night employ'd,
   His heritage they toil to clear.

4 The love of Christ their hearts constrains,
   And strengthens their unwearied hands;

They spend their sweat, and blood, and pains,
  To cultivate Immanuel's lands.

5 Jesus their toil delighted sees,
  Their industry vouchsafes to crown :
He kindly gives the wish'd increase,
  And sends the promised blessing down.

6 The sap of life, the Spirit's powers,
  He rains incessant from above ;
He all his gracious fulness showers
  To perfect their great work of love.

7 O multiply thy sowers' seed,
  And fruit they every hour shall bear :
Throughout the world thy gospel spread,
  Thine everlasting truth declare !

8 We then in perfect love renew'd,
  Shall know the greatness of thy pow'rs.
Stand in the temple of our God
  As pillars, and go out no more.

51 L. M. *Solemnity.*

1 WHEN Jesus did from heav'n descend,
  He came to be the sinners friend ;
Was moved with pity, love and grace,
To save the human fallen race.

2 It was the kindness of our God,
A precious gift on us bestow'd
To let us know that Jesus is
Our life, our way, our righteousness.

3 A doctrine of the greatest worth:
The Son of God appeared on earth.

When he assumed our flesh and blood,
And sacrificed himself to God.

4 Was it the angels' great delight,
To view that wondrous, glorious Light,
The Son of God in flesh array'd,
To which both kings and prophets pray'd?

5 How highly thankful then ought we
To him, our gracious Savior, be!
Who is our life and righteousness,
Our everlasting joy and peace.

52   C. M.   *Peterborough.*

1 COME ye that love the Savior's name,
   And join to make it known;
The Sov'reign of your heart proclaim,
   And bow before his throne.

2 Behold your King, your Savior crown'd
   With glories all divine;
And tell the wond'ring nations round,
   How bright those glories shine.

3 Infinite power and boundless grace,
   In him unite their rays;
You that have e'er beheld his face,
   Can you forbear his praise?

4 When in his earthly courts we view
   The glories of our King,
We long to love as angels do,
   And wish like them to sing.

5 And shall we long and wish in vain?
   Lord, teach our songs to rise!

    Thy love can animate the strain,
      And bid it reach the skies.

6 Oh, happy period! glorious day!
      When heav'n and earth shall raise,
    With all their pow'rs the raptur'd lay,
      To celebrate thy praise.

53   L. M.   *Tender Thought.*

1 COME weary souls with sins distrest;
    Come, and accept the promised rest:
The Savior's gracious call obey,
And cast your gloomy fears away.

2 Oppress'd with guilt a painful load;
   O come, and spread your woes abroad:
Divine compassion, mighty love,
Will all the painful load remove.

3 Here mercy's boundless ocean flows,
To cleanse your guilt and heal your woes:
Pardon, and life, and endless peace,
How rich the gift, how free the grace!

4 Lord, we accept with thankful heart,
The hope thy gracious words impart:
We come with trembling, yet rejoice,
And bless the kind inviting voice.

5 Dear Savior! let thy powerful love
Confirm our faith, our fears remove;
And sweetly influence every breast,
And guide us to eternal rest.

PUBLIC WORSHIP.

54   Metre 17.   *Sabbath.*

1 SAFELY through another week,
  God has brought us on our way;
Let us now a blessing seek,
Waiting in his courts to-day,
Day of all the week the best,
Emblem of eternal rest.

2 While we seek supplies of grace
Through the dear Redeemer's name,
Show thy reconciling face,
Take away our sin and shame—
From our worldy cares set free,
May we rest this day in thee.

3 Here we're come thy name to praise,
Let us feel thy presence near;
May thy glory meet our eyes,
While we in thy house appear.
Here afford us, Lord, a taste
Of our everlasting feast.

4 May the gospel's joyful sound,
Conquer sinners, comfort saints;
Make the fruits of grace abound,
Bring relief for all complaints:
Such let all our Sabbaths prove,
Till we join the church above.

PUBLIC WORSHIP.

55 C. M. *Primrose.*

1 SALVATION! O the joyful sound,
'Tis pleasure to our ears;
A sov'reign balm for every wound,
A cordial for our fears.

2 Buried in sorrow and in sin,
At hell's dark door we lay;
But we arise by grace Divine,
To see a heavenly day.

3 Salvation! let the echo fly,
The spacious earth around,
While all the armies of the sky
Conspire to raise the sound.

56 L. M. *Tender Thought.*

1 DISMISS us with thy blessing Lord—
Help us to feed upon thy word;
All that has been amiss forgive,
And let thy truth within us live.

2 Though we are guilty, thou art good—
Wash all our works in Jesus' blood;
Give every fettered soul release,
And bid us all depart in peace.

57 METRE 7. *Seraph's Harp.*

1 LORD, dismiss us with thy blessing—
Fill our hearts with joy and peace;

Let us each thy love possessing,
  Triumph in redeeming grace;
    Oh, refresh us!
  Travelling through this wilderness.

2 Thanks we give and adoration,
    For the gospel's joyful sound;
  May the fruits of thy salvation
    In our hearts and lives abound;
      May thy presence
    With us evermore be found.

3 So, when e'er the signal's given,
    Us from earth to call away;
  Borne on angels' wings to heaven,
    Glad to leave our cumbrous clay.
      May we, ready,
    Rise and reign in endless day.

58   S. M.   *Ninety-Third.*

1 ONCE more before we part,
    Oh bless the Savior's name!
  Let every tongue and every heart
    Adore and praise the same.

2 Lord, in thy grace we came.
    That blessing still impart,
  We met in Jesus' sacred name,
    In Jesus' name we part.

3 Still on thy holy word
    We'll live, and feed, and grow;
  And still go on to know the Lord,
    And practice what we know.

PUBLIC WORSHIP.

4 Now Lord, before we part,
  Help us to bless thy name;
Let every tongue and every heart,
  Adore and praise the same.

59   S. M.   *New Hope.*

1 THE swift declining day,
  How fast its moments fly!
While evening's broad and gloomy shade
  Gains on the western sky.

2 Ye mortals, mark its pace,
  And use the hours of light;
For know its Maker can command
  An instant, endless night.

3 Give glory to the Lord,
  Who rules the rolling sphere;
Submissive at his footstool bow,
  And seek salvation there.

4 Then shall new lustre break
  Through all the horrid gloom,
And lead you to unchanging light,
  In your celestial home.

60   METRE 4.   *Female Pilgrim.*

1 PRINCE of Peace, be ever near us,
  Fix in all our hearts thy home;
With thy blessed presence cheer us,
  Let thy sacred kingdom come.
Raise to heav'n our expectation;
  Give our favor'd souls to prove
Glorious and complete salvation,
  In the realms of bliss above.

2 May the grace of Christ our Savior,
   And the Father's boundless love,
With the Holy Spirit's favor,
   Rest upon us from above.
Thus may we abide in union
   With each other and the Lord;
And possess, in sweet communion,
   Joys which earth cannot afford.

61   Metre 4.   *Olney.*

1 JESUS, grant us all a blessing,
   Send it down, Lord, from above,
May we all go home a praying,
   And rejoicing in thy love!
Farewell brethren, farewell sisters,
   Till we all shall meet above.

2 Jesus, pardon all our follies,
   While together we have been;
Make us humble, make us holy,
   Cleanse us all from every sin!
Farewell brethren, farewell sisters,
   Till we all shall meet again.

3 May thy blessing, Lord, go with us,
   To each one's respective home,
And the presence of our Jesus
   Rest upon us ev'ry one!
Farewell brethren, farewell sisters,
   Till we all shall meet at home.

62   L. M.   *Windham.*

1 ALMIGHTY Father! bless the word,
   Which thro' thy grace we now have heard,

O may the precious seed take root,
Spring up, and bear abundant fruit.

2 We praise thee for the means of grace,
Thus in thy courts to seek thy face:
Grant, Lord, that we who worship here,
May all at length in heav'n appear.

NATIVITY OF CHRIST.

63   C. M.   *Augusta.*

1 ON Judah's plains as shepherd sat,
    Watching their flocks by night,
The angel of the Lord appear'd,
    Clad in celestial light.

2 Awe-struck, the vision they regard,
    Appall'd with trembling fear;
When thus a cherub-voice divine
    Breathed sweetly on their ear.

3 "Shepherds of Judah! cease your fears,
    And calm your troubled mind;
Glad tidings of great joy I bring
    To you and all mankind.

4 "This day Almighty love fulfils
    Its great eternal word:
This day is born in Bethlehem
    A Savior—Christ the Lord.

5 "There you shall find the heav'nly Babe
    In humble weeds array'd;
  All meanly wrapped in swaddling clothes,
    And in a manger laid."

6 He ceased, and sudden all around
    Appeared a radiant throng
  Of angels, praising God, and thus
    Warbling their choral song.

7 "Glory to God, from whom on high
    All-gracious mercies flow!
  Who sends his heaven-descended peace
    To dwell with man below."

54.　　　C. M.　　　*Rockingham.*

1 HARK, the glad sound, the Savior comes,
    The Savior promised long!
  Let every heart prepare a throne,
    And every voice a song.

2 On him the the Spirit largely pour'd,
    Exerts his sacred fire;
  Wisdom and might, and zeal and love
    His holy breast inspire.

3 He comes the pris'ners to release,
    In Satan's bondage held,
  The gates of brass before him burst,
    The iron fetters yield.

4 He comes from thickest films of vice
    To clear the inward sight;
  And on the eyes obscured by sin,
    To pour celestial light.

NATIVITY OF CHRIST.

5 He comes the broken heart to bind,
　The bleeding soul to cure;
And with the treasures of his grace
　T' enrich the humble poor.

6 Our glad hosannas, Prince of Peace,
　Thy welcome shall proclaim,
And heav'n's eternal arches ring
　With thy beloved name.

65　　　　　S. M.　　　　*Ninety-Third.*

1 REJOICE in Jesus' birth!
　To us a Son is giv'n,
To us a child is born on earth,
　Who made both earth and heav'n.

2 He reigns above the sky,
　This universe sustains—
The God Supreme—the Lord most high,
　The King Messiah reigns!

3 Th' Almighty God, is he,
　Author of heavenly bliss!
The Father of Eternity,
　The glorious Prince of Peace!

4 His government shall grow,
　From strength to strength proceed;
His righteousness the church o'erflow,
　And all the earth o'erspread.

66　　　　8's & 7's　　*Babe of Bethlehem.*

1 YE nations all, on you I call,
　Come hear this declaration,

NATIVITY OF CHRIST. 57

And don't refuse the glorious news
   Of Jesus and salvation.
To royal Jews came first the news
   Of Christ the great Messiah,
As was foretold by prophets old,
   Isaiah, Jeremiah.

2 To Abraham the promise came,
   And to his seed for ever,
A light to shine in Isaac's line,
   By Scripture we discover;
Hail, promised morn! the Savior's born,
   The glorious Mediator—
God's blessed Word made flesh and blood,
   Assumed the human nature.

3 His parents poor in earthly store,
   To entertain the Stranger
They found no bed to lay his head,
   But in the ox's manger:
No royal things, as used by kings,
   Were seen by those that found him,
But in the hay the Stranger lay,
   With swaddling bands around him.

4 On the same night a glorious light
   To shepherds there appeared,
Bright angels came in shining flame,
   They saw and greatly feared;
The angels said—"Be not afraid,
   Although we much alarm you,
We do appear, good news to bear,
   As now we will inform you.

5 "The city's name is Bethlehem,
   In which God hath appointed,

NATIVITY OF CHRIST.

This glorious morn a Savior's born,
　For him God hath anointed;
By this you'll know, if you will go,
　To see this little Stranger,
His lovely charms in Mary's arms,
　Both lying in a manger."

6　When this was said straightway was made
　　A glorious sound from heaven,
Each flaming tongue an anthem sung,
　"To men a Savior's given,
In Jesus' name the glorious theme,
　We elevate our voices,
At Jesus' birth be peace on earth,
　Meanwhile all heaven rejoices."

7　Then with delight they took their flight,
　　And wing'd their way to glory,
The shepherds gazed and were amazed,
　To hear the pleasing story;
To Bethlehem they quickly came,
　The glorious news to carry,
And in the stall they found them all,
　Joseph, the Babe and Mary.

8　The shepherds then return'd again
　　To their own habitation,
With joy of heart they did depart,
　Now they have found salvation.
Glory, they cry, to God on high,
　Who sent his Son to save us;
This glorious morn the Savior's born,
　His name it is CHRIST JESUS.

NATIVITY OF CHRIST.

67   Metre. 33.   *Star in the East.*

1 HAIL the blest morn when the great Mediator
   Down from the regions of glory descends;
Shepherds, go worship the Babe in the manger,
   Lo! for his guard the bright angels attend.

2 Brightest and best of the sons of the morning,
   Dawn on our darkness and lend us thine aid:
Star of the East, the horizon adorning,
   Guide where our Infant Redeemer is laid.

3 Cold on his cradle the dew drops are shining,
   Low lies his bed with the beasts of the stall:
Angels adore him in slumber reclining,
   Maker, and Monarch, and Savior of all.

4 Say, shall we yield him, in costly devotion,
   Odors of Edom and off'rings divine —
Gems of the mountain and pearls of the ocean,
   Myrrh from the forest and gold from the mine?

5 Vainly we offer each ample oblation,
   Vainly with gold would his favor secure;
Richer by far is the heart's adoration—
   Dearer to God are the prayers of the poor.

68   C. M.   *Awful Majesty.*

1 WHILE shepherds watched their flocks by night,
   All seated on the ground,
The angel of the Lord came down,
   And glory shone around.

2 "Fear not," said he, (for mighty dread
   Had seiz'd their troubled mind,)
"Glad tidings of great joy I bring
   To you and mankind.

NATIVITY OF CHRIST.

3 "To you, in David's town, this day,
　　Is born of David's line,
　The Savior, who is Christ the Lord;
　　And this shall be the sign:

4 "The heavenly Babe you there shall find
　　To human view display'd,
　All meanly wrapp'd in swathing bands,
　　And in a manger laid."

5 Thus spake the seraph, and forthwith
　　Appear'd a shining throng
　Of angels praising God on high,
　　And thus address'd their song:

6 "All glory be to God on high,
　　And to the earth be peace;
　Good will henceforth, from heav'n to men,
　　Begin and never cease."

69   C. M.   *Christmas.*

1 HARK from on high those blissful strains!
　　Whence can such sweetness be?
　Have angels waked their golden harps
　　With heav'ns own minstrelsy?

2 Or do we hear the cherub voice
　　Of infant bands, who raise,
　Soaring from earth, celestial notes
　　In their Creator's praise?

3 Thus spake the shepherds — yet with dread,
　　So strange the sounds they heard,
　While o'er their slumb'ring flocks they kept
　　Their wonted nightly guard.

NATIVITY OF CHRIST.

4 And soon they saw a dazzling light
 Beam through the starry way,
 And shining seraphs clustering where
 The infant Jesus lay.

5 They came a Savior's birth to tell,
 And tunes of rapture sing;
 Hence the glad notes that filled the air—
 Each swept his loudest string.

6 But now, in accents soft and kind,
 The chieftain angel said,
 "Heaven's tidings of great joy we bear—
 Shepherds, be not afraid."

7 Then suddenly th' angelic choir
 Renew'd the rapturous song;
 While heav'n's wide portals caught the sound,
 And echoed it along.

70.   Metre 5.   *Sovereign Grace.*

1 HARK! the herald-angels sing
 "Glory to the new-born king;
 Peace on earth and mercy mild;
 God and sinners reconciled;"
 Joyful all ye nations rise,
 Join the triumphs of the skies;
 With th' angelic host proclaim,
 "Christ is born in Bethlehem."

2 Christ by highest heaven adored,
 Christ the everlasting Lord;
 Late in time behold him come,
 Offspring of a virgin's womb;

NATIVITY OF CHRIST.

Vail'd in flesh, the Godhead see,
Hail th' Incarnate Deity!
Pleased as man with men t' appear,
Jesus our Immanuel here.

3 Hail the heav'n-born Prince of Peace!
Hail, the Sun of Righteousness!
Light and life to all he brings,
Ris'n with healing in his wings:
Mild he lays his glory by,
Born that man no more may die;
Born to raise the sons of earth?
Born to give them second birth.

4 Come, DESIRE OF NATIONS, come!
Fix in us thy humble home;
Rise, the woman's conquering seed,
Bruise in us the serpent's head;
Adam's likeness now efface,
Stamp thine image in its place:
Second Adam from above,
Reinstate us in thy love.

71 METRE 4. *Charleston.*

1 HARK!—what mean those holy voices,
Sweetly sounding through the skies?
Lo! the angelic host rejoices;
Heavenly hallelujahs rise.

2 Hear them tell the wondrous story,
Hear them chant in hymns of joy,
"Glory in the highest—glory!
Glory be to God most high!

3 "Peace on earth—good will from heaven,
Reaching far as man is found."

NATIVITY OF CHRIST.

"Souls redeemed and sins forgiven"—
　Loud our golden harps shall sound.

4 Christ is born the great Anointed;
　Heaven and earth his praises sing!
Oh receive whom God appointed,
　For your Prophet, Priest and King.

5 Haste, ye mortals, to adore him;
　Learn his name, and taste his joy;
Till in heaven ye sing before him,
　Glory be to God most high!

72　　　Metre 7.　　　*Seraph's Harp.*

1 ANGELS! from the realms of glory,
　Wing your flight o'er all the earth;
Ye, who sang creation's story,
　Now proclaim Messiah's birth:
Come and worship—Come and worship
　Worship Christ, the new-born King.

2 Shepherds! in the field abiding,
　Watching o'er your flocks by night:
God with man is now residing,
　Yonder shines the heavenly light:
Come and worship—
　Worship Christ, the new-born King.

3 Saints! before the altar bending,
　Watching long in hope and fear,
Suddenly the Lord, descending,
　In his temple shall appear;
Come and worship—
　Worship Christ, the new-born King.

4 Sinners! wrung with true repentance,
    Doomed for guilt to endless pains,
Justice now revokes the sentence,
    Mercy calls you, break your chains:
Come and worship—
Worship Christ, the new-born King.

NEW - YEAR.

73   Metre 32.   *New-Year.*

1 COME, let us anew, our journey pursue,
    Roll round with the year,
And never stand still till the Master appear!
His adorable will let us glady fulfill,
    And our talents improve;
By the patience of hope, and the labor of love.

2 Our life as a dream, our time as a stream
    Glides swiftly away:
And the fugitive moment refuses to stay.
The arrow is flown, the moment is gone;
    The millenial year
Rushes on to our view, and eternity's here.

3 O that each in the day of His coming may say,
    "I have fought my way through;
I have finish'd the work thou didst give me to do!
O that each from his Lord may receive the glad word,
    "Well and faithfully done!
Enter into my joy and sit down on my throne."

74   C. M.   *Peterborough.*

1 NOW, gracious Lord, thine arm reveal,
   And make thy glory known;
Now let us all thy presence feel,
   And soften hearts of stone.

2 From all the guilt and former sin,
   May mercy set us free;
And let the year we now begin,
   Begin and end with thee.

3 Send down thy Spirit from above,
   That saints may love thee more;
And sinners now may learn to love,
   Who never loved before.

4 And when before thee we appear,
   In one eternal home,
May growing numbers worship here,
   And praise thee in our room.

75   C. M.   *Barby.*

1 SING to the great Jehovah's praise!
   All praise to him belongs,
Who kindly lengthens out our days,
   Demands our choicest songs:
His providence has brought us through
   Another various year;
We all with vows and anthems new
   Before our God appear.

2 Father, thy mercies past we own,
   Thy still continued care;

NEW-YEAR.

To thee presenting, through thy Son,
  Whate'er we have or are:
Our lips and lives shall gladly show
  The wonders of thy love,
While on in Jesus' steps we go
  To seek thy face above.

3 Our residue of days or hours,
  Thine, wholly thine, shall be;
And all our consecrated powers,
  A sacrifice to thee:
Till Jesus in the clouds appear,
  To saints on earth forgiv'n,
And bring the grand sabbatic year,
  The jubilee of heav'n.

76   METRE 9.   *Lenox.*

1 THE Lord of earth and sky,
    The God of ages praise!
  Who reigns enthroned on high,
    Ancient of endless days!
  Who lengthens out our trials here,
  And spares us yet another year.

2 Barren and withered trees,
    We cumbered long the ground!
  No fruit of holiness
    On our dead souls was found;
  Yet doth he us in mercy spare
  Another and another year.

3 When justice bared the sword,
    To cut the fig tree down,
  The pity of the Lord
    Cries, "let it still alone!"

NEW-YEAR.

The Father mild inclines his ear,
And spares us yet another year.

4 Jesus, thy speaking blood,
  From God obtain'd the grace;
Who therefore hath bestow'd
  On us a longer space;
Thou didst in our behalf appear,
And lo! we see another year!

5 Then dig about the root,
  Break up their fallow ground,
And let our gracious fruit
  To thy great praise abound;
O let us all thy praise declare,
And fruit unto perfection bear.

77   C. M.   Rochester.

1 OUR life is ever on the wing,
    And death is ever nigh;
  The moment when our lives begin,
    We all begin to die.

2 Yet, mighty God, our fleeting days
    Thy lasting favors share;
  Yet with the bounties of thy grace,
    Thou load'st the rolling year.

3 'Tis sov'reign mercy finds us food,
    And we are clothed with love;
  While grace stands pointing out the road
    That leads our souls above.

4 His goodness runs an endless round,
    All glory to the Lord!

5*

NEW-YEAR.

His mercy never knows a bound,
And be his name adored!

5 Thus we begin the lasting song,
And when we close our eyes,
Let future ages praise prolong,
Till time and nature dies.

78 C. M. Hockingham.

1 AND now my soul, another year
Of this short life is past;
I cannot long continue here,
And this may be my last.

2 Much of my dubious life is gone,
Nor will return again,
And swift my passing moments run,
The few that yet remain.

3 Awake, my soul, with utmost care
Thy true condition learn,
What are thy hopes, how sure, how fair,
And what thy great concern?

4 Now a new scene of time begins,
Set out afresh for heav'n!
Seek pardon for thy former sins,
In Christ so freely giv'n.

5 Devoutly yield thyself to God,
And on his grace depend,
With zeal pursue the heavenly road,
Nor doubt a happy end.

CRUCIFIXION.

79   L. M.   *Retirement.*

1 WHEN I survey the wondrous cross,
On which the Prince of glory died,
My richest gain I count but loss,
And pour contempt on all my pride.

2 Forbid it, Lord, that I should boast,
Save in the death of Christ, my God;
All the vain things that charm me most,
I sacrifice them to his blood.

3 See from his head, his hands, his feet,
Sorrow and love flow mingled down,
Did e'er such love and sorrow meet,
Or thorns compose so rich a crown?

4 [His dying crimson, like a robe,
Spreads o'er his body on the tree;
Then am I dead to all the globe,
And all the globe is dead to me.]

5 Were the whole realm of nature mine,
That were a present far too small;
Love so amazing, so divine,
Demands my soul, my life, my all.

80   L. M.   *Salem.*

1 HE dies! the friend of sinners dies,
Lo! Salem's daughters weep around!
A solemn darkness vails the skies!
A sudden trembling shakes the ground.

CRUCIFIXION.

2 Come, saints, and drop a tear or two,
  For him who groan'd beneath your load:
  He shed a thousand drops for you,
  A thousand drops of richer blood.

3 Here's love and grief beyond degree—
  The Lord of glory dies for men!
  But lo! what sudden joys we see!
  Jesus the dead—revives again!

4 The rising God forsakes the tomb!
  Up to his Father's courts he flies!
  Cherubic legions guard him home,
  And shout him welcome to the skies!

5 Break off your tears, ye saints, and tell
  How high your great deliv'rer reigns;
  Sing how he spoiled the hosts of hell,
  And led the tyrant, death—in chains.

6 Say, "live forever, glorious King,
  Born to redeem, and strong to save!"
  Then ask, "oh death! where is thy sting?"
  And where thy vict'ry, boasting grave?"

81   C. M.   *Liberty Hall.*

1 ALAS! and did my Savior bleed,
    And did my Sov'reign die?
  Would he devote that sacred head
    For such a worm as I?

2 [Thy body slain, sweet Jesus, thine,
    And bathed in its own blood,
  While all exposed to wrath divine,
    The glorious Suff"rer stood!]

CRUCIFIXION.

3 Was it for crimes that I had done
   He groan'd upon the tree?
Amazing pity, grace unknown!
   And love beyond degree!

4 Well might the sun in darkness hide,
   And shut his glories in,
When God the mighty Maker died,
   For man the creature's sin.

5 Thus might I hide my blushing face,
   While his dear cross appears,
Dissolve my heart in thankfulness,
   And melt my eyes to tears.

6 But drops of grief can ne'er repay
   The debt of love I owe:
Here, Lord, I give myself away,
   'Tis all that I can do.

---

82   L. M.   *Solemnity.*

1 'TWAS on that dark, that doleful night,
   When powers of earth and hell arose
Against the Son of God's delight,
And friends betray'd him to his foes.

2 Before the mournful scene began,
He took the bread, and bless'd and brake.
What love through all his actions ran!
What wondrous words of grace he spake!

3 "This is my body broke for sin,
Receive and eat the living food;"
Then took the cup and bless'd the wine;
"'Tis the new cov'nant in my blood."

CRUCIFIXION.

4 [For us his flesh with nails was torn,
He bore the scourge, he felt the thorn:
And justice pour'd upon his head
In heavy vengeance in our stead.]

5 For us his vital blood was spilt,
To buy the pardon of our guilt,
When for black crimes of biggest size,
He gave his soul a sacrifice.

6 "Do this," he cried, "till time shall end,
"In mem'ry of our dying Friend;
"Meet at my table, and record
"The love of your departed Lord."

7 [Jesus, thy feast we celebrate,
We show thy death, we sing thy name,
Till thou return, and we shall eat
The marriage supper of the Lamb.]

83   METRE 4.   *Olney.*

1 HAIL! thou once despised Jesus,
   Hail! thou Galilean King!
Thou did'st suffer to release us;
   Thou did'st free salvation bring:
Hail, thou agonizing Savior,
   Bearer of our sin and shame!
By thy merits we find favor;
   Life is given through thy name.

2 Paschal Lamb, by God appointed,
   All our sins on thee were laid:
By almighty love anointed,
   Thou hast full atonement made.

CRUCIFIXION.

All thy people are forgiven
  Through the virtue of thy blood ;
Open'd is the gate of heav'n ;
  Peace is made 'twixt man and God.

3 Jesus hail ! enthroned in glory,
  There forever to abide !
All the heav'nly hosts adore thee,
  Seated at thy Father's side :
There for sinners thou art pleading :
  There thou dost our place prepare :
Ever for us interceding,
  Till in glory we appear.

4 Worship, honor, pow'r and blessing,
  Thou art worthy to receive ;
Loudest praises without ceasing,
  Meet it is for us to give :
Help, ye bright, angelic spirits !
  Bring your sweetest, noblest lays !
Help to sing our Savior's merits ;
  Help to chant Immanuel's praise.

84   C. M.   *The Dying Penitent.*

1 AS on the cross the Savior hung,
    And wept, and bled, and died,
  He pour'd salvation on a wretch,
    That languished at his side.

2 His crimes with inward grief and shame,
    The penitent confess'd ;
  Then turned his dying eyes to Christ,
    And thus his pray'r address'd :

3 "Jesus, thou Son and Heir of heav'n,
    Thou spotless Lamb of God ;

CRUCIFIXION.

I see thee bath'd in sweat and tears,
  And welt'ring in thy blood.

4 "Yet quickly from these scenes of woe,
    In triumph shalt thou rise,
  Burst through the gloomy shades of death,
    And shine above the skies.

5 "Amid the glories of that world,
    Dear Savior, think on me,
  And in the victories of thy death,
    Let me a sharer be."

6 His prayer the dying Jesus hears,
    And instantly replies—
  "To-day thy parting soul shall be
    With me in Paradise."

85   METRE 17.   *Mount Calvary.*

1 HEARTS of stone, relent, relent,
    Break, by Jesus' cross subdued;
  See his body, mangled—rent,
    Covered with a gore of blood:
  Sinful soul, what hast thou done!
  Murder'd God's eternal Son.

2 Yes, our sins have done the deed,
    Drove the nails that fixed him there;
  Crown'd with thorns his sacred head,
    Pierc'd him with a soldier's spear;
  Made his soul a sacrifice,—
  For a sinful world he dies.

3 Will you let him die in vain,
    Still to death pursue your Lord;

CRUCIFIXION.

Open tear his wounds again,
  Trample on his precious blood?
No! with all my sins I'll part,
  Savior, take my broken heart.

86   METRE 29.   *Lena.*

1 SEE the Lord of glory dying!
  See him gasping, hear him crying!
    See his burden'd bosom heave;
  Look ye sinners, ye that hung him,
  Look how deep your sins have stung him,
    Dying sinners, look and live.

2 See the rocks and mountains shaking,
  Earth unto her centre quaking—
    Nature's groans awake the dead:
  Look on Phebus struck with wonder,
  Whilst the peals of legal thunder
    Smote the dear Redeemer's head.

3 Heaven's bright melodious legions,
  Chanting through the tuneful regions,
    Cease to trill the quiv'ring string:
  Songs seraphic all suspended,
  'Till the mighty war is ended,
    By the all-victorious King.

4 Hell and all the powers infernal
  Vanquished by the King Eternal,
    When he pour'd his vital flood;
  By his groans which shook creation,
  Lo! we found a proclamation,
    Peace and pardon by his blood.

5 Shout, ye saints, with adoration,
  Fill with praise the wide creation,

Since He's risen from the grave;
Shout with joyful acclamation,
To the Rock of our salvation,
Who alone has power to save.

87   10, 7, 14, 9.   *Crucifixion.*

1 SAW ye my Savior, saw ye my Savior?
    Saw ye my Savior and God?
  O! he died on Calvary, to atone for you and me,
And to purchase our pardon with blood.

2 He was extended! He was extended!
    Shamefully nailed to the cross:
  Oh! he bow'd his head and died, thus my Lord was crucified,
To atone for a world that was lost.

3 Jesus hung bleeding! Jesus hung bleeding!
    Three dreadful hours in pain:
  Oh! the sun refused to shine, when the Majesty divine,
Was derided, insulted, and slain.

4 Darkness prevailed! Darkness prevailed!
    Darkness prevail'd o'er the land,
  Oh! the solid rocks were rent, thro' creation's vast extent,
When the Jews crucified the God-Man.

5 When it was finish'd! When it was finish'd!
    And the atonement was made,
  He was taken by the great, and embalmed in spices sweet,
And in a new sepulchre was laid.

CRUCIFIXION.

6 Hail, mighty Savior! hail mighty Savior!
   Prince and the author of peace,
  Oh, he burst the bars of death, and triumph-
      ing, left the earth,
 He ascended to mansions of bliss.
7 Now interceding, now interceding,
   Pleading that sinners might live;
  Saying, Father, I have died, (Oh behold my
      hands and side!)
 To redeem them, I pray thee forgive.
8 I will forgive them, I will forgive them,
   When they repent and believe;
  Let them now return to thee, and be recon-
      ciled to me,
 And salvation they all shall receive.

88   C. M.   Fiducia.

1 ANGELS in shining order stand,
   Around the Savior's throne;
  They bow with rev'rence at his feet,
   And make his glories known.
  Those happy spirits sing his praise,
   To all eternity,
  But I can sing redeeming grace,
   For Jesus died for me.

2 The cross of Christ inspires my heart,
   To sing redeeming grace;
  Awake my soul, and bear a part
   In my Redeemer's praise.
  O! what can be compared to him,
   Who died upon the tree!
  This is my dear delightful theme,
   That Jesus died for me.

CRUCIFIXION.

3 When at the table of the Lord
   We humbly take our place;
The death of Jesus we record,
   With love and thankfulness.
These emblems bring my Lord to view,
   Upon the bloody tree,
My soul believes and feels it 's true,
   That Jesus died for me.

4 His body broken, nail'd and torn,
   And stain'd with streams of blood,
His spotless soul was left forlorn,
   Forsaken of his God.
'T was then his Father gave the stroke,
   That justice did decree:
All nature felt the dreadful stroke,
   When Jesus died for me.

5 Eli lama sabachthani,
   My God, my God, he cried,
Why hast thou thus forsaken me?
   And thus my Savior died.
But why did God forsake his Son?
   When bleeding on the tree?
He did for sins, but not his own,
   For Jesus died for me.

6 My guilt was on my Surety laid,
   And therefore he must die;
His soul a sacrifice was made,
   For such a worm as I.
Was ever love so great as this?
   Was ever grace so free?
This is my glory, joy, and bliss,
   That Jesus died for me.

CRUCIFIXION.

7 He took his meritorious blood,
  And rose above the skies,
And in the presence of his God,
  Presents his sacrifice.
His intercession must prevail
  With such a glorious plea;
My cause can never, never fail,
  For Jesus died for me.

8 Angels in shining order sit
  Around my Savior's throne;
They bow with rev'rence at his feet,
  And make his glories known.
Those happy Spirits sing his praise,
  To all eternity;
But I can sing redeeming grace,
  For Jesus died for me.

9 O! had I but an angel's voice
  To bear my heart along,
My flowing numbers soon would raise
  To an immortal song.
I'd charm their harps and golden lyres
  In sweetest harmony,
And tell to all the heavenly choirs,
  That Jesus died for me.

89   8,8,8,6,8,8,8,6.   *Messiah.*

1 THE Son of man they did betray,
  He was condemned and led away;
Think, O my soul, that mournful day,
  Look on Mount Calvary!
Behold him, Lamb-like led along,
Surrounded by a wicked throng,
Accused by each lying tongue.

CRUCIFIXION.

And thus the Lamb of God was hung,
  Upon the shameful tree.

2 'T was thus the glorious Sufferer stood,
With hands and feet nail'd to the wood:
From ev'ry wound a stream of blood
  Came trickling down amain:
His bitter groans all nature struck,
And at his voice the rocks were broke,
And sleeping saints their graves forsook.
The spiteful Jews had round him mock'd,
  And laughed at his pain.

3 Thus hung between the earth and skies,
Behold him tremble as he dies,
O sinners hear his mournful cries;
  Behold his torturing pain.
The mourning sun withdrew his light,
Blush'd and refus'd to own his sight,
All azure clothed in robes of night,
All nature mourned and stood affright,
  When Christ the Lord was slain.

4 Ye men and angels, hear the Son,
He cries for help, but there in none:
He treads the wine-press all alone,
  His garments stained with blood.
In lamentations hear him cry,
Eli lama sabachthani;
Tho' death may close these languid eyes,
He soon will mount the upper skies,
  The conquering Son of God.

5 Both Jews and Romans in a band,
With hearts like steel around him stand,
Say'ng if you're come to save the land,
  Now try yourself to free.

CRUCIFIXION.

A soldier pierced him when he died,
And healing streams came from his side,
And thus my Lord was crucified,
Stern Justice now is satisfied,
   Sinners, for you and me.

6 Behold him mount a throne of state,
He fills the mediatorial seat,
While millions bowing at his feet,
   In loud hosannas tell;
How he endured exquisite pains,
And led the monster death in chains;
Ye seraphs raise your highest strains,
While music fills bright Salem's plains.
   He has conquered death and hell.

7 'Tis done, the dreadful debt is paid,
The great atonement now is made;
Sinners on me your guilt was laid,
   For you I spilt my blood;
For you my tender soul did move.
For you I left my courts above,
That you the length and breadth might prove,
The depth and height of perfect love,
   In Christ your smiling God.

8 All glory be to God on high,
Who reigns enthroned above the sky,
Who sent his Son to bleed and die,
   Glory to him be given.
While heaven above his praise resounds,
Zion shall sing his grace abounds,
I hope to sing eternal rounds,
In flaming love which knows no bounds,
   When carried up to heav'n.

CRUCIFIXION.

90   Metre 4.   *Advocate—Disciple.*

1 GREAT High Priest, we view thee stooping
   With our names upon thy breast,
In the garden groaning, drooping,
   To the ground with sorrow prest,
Weeping angels stood confounded,
   To behold their Maker thus,
And shall we remain unwounded,
   When we know 'twas all for us.

2 On the cross thy body broken
   Cancels every penal-tie;
Tempted souls, produce this token,
   All demands to satisfy.
All is finished; do not doubt it,
   But believe your dying Lord;
Never reason more about it,
   Only take him at his word.

3 Come, behold your Savior bleeding,
   Streams of mercy from him flow,
Whilst before his Father pleading
   For those men who wrought his woe.
Lo, he cried, Father forgive them,
   Tho' they do my life pursue,
I am willing to receive them,
   For they know not what they do.

4 Come thou everlasting Spirit,
   Bring to every thankful mind,
All the Savior's dying merit,
   All his suff'rings for mankind.
True recorder of his passion,
   Now thy living fire impart,

CRUCIFIXION.

Now revealed thy great salvation,
  Preach his gospel to our heart.

5 Lord, we fain would trust thee solely;
  'T was for us thy blood was spilt;
Gracious Savior, take us wholly,
  Take and make us what thou wilt,
Grant us now thy heavenly blessing,
  Let thy love our songs employ;
Then we'll find, thy peace possessing,
  In thy service all our joy.

91.   C. M.   Walsal.

1 BEHOLD the Savior of mankind
    Nail'd to the shameful tree,
  How vast the love that him inclined
    To bleed and die for thee!

2 Hark, how he groans! while nature shakes,
    And earth's strong pillars bend!
  The temple's vail in sunder breaks,
    The solid marbles rend.

3 'T is done! the precious ransom's paid;
    "Receive my soul!" he cries:
  See where he bows his sacred head!
    He bows his head and dies!

4 But soon he'll break death's envious chain,
    And in full glory shine,
  O Lamb of God! was ever pain,
    Was ever love like thine!

RESURRECTION.

92   C. M.   *Solon.*

1 THIS is the day the Lord hath made,
   He calls the hours his own;
Let heaven rejoice, let earth be glad,
   And praise surround the throne.

2 To-day he rose and left the dead,
   And Satan's empire fell;
To-day the saints his triumph spread,
   And all his wonders tell.

3 Hosanna to th' anointed King,
   To David's holy Son;
Help us, O Lord; descend and bring
   Salvation from thy throne.

4 Bless'd is the Lord, who comes to men
   With messages of grace;
Who comes, in God his Father's name
   To save our sinful race.

5 Hosanna in the highest strains
   The church on earth can raise:
The highest heavens in which he reigns,
   Shall give him nobler praise.

93   C. M.   *Primrose.*

1 HOSANNA to the Prince of light,
   That cloth'd himself in clay;
Enter'd the iron gates of death
   And tore the bars away.

RESURRECTION.

2 Death is no more the king of dread,
  Since our Immanuel rose;
He took the tyrant's sting away,
  And spoil'd our hellish foes.

3 See how the conquerer mounts aloft,
  And to his Father flies
With scars of honor in his flesh,
  And triumph in his eyes.

4 There our exalted Savior reigns,
  And scatters blessings down:
Our Jesus fills the middle seat
  Of the celestial throne.

5 [Raise your devotion, mortal tongues,
  To reach his bless'd abode:
Sweet be the accents of your songs
  To our incarnate God.

6 Bright angels, strike you loudest strings,
  Your sweetest voices raise;
Let heaven, and all created things,
  Sound our Immanuel's praise.

94   C. M.   *Youthful Piety.*

1 YE humble souls that seek the Lord,
    Chase all your fears away,
And bow with pleasure down to see
    The place where Jesus lay.

2 Thus low the Lord of life was brought:
    Such wonders love can do!
Thus cold in death that bosom lay,
    Which throbb'd and bled for you.

RESURRECTION.

3 A moment give aloose to grief—
   Let grateful sorrows rise;
And wash the bloody stains away
   With torrents from your eyes.

4 Then dry your tears and tune your songs,
   The Savior lives again;
Not all the bolts and bars of death
   The Conq'ror could detain.

5 High o'er th' angelic bands he rears
   His once dishonor'd head;
And thro' unnumber'd years he reigns,
   Who dwelt among the dead.

6 With joy like his shall every saint
   His empty tomb survey;
Then rise, with his ascending Lord,
   To realms of endless day.

95   METRE 5.   *Resurrection.*

1 ANGELS! roll the rock away,
  Death! yield up thy mighty prey,
See! he rises from the tomb,
Glowing with immortal bloom.

2 'Tis the Savior! angels, raise
Fame's eternal trump of praise!
Let the earth's remotest bound
Hear the joy-inspiring sound.

3 Now, ye saints, lift up your eyes!
Now to glory see him rise,
In long triumph up the sky—
Up to waiting worlds on high.

4 Praise him, all ye heavenly choirs!
  Praise, and sweep your golden lyres!
  Shout, O earth, in rapt'rous song,
  Let the strains be sweet and strong!

THE WORD OF GOD.

96   C. M.   *Rockingham.*

1 FATHER of mercies! in thy word
   What endless glory shines!
 For ever be thy name ador'd,
   For these celestial lines.

2 Here may the wretched sons of want
   Exhaustless riches find;
 Riches above what earth can grant,
   And lasting as the mind.

3 Here, the fair tree of knowledge grows
   And yields a free repast:
 Sublimer sweets than nature knows
   Invite the longing taste.

4 Here the Redeemer's welcome voice
   Spreads heavenly peace around;
 And life, and everlasting joys,
   Attend the blissful sound.

5 O may these heavenly pages be
   My ever dear delight:
 And still new beauties may I see,
   And still increasing light.

THE WORD OF GOD.

6 Divine instructor, gracious Lord!
  Be thou forever near;
Teach me to love thy sacred word.
  And view my Savior there!

97   C. M.   *Awful Majesty*

1 HOW shall the young secure their hearts,
    And guard their lives from sin?
  Thy word the choicest rules imparts,
    To keep the conscience clean.

2 When once it enters to the mind,
    It spreads such light abroad,
  The meanest souls instruction find,
    And raise their thoughts to God.

3 'Tis like the sun, a heavenly light,
    That guides us all the day;
  And through the dangers of the night,
    A lamp to lead our way.

4 The men that keep thy law with care,
    And meditate thy word,
  Grow wiser than their teachers are,
    And better know the Lord.

5 Thy precepts make me truly wise;
    I hate the sinner's road;
  I hate my own vain thoughts that rise,
    But love thy law, my God.

6 The starry heav'ns thy rule obey,
    The earth maintains her place,
  And these thy servants, night and day,
    Thy skill and power express.

THE WORD OF GOD.

7 [But still thy law and gospel, Lord,
   Have lessons more divine;
Not earth stands firmer than thy word,
   Nor stars so nobly shine.]

8 Thy word is everlasting truth,
   How pure is every page!
That holy book shall guide our youth,
   And well support our age.

98 S. M. *Idumea—Shireland.*

1 LET sinners take their course,
   And choose the road to death;
But in the worship of my God
   I'll spend my daily breath.

2 My thoughts address his throne
   When morning brings the light;
I seek his blessings every noon,
   And pay my vows at night.

3 Thou wilt regard my cries,
   O my eternal God,
While sinners perish in surprise
   Beneath thine angry rod.

4 Because they dwell at ease,
   And no sad changes feel,
They neither fear nor trust thy name,
   Nor learn to do thy will.

5 But I, with all my cares,
   Will lean upon the Lord;
I'll cast my burdens on his arm,
   And rest upon his word.

THE WORD OF GOD.

6 His arm shall well sustain
  The children of his love:
The ground on which their safety stands,
  No earthly power can move.

99   C. M.   *Solon—Balerma.*

1 LET the whole race of creation lie
    Abased before their God:
  Whate'er his sov'reign voice has form'd,
    He governs with a nod.

2 [Ten thousand ages ere the skies
    Were into motion brought,
  All the long years and worlds to come,
    Stood present to his thought.

3 There's not a sparrow or a worm,
    But 's found in his decrees;
  He raises monarchs to their throne,
    And sinks them as he please.]

4 If light attends the course I run,
    'Tis he provides those rays;
  And 'tis his hand that hides my sun,
    If darkness cloud my days.

5 Yet I would not be much concern'd,
    Nor vainly long to see
  The volumes of his deep decrees,
    What months are writ for me.

6 When he reveals the book of life,
    O, may I read my name
  Among the chosen of his love,
    The followers of the Lamb.

FAITH AND REPENTANCE.

100   C. M.   *Mear.*

1 WHAT glory gilds the sacred page!
    Majestic, like the sun,
It gives a light to every age,
    It gives, but borrows none.

2 His hand that gave it, still supplies
    The gracious light and heat;
His truths upon the nations rise;
    They rise, but never set.

3 Let everlasting thanks be thine,
    For such a bright display,
As makes a world of darkness shine,
    With beams of heavenly day.

4 My soul rejoices to pursue
    The paths of truth and love;
Till glory breaks upon my view
    In brighter worlds above.

FAITH AND REPENTANCE.

101   L. M.   *Devotion.*

1 BLESS'D are the humble souls, that see
    Their emptiness and poverty;
Treasures of grace to them are given,
And crowns of joy laid up in heaven.

2 Bless'd are the men of broken heart,
    Who mourn for sin with inward smart;

FAITH AND REPENTANCE.

 The blood of Christ divinely flows
 A healing balm for all their woes.

3 Bless'd are the meek who stand afar
From rage and passion, noise and war:
God will secure their happy state,
And plead their cause against the great.

4 Bless'd are the souls that thirst for grace,
Hunger and long for righteousness;
They shall be well supplied and fed
With living streams and living bread.

5 Bless'd are the men whose bowels move
And melt with sympathy and love;
From Christ the Lord shall they obtain
Like sympathy and love again.

6 Bless'd are the pure, whose hearts are clean
From the defiling power of sin;
With endless pleasure they shall see
A God of spotless purity.

7 Bless'd are the men of peaceful life,
Who quench the coals of growing strife;
They shall be called the heirs of bliss,
The sons of God, the God of peace.

8 Bless'd are the suff'rers, who partake
Of pain and shame for Jesus' sake;
Their souls shall triumph in the Lord,
Glory and joy are their reward.

102 C. M. *Liberty Hall—Dublin.*

1 OH! if my soul were formed for woe,
 How would I vent my sighs!

FAITH AND REPENTANCE.

 Repentance should, like rivers flow
  From both my streaming eyes.

2 'T was for my sins, my dearest Lord
  Hung on the cursed tree,
 And groan'd away a dying life
  For thee, my soul, for thee.

3 Oh! how I hate those lusts of mine,
  That crucified my God!
 Those sins that pierc'd and nail'd his flesh
  Fast to the fatal wood.

4 Yes, my Redeemer, they shall die,
  My heart has so decreed:
 Nor will I spare the guilty things
  That made my Savior bleed.

5 Whilst with a melting, broken heart,
  My murder'd Lord I view,
 I raise revenge against my sins,
  And slay the murd'rers too.

103   L. M.   *Supplication.*

1 O THOU that hear'st when sinners cry,
 Though all my crimes before thee lie,
Behold them not with angry look,
But blot their mem'ry from thy book.

2 Create my nature pure within,
 And from my soul averse to sin;
Let thy good Spirit ne'er depart,
Nor hide thy presence from my heart.

3 I cannot live without thy light,
 Cast out and banished from thy sight;

BAPTISM.

Thine holy joys, my God, restore,
And guard me that I fall no more.

4 Though I have grieved thy Spirit, Lord.
Thy help and comfort still afford,
And let a wretch come near thy throne.
To plead the merits of thy Son.

5 A broken heart, my God, my King,
Is all the sacrifice I bring:
The God of grace will ne'er despise
A broken heart for sacrifice.

6 My soul lies humble in the dust,
And owns the dreadful sentence just:
Look down O Lord, with pitying eye.
And save the soul condemned to die.

7 Then will I teach the world thy ways:
Sinners shall learn thy sovereign grace:
I'll lead them to my Savior's blood,
And they shall praise a pard'ning God.

8 O may thy love inspire my tongue!
Salvation shall be all my song;
And all my powers shall join to bless
The Lord, my strength and righteousness.

BAPTISM.

104   C. M.   *Rochester.*

1 IF glorious angels do rejoice,
When sinners turn to God,

BAPTISM.

Let us unite with cheerful voice,
  To spread his praise abroad.

2 When Jesus unto Jordan came,
    And was baptized of John,
  A voice from heaven did proclaim—
    "He's my Beloved Son."

3 His ministers he sent about
    To preach the word of grace,
  And to baptize the world throughout,
    Who should his truth embrace.

4 Lord, we have here before our eyes,
    Some that have set their hands
  To serve thee and to be baptized,
    As thou did'st give command.

5 Glory to God who reigns above,
    For his abounding grace,
  In this the token of his love,
    To us a guilty race.

6 Let us employ our tongues to sing,
    The praises of the Lord,
  For calling sinners home to him
    By his all-powerful word.

105. C. M. *Solon.*

1 COME in ye blessed of the Lord,
    And join his children here;
  Wash'd in the Savior's cleansing blood.
  For him, your Lord, appear.

2 Stay not within the wilderness,
    Nor waiting at the door;

BAPTISM.

For Jesus can your woes redress,
  Were they ten thousand more.

3 Though fearing, trembling, rise and come.
  Yield to the Savior's voice,
For hung'ring, thirsting souls there's room
  O make the blissful choice!

4 Room in the Savior's gracious breast,
  That breast which glows with love—
Room in the church, his chosen rest,
  And room in heaven above.

5 Why will you longer lingering stay,
  When Jesus says "There's room?"
Now is the time, th' accepted day;—
  Arise, he bids you come.

106   L. M.   *Portugal.*

1 'TWAS the commission of our Lord—
  "Go, teach the nations and baptize,"
The nations have received the word,
  Since he ascended to the skies.

2 He sits upon th' eternal hills,
  With grace and pardon in his hands,
And sends his cov'nant with the seals,
  To bless the distant Christian lands.

3 "Repent and be baptized," he saith,
  "For the remission of your sins;"
And thus our sense assists our faith,
  And shows us what the gospel means.

4 Our souls he washes in his blood,
  As water makes the body clean;

BAPTISM.

  And the good Spirit from our God
    Descends like purifying rain.

3 Thus we engage ourselves to thee,
    And seal our covenant with the Lord:
  O may the great eternal Three
    In heaven our solemn vows record.

107   11,9,11,9.   PECULIAR.

1 THE NAME of the Lord is a fountain of life,
    Its waters are sweeter than honey,
  No taste of the gall of terrestrial strife,
    Come buy without price, without money.

2 The NAME of the Lord is a full flowing stream,
    From Zion's immovable mountain,
  Its currents with virtues unspeakably teem,—
    Come, come to the life-giving fountain.

3 The NAME of the Lord is a river of grace,
    Whose waters as soon as they're tasted,
  New energy give to the sons of a race,
    With passion enfeebled and wasted.

4 Then come to its banks, all ye tribes of mankind,
    And drink of the stream of salvation,
  Its course is no longer to Judah confined,
    It flows through the guiltiest nation.

5 Come, drink living waters, though Jesus is gone,
    His NAME still conveys absolution;
  Come drink where the stream of remission flows
      down,
    Through a rite of his own institution.

108   C. M.   *Augusta.*

1 WHEN Jesus Christ the Virgin's Son,
　Of David's royal race,
His brilliant course of works begun,
　And preach'd the reign of grace—

2 He call'd on Abraham's seed in vain,
　His mission to believe:
To own his right to rule and reign,
　His NAME as Prince receive.

3 This NAME the scribes refused to wear,
　And spurned the Nazarene,
Would not the fame of Jesus share,
　Or in his train be seen.

4 What lofty names could Jesus bring
　His princely birth to show?
Could Gallilee produce a king?
　Or good from Naz'reth flow?

5 They taunted thus the birth obscure
　Of chaste Maria's Son,
And scorn'd his favor to secure,
　His NAME by putting on.

6 But found at length, without disguise
　This NAME they must receive,
No other known beneath the skies,
　Could life eternal give.

7 And skillful men of later days,
　Have splendid systems built,
To shun its use by various ways
　Of cleansing souls from guilt.

But they too, like the Jews of old,
   Would they salvation win,
Must come and be with Christ enroll'd
   And wash away their sin.

Then let us all to Christ repair,—
   To Christ the virgin's Son,
His NAME our badge of glory wear,
   And put his armor on.

109   C. M.   *Mear*

1 THE Lord's disciples when they spread
   O'er Judah's sacred plains;
Relieved the sick, restored the dead,
   And cast out plagues and pains.

2 They pour no drugs through Palestine,
   No medicines they had,
They only used the NAME divine,
   Its power alone display'd.

3 And strange the virtues of that NAME,
   From which diseases fled,
The devils trembled where it came,
   And spirits foul obey'd.

4 And still, O Lord, thy name conveys,
   To Adam's ruined race,
If used in thy appointed ways,
   A sure and real grace.

5 No useless mark, no naked sign,
   It so renews the soul,
As long ago in Palestine,
   It made the sinner whole.

7*

BAPTISM.

110   Metre 12.   *Deliverance.*

1 WHEN sinners awake and perceive,
   What desperate creatures they are,
How shall they obtain a relief.
From misery, guilt and despair?
In vain is our search and our cry,
Till we in submission and zeal.
The words of our Savior apply,
"To do his adorable will."

2 God will not be pleased with our prayer,
If we disobey his command,
But if we obedient are,
Will bring us unto his right hand.
Sincerely believe in his word,
Put on his adorable name.
Salvation in Jesus our Lord,
The penitent then shall obtain.

3 Thus Peter to inquiring Jews,
Convinced in their hearts as they were;
Their interest in Jesus should lose,
Eternal damnation must bear,
"He said that they all should repent,
"Be baptized in Jesus' name.
"Then shall his good Spirit be sent.
"They all shall be bless'd with the same.

4 "This promise is even to you,—
"And all that are yet afar off,
"For Jesus' commands we pursue,
"Though infidel mockers may scoff,
"The Lord will yet bring many nigh.
"His house and his mansions to fill,

BAPTISM. 101

"To share in his ample supply,
"Who meekly submit to his will."

111   L. M.   *Tender Thought.*

1 AS the apostles sat at meat,
    Before our Savior did ascend,
He did them with his presence greet,
And gave to them his last command.

2 Upbraided them with unbelief,
And hardness of each stubborn heart:
His counsel we must all receive,
Else we with Christ can have no part.

3 "Go, preach my gospel," Jesus saith,
"And bring them all unto the host,
"Baptize believers in the name
"Of Father, Son, and Holy Ghost."

4 "He that believes and is baptized,
Shall dwell in realms of joy above,—
Who don't believe the words of Christ,
Shall never taste redeeming love."

PRAYER AND SUPPLICATION.

112   C. M.   *Standish*

1 COME Holy Spirit, heavenly Dove,
    With all thy quick'ning powers:
Kindle a flame of sacred love
    In these cold hearts of ours.

2 Look how we grovel here below,
   Fond of these trifling toys,
 Our souls can neither fly nor go
   To reach eternal joys.

3 In vain we tune our formal songs,
   In vain we strive to rise,
 Hosannas languish on our tongues,
   And our devotion dies.

4 Dear Lord! and shall we ever live
   At this poor dying rate?
 Our love so faint, so cold to thee,
   And thine to us so great?

5 Come Holy Spirit, heavenly Dove,
   With all thy quick'ning powers:
 Come shed abroad a Savior's love,
   And that shall kindle ours.

113   L. M.   *Alfreton.*

1 O THOU to whose all searching sight,
   The darkness shineth as the light.
 Search, prove my heart, it pants for thee,
 O burst these bonds and set it free.

2 Wash out its stains, refine its dross,
 Nail my affections to the cross:
 Hallow each thought, let all within
 Be clean, as thou my Lord art clean.

3 If in this darksome wild I stray,
 Be thou my light, be thou my way:
 No foes, no violence I fear,
 No fraud, while thou my God art near.

SUPPLICATION.

4 When rising floods my soul o'erflow,
When sinks my heart in waves of woe.
Jesus thy timely aid impart,
And raise my head, and cheer my heart.

5 Savior, where'er thy steps I see,
Dauntless, untired, I follow thee;
O let thy hand support me still,
And lead me to thy holy hill.

6 If dark and thorny be the way,
My strength proportion to my day;
Till toil, and grief, and pain shall cease,
Where all is calm, and joy, and peace.

114   C. M.   *St. Olave.*

1 FATHER, I stretch my hands to thee,
   No other help I know;
If thou withdraw thyself from me,
   Ah, whither shall I go?

2 What did thine only Son endure,
   Before I drew my breath!
What pain, what labor to secure
   My soul from endless death!

3 O Jesus, could I this believe,
   I now should feel thy power;
Now my poor soul thou wouldst retrieve,
   Nor let me wait one hour.

Author of faith, to thee I lift
   My weary, longing eyes;
O let me now receive that gift,
   My soul without it dies.

5 Surely thou canst not let me die;
  O speak, and I shall live;
And here I will unwearied lie,
  Till thou thy Spirit give.

6 The worst of sinners would rejoice,
  Could they but see thy face;
O let me hear thy quickening voice,
  And taste thy pard'ning grace.

115   C. M.   *Burstall—Dublin.*

1 O FOR a closer walk with God,
  A calm and heavenly frame;
A light to shine upon the road,
  That leads me to the Lamb.

2 Where is the blessedness I knew,
  When first I saw the Lord?
Where is the soul-refreshing view
  Of Jesus and his word?

3 What peaceful hours I once enjoy'd,
  How sweet their mem'ry still!
But they have left an aching void,
  The world can never fill.

4 Return, O holy dove, return,
  Sweet messenger of rest:
I hate the sins that made thee mourn,
  And drove thee from my breast.

5 The dearest idol I have known,
  Whate'er that idol be,
Help me to tear it from thy throne,
  And worship only thee.

SUPPLICATION. 105

6 So shall my walk be close with God.
   Calm and serene my frame:
So purer light shall mark the road,
   That leads me to the Lamb.

116   L. M.   *Supplication.*

1 SHOW pity Lord, O Lord, forgive,
   Let a repenting rebel live:
Are not thy mercies large and free?
May not a sinner trust in thee?

2 My crimes are great, but can't surpass
The power and glory of thy grace:
Great God, thy nature hath no bound,
So let thy pard'ning love be found.

3 Oh, wash my soul from every sin,
And make my guilty conscience clean:
Here on my heart the burden lies,
And past offences pain my eyes.

4 My lips with shame my sins confess
Against thy law, against thy grace;
Lord, should thy judgments grow severe,
I am condemned, but thou art clear.

5 Should sudden vengeance seize my breath,
I must pronounce thee just in death:
And if my soul were sent to hell,
Thy righteous law approves it well.

6 Yet save a trembling sinner, Lord,
Whose hope still hov'ring round thy word,
Would light on some sweet promise there,
Some sure support against despair.

117   C. M.   Dublin.

1 I'LL bless the Lord from day to day:
    How good are all his ways!
  Ye humble souls that use to pray,
    Come help my lips to praise.

2 Sing to the honor of his name,
    How a poor suff'rer cried;
  Nor was his hope exposed to shame,
    Nor was his suit denied.

3 When threat'ning sorrows round me stood,
    And endless fears arose,
  Like the loud billows of a flood,
    Redoubling all my woes.

4 I told the Lord my sore distress,
    With heavy groans and tears:
  He gave my sharpest torments ease,
    And silenced all my fears.

5 O sinners, come and taste his love;
    Come, learn his pleasant ways;
  And let your own experience prove
    The sweetness of his grace.

6 He bids his angels pitch their tents
    Round where his children dwell;
  What ills their heavenly care prevents
    No earthly tongue can tell.

7 O love the Lord, ye saints of his;
    His eye regards the just:
  How richly bless'd their portion is
    Who make the Lord their trust.

SUPPLICATION.

8 Young lions, pinch'd with hunger, roar,
  And famish in the wood:
But God supplies his holy poor
  With every needful good.

118   C. M.   *Salvation.*

1 COME humble sinner, in whose breast
    A thousand thoughts revolve;
  Come with your guilt and fears opprest,
    And make this last resolve.

2 "I'll go to Jesus, though my sins
    Have like a mountain rose:
  I know his courts, I'll enter in,
    Whatever may oppose.

3 "Prostrate I'll lie before his throne,
    And there my guilt confess;
  I'll tell him I'm a wretch undone
    Without his sov'reign grace.

4 "I'll to the gracious King approach,
    Whose sceptre pardon gives;
  Perhaps he will command my touch,
    And then the suppliant lives.

5 "Perhaps he will admit my plea,
    Perhaps will hear my prayer;
  But if I perish I will pray,
    And perish only there.

6 "I can but perish if I go;
    I am resolved to try;
  For if I stay away, I know
    I must forever die.

7 "But if I die with mercy sought,
  When I the King have tried,
 This were to die (delightful thought!)
  As sinners never died."

119   C. M.   *Bethel.*

1 BESTOW, dear Lord, upon our youth,
  The gift of saving grace:
 And let the seed of sacred truth
  Fall in a fruitful place.

2 Grace is a plant, where'er it grows,
  O pure and heavenly root;
 But fairest in the youngest shows,
  And yields the sweetest fruit.

3 Ye careless ones, O hear betimes
  The voice of sovereign love;
 Your youth is stain'd with many crimes,
  But mercy reigns above.

4 True you are young, but there's a stone
  Within the youngest breast;
 Or half the crimes which you have done
  Would rob you of your rest.

5 For you the public prayer is made,
  O join the public prayer!
 For you the secret tear is shed,
  O shed yourselves a tear!

6 We pray that you may early prove
  The Spirit's power to teach:
 You cannot be too young to love
  That Jesus, whom we preach.

120   L. M.   Kingsbridge.

1 GREAT GOD, indulge my humble claim:
  Thou art my hope, my joy, my rest:
  The glories that compose thy name
  Stand all engaged to make me bless'd.

2 Thou great and good, thou just and wise;
  Thou art my Father and my God;
  And I am thine by sacred ties,
  Thy son, thy servant bought with blood.

3 With heart and eyes, and lifted hands,
  For thee I long, to thee I look,
  As travelers in thirsty lands,
  Pant for the cooling water brook.

4 With early feet I love t' appear
  Among thy saints, and seek thy face:
  Oft have I seen thy glory there,
  And felt the power of sovereign grace.

5 Not fruits nor wines, that tempt our taste,
  No pleasures that to sense belong,
  Could make me so divinely bless'd,
  Or raise so high my cheerful song.

6 My life itself, without thy love,
  No taste or pleasure could afford;
  'Twould but a tiresome burden prove,
  If I were banish'd from the Lord.

7 Amidst the wakeful hours of night,
  When busy cares afflict my head,
  One thought of thee gives new delight
  And adds refreshment to my bed.

3 I'll lift my hands, I'll raise my voice,
While I have breath to pray or praise;
This work shall make my heart rejoice,
And bless the remnant of my days.

121 Metre 8. *Plymouth Rock*

1 JESUS, thy boundless love to me
No thought can reach, no tongue declare
O knit my thankful heart to thee,
And reign without a rival there!
Thine wholly, thine alone I am;
Be thou alone my constant flame.

2 O grant that nothing in my soul
May dwell but thy pure love alone!
O may thy love possess me whole,
My joy, my treasure, and my crown!
Strange flames far from my heart remove;
My every act, word, thought be love.

3 O Love, how cheering is thy ray!
All pain before thy presence flies;
Care, anguish, sorrow, melt away,
Where'er thy healing beams arise:
O Jesus, nothing may I see,
Nothing desire or seek but thee!

Unwearied may I thus pursue,
Dauntless to the high prize aspire;
Hourly within my soul renew
This holy flame, this heavenly fire;
And day and night be all my care
To guard the sacred treasure there.

122   Metre 8.   *Missionary Farewell.*

1 MY Savior, thou my love to me
    In shame, in want, in pain hast show'd
For me on the accursed tree,
    Thou pouredst forth thy guiltless blood!
Thine image on my heart impress,
Nor aught shall the loved stamp efface.

2 More hard than marble is my heart,
    And foul with sins of deepest stain;
But thou the mighty Savior art,
    Nor flow'd thy cleansing blood in vain
Ah, soften, melt this rock, and may
Thy blood wash all these stains away.

3 O that I, as a little child,
    May follow thee, and never rest,
Till sweetly thou hast breath'd thy mild
    And lowly mind into my breast;
Nor ever may we parted be,
Till I one spirit be with thee.

4 Still let thy love point out my way:
    How wondrous things thy love has wrought
Still lead me, lest I go astray:
    Direct my work, inspire my thought;
And if I fall, soon may I hear
Thy voice, and know that love is near.

5 In suff'ring be thy love my peace,
    In weakness be thy love my power;
And when the storms of life shall cease,
    Jesus, in that important hour,
In death as life be thou my guide,
And save me, who for me hast died.

123   C. M.   *Augusta.*

1 WHILST thee I seek, protecting Pow'r!
    Be my vain wishes still'd;
And may this consecrated hour
    With better hopes be fill'd.

2 Thy love the pow'r of thought bestow'd.
    To thee my thoughts would soar;
Thy mercy o'er my life has flow'd;
    That mercy I adore.

3 In each event of life how clear
    Thy ruling hand I see!
Each blessing to my soul most dear,
    Because conferr'd by thee.

4 In every joy that crowns my days,
    In every pain I bear,
My heart shall find delight in praise,
    Or seek relief in pray'r.

5 When gladness wings my favor'd hour,
    Thy love my thoughts shall fill,
Resign'd, when storms of sorrow low'r,
    My soul shall seek thy will.

6 My lifted eye without a tear,
    The gathering storm shall see;
My steadfast heart shall know no fear;
    That heart will rest on thee.

124   METRE 5.   *Frankfort.*

1 LORD, I cannot let thee go,
    Till a blessing thou bestow;
Do not turn away thy face,
Mine's an urgent, pressing case.

2 Dost thou ask me who I am?
Ah! my Lord, thou know'st my name:
Yet the question gives a plea
To support my suit with thee.

3 Thou didst once a wretch behold,
In rebellion blindly bold,
Scorn thy grace, thy pow'r defy;
That poor rebel, Lord, was I.

4 Once a sinner near despair,
Sought thy mercy-seat by pray'r;
Mercy heard and set him free;
Lord, that mercy came to me.

5 Many days have pass'd since then,
Many changes I have seen;
Yet have been upheld till now;
Who could hold me up thou.

6 Thou hast help'd in ev'ry need;
This emboldens me to plead:
After so much mercy past,
Canst thou let me sink at last?

7 No—I must maintain my hold,
'Tis thy goodness makes me bold,
I can no denial take,
When I plead for Jesus' sake.

125   METRE 5.   *Hotham.*

1 JESUS! lover of my soul,
    Let me to thy bosom fly,
While the raging billows roll—,
    While the tempest still is high!

Hide me, O my Savior, hide,
  Till the storm of life is past;
Safe into the haven guide;
  O, receive my soul at last.

2 Other refuge have I none,—
  Hangs my helpless soul on thee;
Leave, ah leave me not alone,
  Still support and comfort me;
All my *trust* on thee is stay'd,
  All my *help* from thee I bring;
Cover my defenceless head
  With the shadow of thy wing.

3 Thou, O Christ, art all I want;
  All in all in thee I find!
Raise the fallen, cheer the faint,
  Heal the sick, and lead the blind,
Just and holy is thy name,
  I am all unrighteousness;
Vile and full of sin I am,
  Thou art full of truth and grace.

4 Plenteous grace with thee is found,
  Grace to pardon all my sins—
Let the healing stream abound;
  Make and keep me pure within;
Thou of life the fountain art,
  Freely let me take of thee:
Spring thou up within my heart,
  Rise to all eternity.

126   L. M.   *Conformity*

1 JESUS, my Savior, let me be
  More perfectly conformed to thee;

SUPPLICATION. 115

Implant each grace, each sin dethrone,
And form my temper like thine own.

2 My foe, when hungry let me feed,
Share in his grief, supply his need:
The haughty frown may I not fear,
But with a lowly meekness bear.

3 Let the envenom'd heart and tongue,
The hand outstretched to do me wrong,
Excite no feelings in my breast,
But such as Jesus once express'd.

4 To others let me always give
What I from others would receive;
Good deeds for evil ones return,
Nor when provoked, with anger burn.

5 This will proclaim how bright and fair
The precepts of the gospel are;
And God himself, the God of love,
His own resemblance will approve.

127   METRE S. *Missionary Farewell.*

1 GO watch and pray, thou canst not tell
   How near the hour of death may be;
Thou canst not know how soon the bell
   May toll its doleful notes for thee:
Death's countless snares beset thy way,
Frail child of dust, go watch and pray.

2 Fond youth, while free from blighting care
   And while thy vig'rous pulse beats high
Do hope's glad visions bright and fair,
   Dilate thy young and sparkling eye.

8*

Soon these must change, must pass away;
Frail child of dust, go watch and pray.

3 Thou aged man, life's wintry storm
　　Hath sear'd thy past and vernal bloom;
　With trembling limbs and wasting form,
　　Now thou art bending o'er the tomb,
And can vain hope lead thee astray?
Go, weary pilgrim, watch and pray.

4 Ambition, stop thy panting breath,
　　Pride humble sink thy lifted eye;
　Behold the caverns dark with death,
　　Which now before you open lie:
The heavenly warning now obey,
Ye sons of pride, go watch and pray.

128　　　Metre 5.　　Divine Inquiry.

1 LORD, we come before thee now,
　At thy feet we humbly bow:
　O! do not our suit disdain;
　Shall we seek thee, Lord, in vain?

2 Lord, on thee our souls depend;
　In compassion now descend;
　Fill our hearts with thy rich grace,
　Tune our lips to sing thy praise.

3 In thine own appointed way,
　Now we seek thee, here we stay;
　Lord, we know not how to go,
　Till a blessing thou bestow.

4 Send some message from thy word,
　That may peace and joy afford;

SUPPLICATION.

Let thy Spirit now impart
Full salvation to each heart.

Comfort those who weep and mourn,
Let the time of joy return;
Those that are cast down, lift up;
Make them strong in faith and hope.

6 Grant that all may seek and find
Thee a gracious God, and kind;
Heal the sick the captive free,
Let us all rejoice in thee.

---

129   S. M.   *Aylesbury.*

1 MY soul, be on thy guard,
  Ten thousand foes arise;
And hosts of sins are pressing hard,
  To draw thee from the skies.

2 O watch, and fight, and pray,
  The battle ne'er give o'er:
Renew it boldly every day,
  And help divine implore.

3 Ne'er think the vict'ry won,
  Nor once at ease sit down:
Thy arduous work will not be done,
  Till thou hast got thy crown.

4 Fight on, my soul, till death
  Shall bring thee to thy God:
He'll take thee at thy parting breath,
  Up to his blest abode.

130 C. M. *Rochester.*

1 APPROACH, my soul, the mercy seat,
   Where Jesus answers prayer;
 There humbly fall before his feet,
   For none can perish there.

2 Thy promise is my only plea,
   With this I venture nigh;
 Thou callest burden's souls to thee,
   And such, O Lord, am I.

3 Bow'd down beneath a load of sin,
   By Satan sorely prest;
 By war without, and fears within,
   I come to thee for rest.

4 Be thou my shield and hiding place!
   That, shelter'd near thy side,
 I may my fierce accuser face,
   And tell him, thou hast died.

5 O wond'rous love to bleed and die,
   To bear the cross and shame;
 That guilty sinners, such as I,
   Might plead thy gracious name.

6 "Poor tempest tossed soul, be still,
   My promised grace receive;"
 'Tis Jesus speaks—I must—I will,
   I can, I do believe.

131 L. M. *Windham.*

1 HOW long O Lord, shall I complain,
   Like one who seeks his God in vain?

Canst thou thy face forever hide,
And I still pray, and be denied?

2 Shall I forever be forgot,
As one whom thou regardest not?
Still shall my soul thy absence mourn?
And still despair of thy return?

3 How long shall my poor troubled breast
Be with these anxious thoughts oppress'd?
And Satan, my malicious foe,
Rejoice to see me sunk so low?

4 Hear, Lord, and grant me quick relief,
Before my death concludes my grief;
If thou withhold'st thy heav'nly light,
I sleep in everlasting night.

5 How will the powers of darkness boast,
If but one praying soul be lost!
But I have trusted in thy grace,
And shall again behold thy face.

6 Whate'er my fears or foes suggest,
Thou art my hope, my joy, my rest;
My heart shall feel thy love, and raise
My cheerful voice to songs of praise.

132   S. M. *Little Marlborough.*

1 WITH humble heart and tongue,
    My God, to thee I pray:
Oh, make me learn, while I am young,
    How I may cleanse my way.

2 Make an unguarded youth
    The object of thy care;

Help me to choose the way of truth,
  And fly from every snare.

3 My heart, to folly prone,
   Renew by pow'r divine;
 Unite it to thyself alone,
   And make me wholly thine.

4 Oh, let thy word of grace
   My warmest thoughts employ;
 Be this, through all my following days,
   My treasure and my joy.

5 To what thy laws impart,
   Be my whole soul inclined;
 Oh, let them dwell within my heart,
   And sanctify my mind.

6 May thy young servant learn,
   By these to cleanse his way;
 And may I here the path discern,
   That leads to endless day.

133   C. M.   *Dublin.*

1 PRAYER is the soul's sincere desire,
   Unuttered or express'd,
 The motion of a hidden fire
   That trembles in the breast.

2 Prayer is the burden of a sigh,
   The falling of a tear;
 The upward glancing of an eye,
   When none but God is near.

3 Prayer is the simplest form of speech
   That infant lips can try;

SUPPLICATION.

 Prayer the sublimest strains that reach
  The majesty on high.

4 Prayer is the Christian's vital breath,
  The Christian's native air,
 His watchword at the gate of death—
  He enters heaven with prayer.

5 Prayer is the contrite sinner's voice
  Returning from his ways,
 While angels in their songs rejoice,
  And say—"Behold he prays."

134   L. M.   *Old Hundred.*

1 WHAT various hind'rances we meet,
  In coming to a mercy-seat!
 Yet who that knows the worth of pray'r
 But wishes to be often there.

2 Pray'r makes the darkened cloud withdraw,
 Pray'r climbs the ladder Jacob saw—
 Gives exercise to faith and love—
 Brings every blessing from above.

3 Restraining pray'r—we cease to fight;
 Pray'r makes the Christian's armor bright;
 And Satan trembles when he sees
 The weakest saint upon his knees.

4 Have you no words?—Ah, think again;
 Words flow apace when you complain,
 And fill your fellow-creature's ear
 With the sad tale of all your care.

5 Were half the breath thus vainly spent,
 To heaven in supplication sent—

Your cheerful song would oft'ner be,
"Hear what the Lord hath done for me!"

135   METRE 5.   *Cookham.*

1 HOLY Jesus, lovely Lamb,
    Thine and only thine I am;
  Take my body, spirit, soul,
  Only thou possess the whole.

2 Thou my dearest object be,
  Let me ever cleave to thee;
  Let me choose the better part,
  Let me give thee all my heart.

3 Whom have I on earth below?
  Only thee I wish to know:
  Whom have I in heav'n but thee?
  Thou art all in all to me.

4 All my treasure is above,
  My best portion is thy love:
  Who the worth of love can tell?
  Infinite, unsearchable!

5 Nothing else may I require;
  Let me thee alone desire;
  Pleased with what thy love provides,
  Wean'd from all the world besides.

136   METRE 16.   *Mendon.*

1 LAMB of God for sinners slain,
    To thee I humbly pray;
  Heal me of my grief and pain,
    O take my sins away.

SUPPLICATION.

From this bondage, Lord, release;
  No longer let me be oppress'd;
Jesus, Master, seal my peace,
  And take me to thy breast.

2 Wilt thou cast a sinner out,
    Who humbly comes to thee?
  No, my God, I cannot doubt,
    Thy mercy is for me:
  Let me then obtain the grace,
    And be of Paradise possess'd:
  Jesus, Master, seal my peace,
    And take me to thy breast.

3 Worldly good I do not want:
    Be that to others giv'n:
  Only for thy love I pant;
    My all on earth or heav'n;
  This the crown I fain would seize,
    The good wherewith I would be blest:
  Jesus, Master, seal my peace,
    And take me to thy breast.

4 This delight I fain would prove,
    And then resign my breath,
  Join the happy few whose love,
    Was mightier than death.
  Let it not my Lord displease,
    That I would die to be thy guest!
  Jesus, Master, seal my peace,
    And take me to thy breast.

137 METRE 12. *Deliverance*

1 HOW shall a lost sinner in pain,
  Recover his forfeited peace?

When brought into bondage again,
  What hope of a second release?
Will mercy itself be so kind
  To spare such a rebel as me?
And O, can I possibly find
  Such plenteous redemption in thee?

2 O Jesus, of thee I inquire,
  If still thou art able to save,
The brand to pluck out of the fire,
  And ransom my soul from the grave?
The help of thy Spirit restore,
  And show me the life-giving blood;
And pardon a sinner once more,
  And bring me again unto God.

O Jesus, in pity draw near,
  Come quickly to help a lost soul,
To comfort a mourner appear,
  And make a poor Lazarus whole:
The balm of thy mercy apply,
  Thou seest the sore anguish I feel;
Save, Lord, or I perish, I die,
  O save, or I sink into hell!

4 I sink if thou longer delay
  Thy pardoning mercy to show:
Come quickly, and kindly display,
  The pow'r of thy passion below:
By all thou hast done for my sake,
  One drop of thy blood I implore:
Now, now let it touch me, and make
  The sinner a sinner no more.

SUPPLICATION.

138 C. M. *Bangor—Balerma.*

1 JESUS, thou art the sinner's friend,
  As such, I look to thee;
Now in the bowels of thy love,
  O Lord, remember me!

2 Remember thy pure word of grace,
  Remember Calvary!
Remember all thy dying groans,
  And then remember me.

3 Thou wondrous Advocate with God,
  I yield myself to thee;
While thou art sitting on thy throne,
  O Lord, remember me!

4 I own I'm guilty, own I'm vile,
  But thy salvation's free;
Then in thy all-abounding grace,
  O Lord, remember me!

5 Howe'er forsaken or distress'd,
  Howe'er oppress'd I be;
Howe'er afflicted here on earth,
  Do thou remember me!

6 And when I close my eyes in death,
  And creature helps all flee,
Then O my great Redeemer God,
  I pray, remember me!

139 C. M. *Dublin.*

1 LORD, teach thy servants how to pray,
  With rev'rence and with fear;
Though dust and ashes, yet we may,
We must to thee draw near.

2 We come, then, God of grace, to thee !
  Give broken, contrite hearts;
Give what thine eye delights to see,
  Truth in the inward parts.

3 Give deep humility—the sense
  Of godly sorrow give;
A strong desiring confidence
  To see thy face and live.

4 Give faith in that one Sacrifice
  Which can for sin atone;
To cast our hopes, to fix our eyes
  On Christ—on Christ alone.

5 Give patience still to wait and weep,
  Though mercy long delay —
Courage our fainting souls to keep,
  And trust thee, though thou slay.

6 Give these—and then thy will be done !
  Thus strengthened with all might,
We, through thy Spirit and thy Son,
  Shall pray, and pray aright.

140   Metre 10.   *Unitia—Stockbridge*

1 COME Lord from above, the mountains remove,
O'erturn all that hinders the course of thy love
My bosom inspire, enkindle the fire,
And wrap my whole soul in the flames of desire.

2 I languish and pine for the comfort divine.
O when shall I say, my Beloved is mine ?
I've chosen the good part, my portion thou art:
O Love, let me find thee, O God, in my heart !

3 For this my heart sighs, nothing else can suffice:
How Lord, can I purchase the pearl of great price?

It cannot be bought; thou know'st I have nought,
Not an action, a word, or a truly good thought.

4 But I hear a voice say, without money you may
Receive it, whoever hath nothing to pay;
Who on Jesus relies, without money or price,
The pearl of forgiveness and holiness buys,

5 The blessing is free, so, Lord, let it be:
I yield that thy love should be given to me:
I freely receive what thou freely dost give,
And consent to thy love, in thine Eden to live

6 The gift I embrace, the Giver I praise,
And ascribe my salvation to Jesus' grace;
It came from above, the foretaste I prove,
And I soon shall receive all thy fulness of love

141.   C. M.   *Suffield.*

1 MY God, consider my distress,
   Let mercy plead my cause;
Though I have sinned against thy grace,
   I ne'er forget thy laws.

2 Forbid, forbid the sharp reproach,
   Which I so justly fear;
Uphold my life, uphold my hope,
   Nor let my shame appear.

3 Be thou a surety, Lord, for me,
   Nor let the proud oppress;
But make thy waiting servant see
   The shinings of thy face.

4 My eyes with expectation fail;
   My heart within me cries.

"When will the Lord his truth fulfill,
 And bid my comforts rise?

5 Look down upon my sorrows, Lord,
 And show thy grace the same;
Thy tender mercies still afford
 To those that love thy name.

142   C. M.   *Liberty Hall.*

1 WITH my whole heart I've sought thy face,
 O let me never stray
From thy commands, O God of grace,
 Nor tread the sinners way.

2 Thy word I've hid within my heart,
 To keep my conscience clean,
And be an everlasting guard
 From every rising sin.

3 I'm a companion of the saints,
 Who fear and love the Lord;
My sorrows rise, my nature faints,
 When men transgress thy word.

4 While sinners do thy gospel wrong,
 My Spirit stands in awe;
My soul abhors a lying tongue,
 But loves thy righteous law.

5 My heart with sacred rev'rence hears
 The threat'nings of thy word;
My flesh, with holy trembling, fears
 The judgments of the Lord.

6 My God, I long, I hope, I wait,
 For thy salvation still;

SUPPLICATION.

While thy whole law is my delight,
  And I obey thy will.

143   L. M.   *Portugal.*

1 JESUS, the spring of joys divine,
    Whence all our hopes and comforts flow;
  Jesus, no other name but thine
  Can save us from eternal woe.

2 In vain would boasting reason find
  The way to happiness and God;
  Her weak directions leave the mind
  Bewildered in a dubious road.

3 No other name will heav'n approve:
  Thou art the true, the living Way,
  Ordained by everlasting love,
  To the bright realms of endless day.

4 Here let our constant feet abide,
  Nor from the heavenly path depart;
  O let thy Spirit, gracious Guide!
  Direct our steps and cheer our heart.

5 Safe lead us through this world of night,
  And bring us to the blissful plains,—
  The regions of unclouded light,
  Where perfect joy forever reigns.

144   L. M.   *Alfreton.*

1 JESUS, my Savior, brother, friend,
    On whom I cast my every care,
  On whom for all things I depend,
  Inspire, and then accept my prayer.

2 If I have tasted of thy grace,
  The grace that sure salvation brings;
  If with me now thy Spirit stays,
  And hov'ring, hides me in his wings.

3 Still let him with my weakness stay,
  Nor for a moment's space depart;
  Evil and danger turn away,
  And keep till he renew my heart.

4 When to the right or left I stray,
  His voice behind me may I hear,
  "Return, and walk in Christ the way,
  Fly back to Christ, for sin is near.

5 His sacred unction from above,
  Be still my comforter and guide,
  Till all the stony he remove,
  And in my loving heart reside.

6 Jesus, I fain would walk in thee,
  From nature's every path retreat;
  Thou art my way, my leader be,
  And set upon the rock my feet.

7 Uphold me, Savior, or I fall;
  O reach me out thy gracious hand!
  Only on thee for help I call,
  Only by faith in thee I stand.

145   L. M.   *Bridgewater*

1 COME, gracious Spirit, heav'nly Dove,
  With light and comfort from above,
  Be thou our guardian, thou our guide,
  O'er ev'ry thought and step preside.

SUPPLICATION.

2 Conduct us safe, conduct us far
From every sin and hurtful snare;
Lead to thy word that rules must give,
And teach us lessons how to live.

3 The light of truth to us display,
And make us know and choose thy way;
Plant holy fear in every heart,
That we from God may ne'er depart.

4 Lead us to holiness the road
That we must take to dwell with God;
Lead us to Christ, the living Way,
Nor let us from his pastures stray.

5 Lead us to God, our final rest,
In his enjoyment to be bless'd;
Lead us to heav'n, the seat of bliss,
Where pleasure in perfection is.

INVITATION.

146   Metre 5.   *Sincerity.*

1 JESUS' precious name excels
Jordan's streams and Salem's wells;
Thirsty sinners, come and draw,
Quench the flames of Sinai's law.

2 Fearful sinners, come and try;
Draw and drink a sweet supply;
Christ is ever full and free;
Sinner, come, where'er you be.

3 See the waters springing up,
  To revive your languid hope;
  Fill your vessels as it rolls,
  And refresh your weary souls.

4 Lo! the Spirit now invites!
  Lo! the cheerful bride unites:
  Jesus calls, be not afraid,
  Lo! for you the well was made.

5 Haste you to the Lamb of God,
  Seek salvation in his blood:
  In it there is boundless store
  For ten thousand thousand more.

6 Let us still our vessels bring
  To the soul-refreshing spring:
  Constant let our praises rise,
  Till we drink above the skies.

147   C. M.   *Christ's Invitation.*

1 AMAZING sight! the Savior stands,
    And knocks at every door!
  Ten thousand blessings in his hands
    To satisfy the poor.

2 "Behold," he saith, "I bleed and die
    To bring you to my rest:—
  Hear, sinner, while I'm passing by,
    And be forever blest.

3 "Will you despise my bleeding love,
    And choose the way to hell?
  Or in the glorious realms above,
    With me forever dwell?

4 "Not to condemn your wretched race
    Have I in judgment come;
But to display unbounded grace,
    And bring lost sinners home.

5 "Will you go down to endless night,
    And bear eternal pain?
Or in the glorious realms of light
    With me forever reign?

6 "Say—will you hear my gracious voice,
    And have your sins forgiv'n?
Or will you make that wretched choice,
    And bar yourselves from heav'n?"

148   L. M.   *Bourbon*

1 TO DAY, if ye will hear his voice,
    Now is the time to make your choice:
Say, will you to Mount Zion go?
Say, will you have this Christ or no?

2 Ye wandering souls, who find no rest,
Say, will you be forever blest?
Will you be saved from sin and hell?
Will you with Christ in glory dwell?

3 Come now, dear youth, for ruin bound,
Obey the gospel's joyful sound;
Come, go with us, and you shall prove
The joy of Christ's Redeeming love.

4 Once more we ask you in his name—
For yet his love remains the same—
Say, will you to Mount Zion go?
Say, will you have this Christ or no?

5 Leave all your sports and glittering toys,
Come share with us eternal joys;
Or must we leave you bound to hell—
Then, dear young friends, a long farewell.

149   Metre 60.   *Healing Fountain.*

1 SEE the Fountain open'd wide,
That from pollution frees us,
Flowing from the wounded side
Of our Immanuel Jesus?

CHORUS
Ho! every one that thirsts,
Come ye to the waters;
Freely drink and quench your thirst,
With Zion's sons and daughters.

2 Sinners, hear the Savior's call,
Consider what you're doing:
Jesus Christ can cleanse you all,
Will you not come unto him?

Ho! every one that thirsts, &c.

3 Dying sinners, come and try;
These waters will relieve you:
Without money come and buy,
For Christ will freely give you.

Ho! every one that thirsts, &c.

4 He who drinks shall never die;
These waters fail him never;
Sinners come, and now apply,
And drink, and live forever.

Ho! every one that thirsts, &c.

INVITATION.

5 Weeping Mary, full of grief,
   Came begging for these waters:
Jesus gave her full relief,
   With Zion's sons and daughters.
     Ho! every one that thirsts, &c.

6 See the woman at the well,
   Conversing with the Savior;
Soon she found that he could tell
   The whole of her behavior.
     Ho! every one that thirsts, &c.

7 When she asked, and thus obtain'd
   A drink, her heart was flaming;
Thus the gift divine she gain'd,
   And ran to town proclaiming,
     Ho! every one that thirsts, &c.

8 The thief had only time to think,
   And tell the doleful story;
Jesus gave him leave to drink,—
   He drank, and fled to glory.
     Ho! every one that thirsts, &c.

9 Christians, you can fully tell
   The virtue of these waters;
You were once the heirs of hell,
   But now are sons and daughters.
     Ho! every one that thirsts, &c.

---

150   METRE 10.   *Stockbridge.*

1 O ALL that pass by, to Jesus draw near;
   He utters a cry, ye sinners, give ear!
From hell to retrieve you he spreads out his hands
Now, now to receive you he graciously stands.

2 If any man thirst and happy would be,
 The vilest and worst may come unto me;
 May drink of my Spirit, excepted is none,
 Lay claim to my merit, and take for his own.

3 Whoever receives the life-giving word,
 In Jesus believes, his God and his Lord;
 In him a pure river of life shall arise;
 Shall in the believer spring up to the skies.

4 My God and my Lord! thy call I obey,
 My soul on thy word of promise I stay:
 Thy kind invitation I gladly embrace,
 Athirst for salvation, salvation by grace.

5 O hasten the hour, send down from above
 The Spirit of power, of health and of love:
 Of filial fear, of knowledge and grace;
 Of wisdom and prayer, of joy and of praise:

6 The Spirit of faith, of faith in thy blood,
 Which saves us from wrath and brings us to God;
 Removes the huge mountain of indwelling sin,
 And opens a fountain that washes us clean.

151 METRE II. *Watchman's Call.*

1 WHY sleep we, my brethren! come let us arise.
 O why should we slumber in sight of the prize;
 Salvation is nearer, our days are far spent.
 O let us be active; awake and repent.

2 Oh how can we slumber! the Master is come.
 And calling on sinners to seek them a home;
 The Spirit and Bride now in concert unite,
 The weary they welcome, the careless invite.

INVITATION. 137

3 O, how can we slumber, our foes are awake :
To ruin poor souls every effort they make,
T' accomplish their object no means are untried,
The careless they comfort, the wakeful misguide.

4 O, how can we slumber when so much was done
To purchase salvation by Jesus the Son !
Now mercy is proffered, and justice display'd.
Now God can be honored and sinners be saved.

5 O, how can we slumber, when death is so near,
And sinners are sinking to endless despair :
Now prayers may avail and gain the high prize.
Before they in torment shall lift up their eyes.

6 O, how can ye slumber, ye sinners, look round.
Before the last trumpet your hearts shall confound ;
O, fly to the Savior, he calls thee to-day :
While mercy is waiting, O make no delay.

152   Metre 10.   *Stockbridge.*

1 YE thirsty for God, to Jesus give ear.
And take, through his blood, a power to draw near ;
His kind invitation, ye sinners, embrace.
Accepting salvation, salvation by grace.

2 Send down from above, who governs the skies.
In vehement love, to sinners, he cries,
"Drink into my Spirit who happy would be,
And all things inherit by coming to me."

3 O Savior of all, thy word we believe,
And come at thy call, thy grace to receive ;
The blessing is given wherever thou art :
The earnest of heaven is love in the heart.

4 To us at thy feet, the Comforter give;
Who gasp to admit thy Spirit and live;
The weakest believers acknowledge for thine,
And fill us with rivers of water divine.

153 METRE 33. *Star in the East.*

1 RESTLESS thy Spirit, poor wandering sinner,
 Restless and roving—O come to thy home!
Return to the arms—to the bosom of mercy;
The Savior of sinners invites thee to come.

2 Darkness surrounds thee, and tempes's are rising
Fearful and dangerous the path thou hast trod:
But mercy shines forth in the rainbow of promise,
To welcome the wanderer home to his God.

3 Peace to the storm in thy soul shall be spoken
Guilt from thy bosom be banish'd away;
And heav'n's sweet breezes, o'er death's rolling billows,
Shall waft thee at last to the regions of day.

4 But oh, if regardless of God's gracious warning
Afar from his favor your soul must remove;
May you never hear—never feel the dread sentence;
But live to his glory, and die in his love.

154 L. M. *Abingdon.*

1 HARK! the Redeemer, from on high,
 Sweetly invites his favorites nigh;
From caves of darkness and of doubt,
He gently speaks and calls us out.

2 "My dove, who hidest in the rock,
　Thine heart almost with sorrow broke;
　Lift up thy face, forget thy fear,
　And let thy voice delight mine ear.

3 "Thy voice to me sounds ever sweet;
　My graces in thy countenance meet;
　Though the vain world thy face despise,
　'Tis bright and comely in mine eyes."

4 Dear Lord, our thankful heart receives
　The hope thine invitation gives;
　To thee our joyful lips shall raise
　The voice of prayer and of praise.

5 I am my Love's and he is mine,
　Our hearts, our hopes, our passions join;
　Nor let a motion nor a word,
　Nor thought, arise to grieve my Lord.

6 My soul to pastures fair he leads,
　Among the lilies where he feeds;
　Among the saints, (whose robes are white
　Washed in his blood) is his delight.

7 Till the day break and shadows flee,
　Till the sweet dawning light I see,
　Thine eyes to me-ward often turn,
　Nor let my soul in darkness mourn.

8 Be like a hart on mountains green,
　Leap o'er the hills of fear and sin;
　Nor guilt, nor unbelief, divide
　My Love, my Savior, from my side.

155   Metre 9.   Lenox.

1 Come, every pious heart,
   That loves the Savior's name,
Your noblest pow'rs exert,
   To celebrate his fame :
Tell all above, and all below,
The debt of love to him you owe.

2 Such was his zeal for God,
   And such his love for you,
He noble undertook
   What Gabriel could not do ;
His every deed of love and grace
All words exceed and thoughts surpass.

3 He left his starry crown,
   And laid his robes aside ;
On wings of love came down,
   And wept, and bled, and died :
What he endured, O who can tell,
To save our souls from death and hell !

4 From the dark grave he rose,
   The mansions of the dead ;
And thence his mighty foes,
   In glorious triumph led :
Up through the sky the Conq'ror rode,
And reigns on high, the Savior God.

5 From thence he'll quickly come,
   His chariot will not stay,
And bear our spirits home
   To realms of endless day :
There shall we see his lovely face,
And ever be in his embrace.

5 Jesus, we ne'er can pay
  The debt we owe thy love,
Yet tell us how we may
  Our gratitude approve:
Our hearts, our all to thee we give:
The gift, though small, thou wilt receive.

156   C. M.   *Divinity.*

1 OH what amazing words of grace
    Are in the gospel found!
  Suited to every sinner's case,
    Who knows the joyful sound.

2 Poor, sinful, thirsty, fainting souls,
    Are freely welcome here;
  Salvation like a river, rolls
    Abundant, free, and clear.

3 Come then, with all your wants and wounds,
    Your every burden bring!
  Here love, unchanging love abounds,
    A deep, celestial spring!

4 Whoever will—O gracious word!
    Shall of this stream partake:
  Come thirsty souls, and bless the Lord,
    And drink for Jesus' sake!

5 Millions of sinners, vile as you,
    Have here found life and peace;
  Come, then, and prove its virtues too,
    And drink, adore, and bless.

157   C. M.   *Rochester.*

1 THE Savior calls—let every ear
    Attend the heav'nly sound:

142 INVITATION.

Ye doubting souls, dismiss your fear,
  Hope smiles reviving round.

2 For every thirsty, longing heart,
  Here streams of bounty flow:
And life, and health, and bliss impart,
  To banish mortal woe.

3 Here springs of sacred pleasure rise,
  To ease your every pain;
(Immortal fountain! full supplies!)
  Nor shall we thirst in vain.

4 Ye sinners, come—'tis mercy's voice,
  The gracious call obey:
Mercy invites to heav'nly joys—
  And can you yet delay?

5 Dear Savior, draw reluctant hearts,
  To thee let sinners fly,
And take the bliss thy love imparts,
  And drink, and never die.

158   L. M.   Hebron.
1 WHILE life prolongs its precious light,
  Mercy is found, and peace is given;
But soon, ah soon! approaching night
  Shall blot out every hope of heaven.

2 While God invites, how blest the day!
  How sweet the gospel's joyful sound!
"Come sinners, haste, oh haste away,
  While yet a pardoning God he's found.

3 Soon, borne on time's most rapid wing,
  Shall death command you to the grave,

INVITATION.

Before his bar your spirits bring,
  And none be found to hear or save.

4 In that lone land of deep despair,
  No Sabbath's heavenly light shall rise;
No God regard your bitter prayer,
  Nor Savior call you to the skies."

5 No wonders to the dead are shown,
  (The wonders of redeeming love;)
No voice his glorious truth makes known,
  Nor sings the bliss of climes above.

6 Silence, and solitude, and gloom,
  In these forgetful realms appear,
Deep sorrows fill the dismal tomb,
  And hope shall never enter there.

159   C. M.   *Awful Majesty.*

1 SINNERS, the voice of God regard;
    'Tis mercy speaks to-day;
  He calls you by his sov'reign word,
    From sin's destructive way.

2 Like the rough sea that cannot rest,
    You live devoid of peace;
  A thousand stings within your breast
    Deprive your souls of ease.

3 Your way is dark and leads to hell;
    Why will you persevere?
  Can you in endless torments dwell,
    Shut up in black despair?

4 Why will you in the crooked ways
    Of sin and folly go?

In pain you travel all your days,
  To reap immortal woe!

5 But he that turns to God shall live,
  Through his abounding grace:
His mercy will the guilt forgive
  Of those that seek his face.

6 Bow to the sceptre of his word,
  Renouncing every sin;
Submit to him your sov'reign Lord,
  And learn his will divine.

7 His love exceeds your highest thoughts;
  He pardons like a God;
He will forgive your num'rous faults,
  Through a Redeemer's blood.

160   L. M.   *Devotion.*

1 THE voice of my Beloved sounds,
  Over the rocks and rising grounds;
O'er hills of guilt, and seas of grief,
He leaps, he flies to my relief.

2 Now, through the vail of flesh, I see,
With eyes of love he looks at me;
Now in the gospel's clearest glass,
He shows the beauties of his face.

3 Gently he draws my heart along,
Both with his beauties and his tongue;
"Rise," saith my Lord, "make haste away,
No mortal joys are worth thy stay.

4 "The Jewish wintry state is gone,
The mists are fled, the spring comes on,

INVITATION.

The sacred turtle-dove we hear
Proclaim the new, the joyful year.

5 "Th' immortal Vine of heavenly root,
Blossoms and buds, and gives her fruit.'
Lo, we are come to taste the wine :
Our souls rejoice and bless the Vine.

6 And when we hear our Jesus say,
"Rise up, my Love and, haste away ;"
Our hearts would fain outfly the wind,
And leave all earthly love behind.

161   METRE 40.   *Boundless Mercy.*

1 DROOPING souls, no longer grieve,
   Heaven is propitious;
If in Christ you do believe,
   You will find him precious;
Jesus now is passing by,
   Calls the mourners to him,
Brings salvation from on high—
   Now look up and view him.

2 From his hands, his feet, his side,
   Runs the healing lotion;
See the consolating tide,
   Boundless as the ocean:
See the healing waters move
   For the sick and dying;
Now resolve to gain his love,
   Or to perish trying.

3 Grace's store is ever free
   Drooping souls to gladden;
Jesus calls, "Come unto me
   Ye weary, heavy laden;

INVITATION.

Though your sins like mountains high.
  Rise and reach to heaven;
Soon as you on me rely,
  All shall be forgiven."

4 Now methinks I hear one say,
  I will go and prove him;
If he takes my sins away,
  Surely I shall love him.
Yes! I see the Father smile.
  Now I lose my burden;
All is grace—for I am vile,
  Yet he seals my pardon.

5 Streaming mercy, how it flows!
  Now I know, I feel it;
Tongue cannot the half disclose,
  Yet I long to tell it.
Jesus' blood has heal'd my wound:
  O the wondrous blessing!
I, through mercy now have found,
  All in him possessing.

162   L. M.   *Tender Thought.*
1 COME hither, all ye weary souls,
    Ye heavy laden sinners, come,
  I'll give you rest from all your toils,
    And bring you to my heav'nly home.

2 "They shall find rest that learn of me:
    I'm of a meek and lowly mind:
  But passion rages like the sea,
    And pride is restless as the wind.

3 "Bless'd is the man whose shoulders take
    My yoke and bear it with delight;

My yoke is easy to his neck,
  My grace shall make the burden light.

4 Jesus, we come at thy command:
  With faith, and hope, and humble zeal,
  Resign our spirits to thy hand,
  To mould and guide us at thy will.

163 METRE 56. *Royal Proclamation.*

1 HEAR the royal proclamation,
  The glad tidings of salvation,
  Publishing to every creature,
  To the ruin'd sons of nature.

CHORUS.

  Jesus reigns, he reigns victorious,
  Over heav'n and earth most glorious.
    Jesus reigns.

2 See the royal banner flying,
  Hear the heralds loudly crying,
  "Rebel sinners, royal favor
  Now is offered by the Savior.
    Jesus reigns.

3 Turn unto the Lord most holy,
  Shun the paths of vice and folly;
  Turn, or you are lost forever;
  Oh! now turn to God the Savior.
    Jesus reigns.

4 Here is wine, and milk, and honey,
  Come and purchase without money;
  Mercy, flowing like a fountain,
  Streaming from the holy mountain.
    Jesus reigns.

INVITATION.

5 For this love, let rocks and mountains,
Purling streams, and crystal fountains,
Roaring thunders, lightning blazes,
Shout the great Messiah's praises.
    Jesus reigns.

164   METRE 7.   *Dresden*

1 COME ye sinners, poor and needy,
  Weak and wounded, sick and sore,
Jesus ready stands to save you,
  Full of pity, love and pow'r;
    He is able,
  He is willing, doubt no more.

2 Now, ye needy, come and welcome,
  God's free bounty glorify;
True belief and true repentance,
  Every grace that brings you nigh,
    Without money
  Come to Jesus Christ and buy.

3 Let not conscience make you linger,
  Nor of fitness fondly dream;
All the fitness he requireth
  Is to feel your need of him;
    This he gives you,
  'Tis the Spirit's glimm'ring beam

Come ye weary, heavy-laden,
  Bruised and mangled by the fall,
If you tarry till you're better,
  You will never come at all,
    Not the righteous,
  Sinners Jesus came to call.

INVITATION.

5 Agonizing in the garden,
  Lo! your Maker prostrate lies!
On the bloody tree behold him,
  Hear him cry before he dies,
    "It is finish'd!"
  Sinners, will not this suffice?

6 Lo! th' incarnate God ascending
  Pleads the merit of his blood;
Venture on him, venture freely;
  Let no other trust intrude:
    None but Jesus,
  Can do helpless sinners good.

7 Saints and angels join in concert,
  Sing the praises of the Lamb,
While the blissful seats of heaven
  Sweetly echo with his name:
    Halielujah!
  Sinners here may do the same.

165   C. M.   *Mear.*

1 YE wretched, hungry, starving poor,
    Behold a royal feast!
  Where mercy spreads her bounteous store,
    For every humble guest.

2 There Jesus stands with open arms;
    He calls—he bids you come:
  Though guilt restrains, and fear alarms,
    Behold, there yet is room.

3 Oh come, and with his children taste
    The blessings of his love;
  While hope expects the sweet repast
    Of nobler joys above.

INVITATION.

4 There, with united heart and voice,
   Before th' Eternal throne,
Ten thousand thousand souls rejoice,
   In songs on earth unknown.

5 And yet ten thousand thousand more
   Are welcome still to come :
Ye longing souls, the grace adore,
   And enter while there's room.

166 S. M. *Aylesbury.*

1 YE sinners, fear the Lord,
   While yet 'tis called to-day ;
Soon will the awful voice of death
   Command your soul away.

2 Soon will the harvest close ;
   The summer soon be o'er ;
And soon your injured, angry God,
   Will hear your prayers no more.

Then while 'tis called to-day,
   O hear the gospel sound ;
Come, sinner, haste—oh haste away,
   While pardon may be found.

COMFORT IN TRIBULATION.

167 C. M. *Augusta.*

1 IF Paul in Cesar's court must stand,
   He need not fear the sea ;

Secured from harm on every hand
  By the divine decree.

2 Although the ship wherein he sail'd,
    By dreadful storm was toss'd;
  The promise over all prevail'd
    And not a life was lost.

3 Jesus, the God whom Paul adored,
    Who saves in time of need
  Was then confess'd by all on board
    A present help indeed.

4 Though neither sun nor stars were seen,
    Paul knew the Lord was near,
  And faith preserved his soul serene,
    When others shook with fear.

5 Believers thus are toss'd about
    On life's tempestuous main,
  But grace assures beyond a doubt,
    They shall their port attain.

6 They must, they shall appear one day,
    Before their Savior's throne;
  The storms they meet with by the way
    But make his power known.

7 Their passage lies across the brink
    Of many a threat'ning wave;
  The world expects to see them sink,
    But Jesus lives to save.

8 Lord, though we are but feeble worms,
    Yet since thy word is past,
  We'll venture through a thousand storms,
    To see thy face at last.

COMFORT IN TRIBULATION.

168　　　C. M.　　　*Solon.*

1 OPPRESS'D with fear, oppress'd with grief,
　　To God I breath'd my cry:
　His mercy brought divine relief,
　　And wiped my tearful eye.

2 His mercy chased the shades of death,
　　And snatch'd me from the grave:
　O may his praise employ that breath
　　Which mercy deigns to save.

3 Come, O ye saints! your voices raise
　　To God in grateful songs:
　And let the memory of his grace
　　Inspire your hearts and tongues.

4 Her deepest gloom, when sorrow spreads,
　　And light and hope depart,
　His smiles celestial morning sheds,
　　And joy revives the heart.

5 Then let my utmost glory be
　　To raise thy honors high:
　Nor let my gratitude to thee
　　In guilty silence die.

6 To thee, my gracious God, I raise
　　My thankful heart and tongue;
　O be thy goodness and thy praise
　　My everlasting song!

169　　　Metre 8.　　*Missionary Farewell.*

1 WOULD Jesus have the sinner die?
　　Why hangs he then on yonder tree?

COMFORT IN TRIBULATION.

What means that strange expiring cry?
  (Sinner, he prays for you and me;)
"Forgive them, Father, O forgive,
They know not that by me they live!"

2 Jesus descended from above,
  Our loss of Eden to retrieve,
Great God of universal love,
  If all the world through thee may live,
In us a quick'ning Spirit be,
And witness thou hast died for me.

3 Thou loving all-atoning Lamb,
  Thee by thy painful agony,
Thy bloody sweat, thy grief and shame,
  Thy cross and passion on the tree,
Thy precious death and life—I pray
Take all, take all my sins away.

4 O let me kiss thy bleeding feet,
  And bathe and wash them with my tears,
The story of thy love repeat
  In every drooping sinner's ears;
That all may hear the quickening sound:
Since I, even I have mercy found.

5 O let thy love my heart constrain,
  Thy love for every sinner free,
That every fallen son of man,
  May taste the grace that found out me;
That all mankind with me may prove,
Thy sovereign, everlasting love.

INFINITE MERCY.

---

170   METRE 5.   *Earnest Call.*

1 DEPTH of mercy! can there be,
  Mercy still reserved for me?
  Can my God his wrath forbear?
  Me, the chief of sinners spare?

2 I have long withstood his grace,
  Long provoked him to his face;
  Would not hearken to his calls,
  Grieved him by a thousand falls.

3 Kindled his relentings are,
  Me he now delights to spare;
  Cries, "How can I give thee up?"
  Lets the lifted thunder drop.

4 There for me the Savior stands:
  Shows his wounds and spreads his hands!
  God is love! I know, I feel;
  Jesus weeps and loves me still.

5 Jesus answer from above,
  Is not all thy nature love?
  Wilt thou not the wrong forget?
  Suffer me to kiss thy feet?

6 Now incline me to repent!
  Let me now my fall lament!
  Now my foul revolt deplore!
  Weep, believe, and sin no more.

171   Metre 11.   *Protection.*

1 HOW firm a foundation, ye saints of the Lord,
Is laid for your faith in his excellent word!
What more can he say than to you he hath said,
Who unto the Savior for refuge have fled?

2 "Fear not, I am with thee, O be not dismay'd,
For I am thy God and will still give thee aid;
I'll strengthen thee, help thee, and cause thee
    to stand,
Upheld by my righteous, omnipotent hand.

3 "When thro' the deep waters I call thee to go,
The rivers of sorrow shall not overflow;
For I will be with thee thy troubles to bless,
And sanctify to thee thy deepest distress.

4 "When thro' fiery trials thy pathway shall lie,
My grace all-sufficient shall be thy supply;
The flames shall not hurt thee—I only design
Thy dross to consume and thy gold to refine.

5 "E'en down to old age my people shall prove,
My sov'reign, eternal, unchangeable love;
And then, when grey hairs shall their temples
    adorn,
Like lambs they shall still in my bosom be borne.

6 "The soul that on Jesus hath lean'd for repose,
I will not, I will not desert to his foes;
That soul, though all hell should endeavor to
    shake,
I'll never, no never, no never forsake.

INFINITE MERCY.

172 C. M. *Rockingham.*

1 HOW condescending and how kind
   Was God's eternal Son!
  Our misery reach'd his heav'nly mind,
   And pity brought him down.

2 When Justice by our sins provoked,
   Drew forth its dreadful sword,
  He gave his soul up to the stroke,
   Without a murm'ring word.

3 He sunk beneath our heavy woes,
   To raise us to his throne;
  There's ne'er a gift his hand bestows,
   But cost his heart a groan.

4 This was compassion like a God,
   That, when the Savior knew
  The price of pardon was his blood,
   His pity ne'er withdrew.

5 Now, though he reigns exalted high,
   His love is still as great:
  Well he remembers Calvary,
   Nor lets his saints forget.

6 Here we behold his bowels roll
   As kind as when he died,
  And see the sorrows of his soul
   Bleed through his wounded side.

7 Here we receive repeated seals
   Of Jesus' dying love;
  Hard is the wretch that never feels
   One soft affection move.

INFINITE MERCY. 157

5 Here let our hearts begin to melt,
  While we his death record,
And, with our joy for pardon'd guilt,
  Mourn that we pierc'd the Lord.

173   Metre 6.   *Refuge*

1 MY God! thy boundless love we praise:
  How bright on high its glories blaze—
    How sweetly bloom below?
  Its streams from thy eternal throne;
  Through heav'n its joys forever run,
    And o'er the earth they flow.

2 'Tis love that gilds the vernal ray,
  Adorns the flowery robe of May;
    Perfumes the breathing gale:
  'Tis love that loads the plenteous plain,
  With blushing fruits and golden grain,
    And smiles o'er every vale.

3 But in thy gospel it appears
  In sweeter, fairer characters,
    And charms the ravished breast:
  There love immortal leaves the skies,
  To wipe the drooping mourner's eyes
    And give the weary rest.

4 There smiles a kind, propitious God,
  There flows a dying Savior's blood,
    The pledge of sins forgiv'n?
  There faith, bright cherub, points the way
  To regions of eternal day,
    And opens all her heav'n.

INFINITE MERCY.

5 Then in redeeming love rejoice,
   My soul!—and hear a Savior's voice,
    That calls thee to the skies;
Above life's empty scenes aspire,
Its sordid cares and mean desire,—
   And seize th' eternal prize.

174.   S. M.   *Ninty-Third.*

1 MY soul, with joy attend,
   While Jesus silence breaks;
No angel's harp such music yields,
   As what my shepherd speaks.

2 "I know my sheep," he cries,
   "My soul approves them well:
Vain is the treach'rous world's disguise,
   And vain the rage of hell.

3 "I freely feed them now
   With tokens of my love;
But richer pastures I prepare,
   And sweeter streams above.

4 "Unnumbered years of bliss
   I to my sheep will give;
And while my throne unshaken stands,
   Shall all my chosen live.

5 "This tried almighty hand,
   Is raised for their defence:
Where is the pow'r shall reach them there?
   Or what shall force them thence."

6 Enough, my gracious Lord,
   Let faith triumphant cry:
My heart can on this promise live,
   Can on this promise die.

THE LOVE OF GOD.

175 L. M. *Devotion.*

1 OF all the joys we mortals know,
   Jesus, thy love exceeds the rest;
Love, the best blessing here below,
   The highest rapture of the blest.

2 While we are held in thine embrace,
   There's not a thought attempts to rove;
Each smile that's seen upon thy face,
   Fixes, and charms, and fires our love.

3 When of thine absence we complain,
   And long, and weep, and humbly pray;
There's a strange pleasure in the pain,
   Those tears are sweet which mourn thy stay.

4 When round thy courts by day we rove,
   Or ask the watchmen of the night
For some kind tidings from above,
   Thy very name creates delight.

5 Jesus, our God, descend and come;
   Our eyes would dwell upon thy face;
'Tis heav'n to see our Lord at home,
   And feel the presence of his grace.

176 L. M. *Kimbolton.*

1 SO let our lives and lips express
   The holy gospel we profess;
So let our works and virtues shine,
   To prove the doctrine all divine.

THE LOVE OF GOD.

2 Thus shall we best proclaim abroad
The honor of our Savior God;
When the salvation reigns within,
And grace subdues the power of sin.

3 Our flesh and sense must be denied;
Passion and envy, lust and pride;
While justice, temperance, truth and love
Our inward piety approve.

4 Religion bears our spirits up,
While we expect that blessed hope,
The bright appearance of the Lord,
And faith stands leaning on his word.

177 L. M. *Bridgewater—Shoel.*

1 WHO is this fair one in distress,
That travels through the wilderness,
And press'd with sorrows and with sins,
On her beloved Lord she leans.

2 This is the spouse of Christ our God,
Bought with the treasure of his blood;
And her request and her complaint,
Is but the voice of every saint.

3 "O let my name engraven stand,
Both on thy heart and on thy hand,
Seal me upon thine arm, and wear
The pledge of love forever there.

4 "Stronger than death thy love is known,
Which floods of wrath could never drown;
And hell and earth in vain combine
To quench a fire so much divine.

5 "But I am jealous of my heart,
　Lest it from thee should once depart;
　Then let thy name be well impress'd,
　As a fair signet on my breast.

6 "Till thou hast brought me to thy home,
　Where fears and doubts can never come,
　Thy count'nance let me often see,
　And often thou shalt hear from me.

7 Come, my beloved, haste away,
　Cut short the hours of thy delay;
　Fly like a youthful hart or roe
　Over the hills where spices grow."

178   Metre 10.   *Unitia.*

1 O TELL me no more of this world's vain store.
　The time for such trifles with me now is o'er;
　A country I've found where true joys abound,
　To dwell I'm determined on that happy ground.

2 The souls that believe, in glory shall live,
　And me in that number will Jesus receive;
　My soul, don't delay—he calls thee away,
　Rise, follow thy Savior, and bless the glad day.

3 No mortal doth know what he can bestow,
　What light, strength & comfort—go after him, go:
　Lo! onward I move to a city above;
　None guesses how wondrous my journey will
　　　prove.

4 Great spoils I shall win from death, hell and sin,
　'Midst outward affliction shall feel Christ within;
　And when I'm to die, receive me, I'll cry,
　For Jesus hath loved me, I cannot tell why.

5 But this I do find, we two are so join'd,
He'll not live in glory and leave me behind,
So this is the race I'm running through grace,
Henceforth, till admitted to see my Lord's face.

6 And now I'm in care, my neighbors may share
These blessings—to seek them will none of you dare?
In bondage, O why! in death will you lie,
When one here assures you free grace is so nigh?

179   Metre 10.   *Stockbridge.*

1 BEGONE unbelief! my Savior is near,
And for my relief will surely appear:
By pray'r let me wrestle, and he will perform,
With Christ in the vessel, I smile at the storm.

2 Though dark be my way, since he is my guide,
'Tis mine to obey, 'tis his to provide:
Though cisterns be broken, and creatures all fail,
The word he has spoken shall surely prevail.

3 His love in time past, forbids me to think
He'll leave me at last in trouble to sink;
Each sweet Ebenezer, I have in review,
Confirms his good pleasure to help me quite thro'.

4 Why should I complain of want and distress?
Temptation or pain?—he told me no less;
The heirs of salvation, I know from his word,
Thro' much tribulation must follow their Lord.

5 Since all that I meet shall work for my good,
The bitter is sweet, the medicine food;
Tho' painful at present, 'twill cease before long,
And then, O how pleasant—the conqueror's song!

THE LOVE OF GOD.

180 METRE 4. *Charleston.*

1 GOD is love; his mercy brightens,
  All the path in which we move:
Bliss he forms, and woe he lightens:
  God is light, and God is love.

2 Chance and change are busy ever;
  Worlds decay, and ages move;
But his mercy waneth never:
  God is light, and God is love.

3 E'en the hour that darkest seemeth
  Will his changeless goodness prove;
From the mist his brightness streameth:
  God is light, and God is love.

4 He with earthly cares entwineth
  Hope and comfort from above;
Every where his glory shineth:
  God is light, and God is love.

181 METRE 21. *Eden of Love.*

1 HOW sweet to reflect on those joys that await me,
In yon blissful region the haven of rest,
Where glorified spirits with welcome shall greet me,
And lead me to mansions prepared for the blest;
Encircled in light, and with glory enshrouded,
My happiness perfect, my mind's sky unclouded,
I'll bathe in the ocean of pleasure unbounded,
And range with delight through the Eden of Love.

THE LOVE OF GOD.

2 While angelic legions, with harps tuned celestial.
  Harmoniously join in the concert of praise,
  The saints, as they flock from the regions terrestrial,
  In loud hallelujahs their voices will raise:
  Then songs of the Lamb shall re-echo through heaven,
  My soul will respond: To Immanuel be given
  All glory, all honor, all might and dominion,
  Who brought us through grace to the Eden of Love.

3 Then hail, blessed state! Hail, ye songsters of glory!
  Ye harpers of bliss, soon I'll meet you above,
  And join your full choir in rehearsing the story,
  "Salvation from sorrow, through Jesus' love."
  Though prisoned in earth, yet by anticipation,
  Already my soul feels a sweet prelibation
  Of joys that await me, when freed from probation:
  My heart's now in heaven, the Eden of Love.

182   Metre 11.   *Conversion.*

1 THY mercy, my God, is the theme of my song,
  The joy of my heart and the boast of my tongue;
  Thy free grace alone, from the first to the last,
  Hath won my affections, and bound my soul fast.

2 Without thy sweet mercy I could not live here:
  Sin soon would reduce me to utter despair:
  But through thy free goodness my spirit revive,
  And he that first made me still keeps me alive.

3 Thy mercy is more than a match for my heart,
  Which wonders to feel its own hardness depart:
  Dissolved by the sunshine, I fall to the ground
  And weep to the praise of the mercy I found.

4 The door of thy mercy stands open all day
  To the poor and the needy who knock by the way:
  No sinner shall ever be empty sent back,
  Who come seeking mercy for Jesus' sake.

5 Thy mercy in Jesus exempts me from hell:
  Its glories I'll sing, and its wonders I'll tell.
  'Twas Jesus, my friend, when he hung on the tree,
  Who open'd the channel of mercy for me.

6 Great Father of Mercies! thy goodness I own,
  And the covenant love of thy crucified Son:
  All praise to the Spirit, whose whisper divine
  Seals mercy, and pardon, and righteousness
      mine!

MORNING HYMNS.

183   L. M.   *Hebron—Devotion.*

1 SWEET is the work, my God, my King,
  To praise thy name, give thanks and sing,
  To show thy love by morning light,
  And talk of all thy truths at night.

2 Sweet is the day of sacred rest;
  No mortal cares shall seize my breast:
  O may my heart in tune be found
  Like David's harp of solemn sound.

3 My heart shall triumph in my Lord,
 And bless his works, and bless his word:
 Thy works of grace, how bright they shine!
 How deep thy counsels! how divine!

4 Fools never raise their thoughts so high;
 Like brutes they live, like brutes they die.
 Like grass they flourish, till thy breath
 Blasts them in everlasting death.

5 But I shall share a glorious part
 When grace hath well refined my heart,
 And fresh supplies of joy are shed
 Like holy oil to cheer my head.

6 Sin (my worst enemy before)
 Shall vex my eyes and ears no more;
 My inward foes shall all be slain,
 Nor Satan break my peace again.

7 Then shall I see, and hear, and know
 All I desired or wish'd below;
 And every power find sweet employ
 In that eternal world of joy.

184.   C. M.   *Consolation.*

1 ONCE more, my soul, the rising day
  Salutes thy waking eyes;
 Once more, my voice, thy tribute pay
  To him that rules the skies.

2 Night unto night his name repeats,
  The day renews the sound,
 Wide as the heaven on which he sits
  To turn the seasons round.

3 'Tis he supports my mortal frame;
   My tongue shall speak his praise:
   My sins would rouse his wrath to flame,
   And yet his wrath delays.

4 On a poor worm thy power might tread,
   And I could ne'er withstand;
   Thy justice might have crushed me dead,
   But mercy held thy hand.

5 A thousand wretched souls are fled
   Since the last setting sun,
   And yet thou lengthenest out my thread,
   And yet my moments run.

6 Dear God, let all my hours be thine,
   Whilst I enjoy the light;
   Then shall my sun in smiles decline,
   And bring a pleasant night.

185   Metre 55.   *Holy Rest.*

1 AGAIN the day returns of holy rest,
   Which, when He made the world, Jehovah blest;
   When, like his own, He bid our labors cease,
   And all be piety, and all be peace.

2 Let us devote this consecrated day,
   To learn his will, and all we learn obey:
   So shall we hear, when fervently we raise
   Our supplication, and our songs of praise.

3 Father of heaven! in whom our hopes confide,
   Whose power defends us, and whose precepts guide;

In life our Guardian—and in death our Friend;
Glory supreme be thine—till time shall end.

186 C. M. *Balerma—Mear.*

1 LORD, in the morning thou shalt hear
My voice ascending high;
To thee will I direct my prayer,
To thee lift up mine eye.

2 Up to the hills where Christ is gone,
To plead for all his saints,
Presenting at his Father's throne,
Our songs and our complaints.

3 Thou art a God, before whose sight
The wicked shall not stand;
Sinners shall ne'er be thy delight,
Nor dwell at thy right hand.

4 But to thy house will I resort,
To taste thy mercies there:
I will frequent thy holy court,
And worship in thy fear.

5 O may thy Spirit guide my feet,
In ways of righteousness,
Make every path of duty straight
And plain before my face.

6 My watchful enemies combine
To tempt my feet astray;
They flatter with a base design
To make my soul their prey.

7 Lord, crush the serpent in the dust.
And all his plots destroy;

MORNING HYMNS. 169

 While those that in thy mercy trust
  For ever shout for joy.

8 The men that love and fear thy name.
  Shall see their hopes fulfill'd;
 The mighty God will compass them
  With favor, as a shield.

187   METRE 5.   *Cookham.*

1 NOW the shades of night are gone;
 Now the morning light is come;
Lord, may I be thine to-day—
Drive the shades of sin away.

2 Fill my soul with heav'nly light,
Banish doubt, and cleanse my sight;
In thy service, Lord, to-day,
Help me labor, help me pray.

3 Keep my haughty passion bound—
Save me from my foes around;
Going out and coming in,
Keep me safe from every sin.

4 When my work of life is past,
Oh! receive me then at last!
Night of sin will be no more,
When I reach the heavenly shore.

188   C. M.   *Liberty Hall.*

1 MY lovely Jesus, while on earth,
 Arose before 'twas day;
And to a solitary place
 Departed, there to pray.

2 I'll do as did my blessed Lord—
  His footsteps I will trace;
I love to meet him in the grove,
  And view his smiling face.

3 Early I'll rise, and sing and pray,
  While I the light enjoy;
May this bless'd work from day to day.
  My heart and tongue employ.

189   C. M.   Dublin.

1 GREAT God, preserved by thine arm,
    I pass the shades of night;
  Serene—and safe from every harm,
    And see returning light.

2 Oh! let the same Almighty care
    My wakeful hours defend;
  From every danger, every snare,
    My heedless steps defend.

3 Smile on my minutes as they roll,
    And guide my future days;
  And let thy goodness fill my soul
    With gratitude and praise.

190   C. M.   Augusta.

1 WHEN we with welcome slumber press'd,
    Had closed our weary eyes,
  A power unseen secured our rest,
    And made us joyful rise.

2 Numbers this night have doubtless met
    Their long eternal doom;

And lost the joy of morning light,
  In death's tremendous gloom.

3 But life to us its light prolongs,
  Let warmest thanks arise;
Great God, accept our morning songs,
  Our willing sacrifice.

191. C. M. *Mear.*

1 GOD of my life, my morning song
  To thee I cheerful raise;
Thy acts of love 'tis good to sing,
  And pleasant 'tis to praise.

2 Preserved by thy Almighty arm,
  I passed the shades of night,
Serene—and safe from every harm.
  To see the morning light.

3 While numbers spent the night in sighs,
  And restless pains and woes,
In gentle sleep I closed my eyes
  And rose from sweet repose.

4 When sleep, death's image, o'er me spread,
  And I unconscious lay,
Thy watchful care was round my bed,
  To guard my feeble clay.

5 O let the same Almighty care
  Through all this day attend;
From every danger, every snare,
  My heedless steps defend.

6 Smile on my minutes as they roll,
  And guide my future days:
And let thy goodness fill my soul
  With gratitude and praise

EVENING HYMNS.

192 S. M. *Shirland*

1 THE day is past and gone,
  The evening shades appear,
O may we all remember well,
  The night of death draws near.

2 We lay our garments by,
  Upon our beds to rest;
So death will soon disrobe us all
  Of what we here possess.

3 Lord, keep us safe this night,
  Secure from all our fears;
May angels guard us while we sleep,
  Till morning light appears.

4 And if we early rise,
  And view th' unwearied sun:
May we set out to win the prize,
  And after glory run!

5 And when our days are past,
  And we from time remove,
O may we in thy bosom rest,
  The bosom of thy love!

193 L. M. *Rockbridge.*

1 GLORY to thee, my God, this night,
  For all the blessings of the light:
Keep me, O keep me, King of kings
Beneath thine own Almighty wings.

EVENING HYMNS. 173

2 Forgive me, Lord, for thy dear Son,
The ill that I this day have done,
That with the world, myself, and thee,
I, ere I sleep, at peace may be.

3 Teach me to live, that I may dread
The grave as little as my bed;
Teach me to die, so that I may
Rise glorious at the awful day.

4 O let my soul on thee repose,
And may sweet sleep mine eyelids close;
Sleep that shall me more vigorous make,
To serve my God when I awake.

5 If in the night I sleepless lie,
My soul with heavenly thought supply:
Let no ill dreams disturb my rest,
No powers of darkness me molest.

194   C. M.   *Liberty Hall.*

1 LORD, thou wilt hear me when I pray;
   I am forever thine:
I fear before thee all the day,
   Nor would I dare to sin.

2 And while I rest my weary head,
   From care and business free,
'Tis sweet conversing on my bed
   With my own heart and thee.

3 I pay this evening sacrifice:
   And when my work is done,
Great God, my faith, my hope relies
   Upon thy grace alone.

4 Thus, with my thoughts composed to peace,
  I'll give mine eyes to sleep;
Thy hand in safety keeps my days
  And will my slumbers keep.

195   C. M.   *Youthful Piety.*

1 DREAD Sovereign, let my evening song.
  Like holy incense, rise;
Assist the offerings of my tongue,
  To reach the lofty skies.

2 Through all the dangers of the day,
  Thy hand was still my guard;
And still to drive my wants away,
  Thy mercy stood prepared.

3 Perpetual blessings from above
  Encompass me around;
But O how few returns of love
  Hath my Creator found!

4 What have I done for him that died
  To save my wretched soul!
How are my follies multiplied,
  Fast at my minutes roll!

5 Lord, with this guilty heart of mine,
  To thy dear cross I flee,
And to thy grace my soul resign,
  To be renewed by thee.

6 Sprinkled afresh with pard'ning blood,
  I lay me down to rest,
As in th' embraces of my God,
  Or in my Savior's breast.

EVENING HYMNS.

196 C. M. *Divinity.*

1 INDULGENT Father, by whose care,
    I've pass'd another day,
  Let me this night thy mercy share,
    And teach me how to pray.

2 Show me my sins, and how to mourn
    My guilt before thy face;
  Direct me, Lord, to Christ alone,
    And save me by thy grace.

3 Let each returning night declare
    The tokens of thy love;
  And every hour thy grace prepare
    My soul for joys above.

4 And when on earth I close mine eyes
    To sleep in death's embrace,
  Let me to heaven and glory rise,
    T' enjoy thy smiling face.

197 C. M. *Awful Majesty.*

1 ALL praise to him who dwells in bliss,
    Who made both day and night:
  Whose throne is darkness in th' abyss
    Of uncreated light.

2 Each thought and deed, his piercing eyes
    With strictest search survey;
  The deepest shades no more disguise,
    Than the full blaze of day.

3 Whom thou dost guard, O King of kings,
    No evil shall molest;

Under the shadows of their wings
  Shall they securely rest.

4 Thy angels shall around their beds
  Their constant stations keep:
Thy faith and truth shall shield their heads,
  For thou dost never sleep.

5 May we with calm and sweet repose,
  And heavenly thoughts refresh'd,
Our eyelids with the morn unclose,
  And bless Thee, ever blest.

198   Metre 12.   *New Jerusalem.*

1 INSPIRER and hearer of prayer,
  Before whom a sinner may bend:
My all to thy covenant care,
  I sleeping or waking commend.

2 If thou art my shield and my sun,
  The night is no darkness to me;
And fast as my moments roll on,
  They bring me but nearer to thee.

From evil secure, and its dread;
  I rest, if my Savior be nigh;
And songs his kind presence indeed,
  Shall in the night season supply.

4 He smiles, and my comforts abound;
  His grace as the dew shall descend:
And walls of salvation surround
  The soul he delights to defend.

EVENING HYMNS.

199   Metre 5.   *Sincerity.*

1 SOFTLY now the light of day
   Fades upon my sight away;
Free from care—from labor free,
Lord, I would commune with thee.

2 Soon for me, the light of day
Shall forever pass away:
Then, from sin and sorrow free,
Take me, Lord, to dwell with thee.

200   C. M.   *Rockingham.*

1 I LOVE to steal awhile away,
   From every cumb'ring care;
And spend the the hours of setting day
   In humble, grateful prayer.

2 I love in solitude to shed
   The penitential tear,
And all His promises to plead,
   Where none but God can hear.

3 I love to think on mercies past,
   And future good implore,
And all my cares and sorrows cast
   On him whom I adore.

4 I love by faith to take a view
   Of brighter scenes in heaven;
The prospect doth my strength renew
   While here by tempest driven.

5 Thus, when life's toilsome day is o'er,
   May its departing ray,
Be calm as this impressive hour,
   And lead to endless day.

FRAILTY OF MAN.

201 C. M. *Dublin.*

1 LORD, what is man, poor, feeble man,
  Born of the earth at first?
 His life a shadow, light and vain,
  Still hast'ning to the dust!

2 Oh what is feeble, dying man,
  Or all his sinful race,
 That God should make it his concern
  To visit him with grace!

3 That God, who darts his lightnings down,
  Who shakes the worlds above,
 What terrors wait his awful frown!
  How wondrous is his love!

202 C. M. *Mear.*

1 OUR God, our help in ages past,
  Our hope for years to come,
 Our shelter from the stormy blast,
  And our eternal home!

2 Beneath the shadow of thy throne
  Thy saints have dwelt secure;
 Sufficient is thy arm alone,
  And my defence is sure.

3 Before the hills in order stood,
  Or earth received her frame,
 From everlasting thou art God,
  To endless years the same.

FRAILTY OF MAN.

4 Thy word commands our flesh to dust.
  "Return, ye sons of men;"
  All nations rose from earth at first,
  And turn to earth again.

5 A thousand ages in thy sight
  Are like an evening gone:
  Short as the watch that ends the night
  Before the rising dawn.

6 The busy tribes of flesh and blood
  With all their lives and cares,
  Are carried downwards by the flood
  And lost in following years.

7 Time like an ever-rolling stream,
  Bears all its sons away:
  They fly forgotten as a dream
  Dies at the opening day,

8 Like flowery fields the nations stand,
  Pleased with the morning light;
  The flowers beneath the mower's hand
  Lie withered ere 'tis night.

9 Our God, our help in ages past,
  Our hope for years to come.
  Be thou our guard while troubles last.
  And our eternal home.

---

203 C. M. *Suffield.*

1 TEACH me the measure of my days,
   Thou Maker of my frame:
  I would survey life's narrow space,
  And learn how frail I am.

*12

2 A span is all that we can boast,
    An inch or two of time;
  Man is but vanity and dust,
    In all his flower and prime.

3 See the vain race of mortals move,
    Like shadows o'er the plain:
  They rage and strive, desire and love,
    But all their noise is vain.

4 Some walk in honor's gaudy show,
    Some dig for golden ore;
  They toil for heirs they know not who,
    And straight are seen no more.

5 What should I wish or wait for then
    From creatures, earth, and dust?
  They make our expectations vain,
    And disappoint our trust.

6 Now I forbid my carnal hope,
    My fond desires recall;
  I give my mortal interest up,
    And make my God my all.

204   S. M.   *Little Marlborough.*

1 LORD, what a feeble piece
    Is this, our mortal frame!
  Our life! how poor a trifle 'tis,
    That scarce deserves the name!

2 Alas, the brittle clay
    That built our bodies first!
  And every month and every day
    'Tis mouldering back to dust.

FUNERAL.

3 Our moments fly apace,
   Our feeble powers decay,
Swift as a flood our hasty days
   Are sweeping us away.

Yet if our days must fly,
   We'll keep their end in sight,
We'll spend them all in wisdom's ways,
   And let them speed their flight.

5 They'll waft us sooner o'er
   This life's tempestuous sea:
Soon we shall reach the peaceful shore
   Of bless'd eternity.

FUNERAL.

205   S. M.   *Aylesbury*

1 AND must this body die?
   This mortal frame decay?
And must these active limbs of mine
   Lie mouldering in the clay?

2 Corruption, earth, and worms,
   Shall but refine this flesh,
Till my triumphant spirit comes,
   To put it on afresh.

3 God, my Redeemer, lives,
   And often from the skies
Looks down, and watches all my dust
   Till he shall bid it rise.

4 Arrayed in glorious grace
 Shall these vile bodies shine,
And every shape, and every face
 Look heavenly and divine.

5 These lively hopes we owe
 To Jesus' dying love;
We would adore his grace below,
 And sing his power above.

6 Dear Lord, accept the praise
 Of these our humble songs,
Till tunes of nobler sound we raise,
 With our immortal tongues.

206   C. M.   *Funeral Thought.*

1 HARK! from the tombs a doleful sound,
 Mine ears attend the cry;
"Ye living men, come view the ground,
 Where you must shortly lie.

2 "Princes, this clay must be your bed,
 In spite of all your towers;
The tall, the wise, the rev'rend head,
 Must lie as low as ours."

3 Great God! is this our certain doom?
 And are we still secure?
Still walking downward to the tomb,
 And yet prepared no more!

4 Grant us the power of quickning grace,
 To fit our souls to fly;
Then, when we drop this dying flesh,
 We'll rise above the sky.

FUNERAL.

207 C. M. *St. Olaves.*

1 LORD, if thine eyes survey our faults,
  And justice grows severe,
Thy dreadful wrath exceeds our thoughts,
  And burns beyond our fear.

2 Thine anger turns our frame to dust;
  By one offence to thee,
Adam, with all his sons, have lost
  Their immortality.

3 Life, like a vain amusement, flies,
  A fable or a song;
By swift degrees our nature dies,
  Nor can our joys be long.

4 'Tis but but a few whose days amount
  To theescore years and ten;
And all beyond that short account
  Is sorrow, toil, and pain.

5 Our vitals, with laborious strife,
  Bear up the crazy load,
And drag these poor remains of life
  Along the tiresome road.

6 Almighty God, reveal thy love,
  And not thy wrath alone;
O let our sweet experience prove
  The mercies of thy throne.

7 Our soul would learn the heavenly art
  T' improve the hours we have,
That we may act the wiser part,
  And live beyond the grave.

FUNERAL.

208   C. M.   *Dublin*

1 WHY do we mourn departing friends,
    Or shake at death's alarms?
'Tis but the voice that Jesus sends
    To call them to his arms.

2 Are we not tending upward too,
    As fast as time can move?
Nor should we wish the hours more slow,
    To keep us from our love.

3 Why should we tremble to convey
    Their bodies to the tomb?
There the dear flesh of Jesus lay.
    And left a long perfume.

4 The graves of all his saints he blest,
    And softened every bed:
Where should the dying members rest,
    But with their dying Head?

5 Thence he arose, ascending high,
    And showed our feet the way;
Up to the Lord our flesh shall fly,
    At the great rising day.

6 Then let the last loud trumpet sound
    And bid our kindred rise;
Awake, ye nations under ground,
    Ye saints, ascend the skies.

209   C. M.   *Blessed Infancy*

1 THY life I read, my dearest Lord,
    With transport all divine;

Thine image trace in every word,—
   Thy love in every line.

2 Methinks I see a thousand charms
   Spread o'er thy lovely face,
While infants in thy tender arms,
   Receive the smiling grace.

3 "I take these little lambs" said he,
   "And lay them in my breast;
Protection they shall find in me,
   In me be ever blest.

4 "Death may the bands of life unloose,
   But can't dissolve my love;
Millions of infant souls compose
   The family above.

5 "Their feeble frames my power shall raise,
   And mould with heavenly skill:
"I'll give them tongues to sing my praise,
   And hands to do my will."

6 His words the happy parents hear
   And shout with joys divine,
Dear Savior, all we have and are
   Shall be forever thine.

210   C. M.   *Salvation.*

1 ATTEND, young friends, while I relate,
   The dangers you are in:
The evils that around you wait,
   While subject unto sin.
Although you flourish like the rose,
   While in its branches green;

Your sparkling eyes in death must close,
　No more will they be seen.

2 In silent shades you must lay down,
　Long in your graves to dwell;
Your friends will then stand weeping round,
　And bid a long farewell.
How small this world will then appear
　At the tremendous hour;
When you Jehovah's voice shall hear,
　And feel his mighty power.

3 In vain you'll mourn, your days are past
　Alas those days are gone;
Your golden hours are spent at last;
　And never to return.
O come this moment and begin,
　While life's sweet moments last,
Turn to the Lord, forsake all sin,
　And he'll forgive what's past.

211.　　　C. M.　　　*Youthful Piety.*

1 DEATH! 'tis a melancholy day
　To those that have no God,
When the poor soul is forced away
　To seek her last abode.

2 In vain to heaven she lifts her eyes;
　But guilt, a heavy chain,
Still drags her downwards from the skies,
　To darkness, fire, and pain.

3 Awake and mourn, ye heirs of hell,
　Let stubborn sinners fear;
You must be driv'n from earth, and dwell
　A long forever there.

FUNERAL. 187

4 See how the pit gapes wide for you,
 And flashes in your face;
And thou, my soul, look downward too,
 And sing recov'ring grace.

5 He is a God of sovereign love,
 Who promised heaven to me,
And taught my thoughts to soar above,
 Where happy spirits be.

6 Prepare me, Lord, for thy right hand;
 Then come the joyful day;
Come death, and some celestial band,
 To bear my soul away.

212   C. M.   *Resignation.*

1 AND let this feeble body fail,
  And let it faint or die;
My soul shall quit the mournful vale,
  And soar to worlds on high:
Shall join the disembodied saints,
  And find its long sought rest
That only bliss for which it pants,
  In the Redeemer's breast.

2 In hope of that immortal crown
  I now the cross sustain:
And gladly wander up and down,
  And smile at toil and pain:
I'll suffer on my threescore years,
  Till my Deliverer come:
And wipe away his servant's tears,
  And take his exile home.

3 O what hath Jesus bought for me!
  Before my ravish'd eyes,

Rivers of life divine I see,
  And trees of Paradise!
I see a world of spirits bright,
  Who taste the pleasure there!
They all are robed in spotless white
  And conq'ring palms they bear.

2 O what are all my sufferings here,
  If, Lord, thou count me meet,
With that enraptured hosts t' appear,
  And worship at thy feet!
Give joy or grief, give ease or pain,
  Take life or friends away:
But let me find them all again
  In that eternal day.

213   METRE 12.   *Deliverance.*

1 HOW blest is our brother, bereft
  Of all that can burden his mind;
How easy the soul that has left
  This wearisome body behind.
Of evil incapable thou,
  Whose relics with envy I see,
No longer in misery now,
  No longer a sinner like me.

2 This earth is affected no more
  With sickness, or shaken with pain;
The war in the members is o'er,
  And never shall vex him again;
No anger, henceforward, or shame,
  Shall redden his innocent clay;
Extinct is the animal flame,
  And passion is vanished away.

FUNERAL.

3 This languishing head is at rest;
    Its thinking and aching are o'er :
This quiet, immovable breast,
    Is heaved by affliction no more:
This heart is no longer the seat
    Of trouble and torturing pain;
It ceases to flutter and beat—
    It never shall flutter again.

4 The lids he so seldom could close,
    By sorrow forbidden to sleep,
Sealed up in eternal repose,
    Have strangely forgotten to weep;
These fountains can yield no supply—
    These hollows from water are free:
The tears are all wiped from these eyes,
    And evils they never shall see.

214   L. M.   Hebron.

1 WHY should we start, and fear to die?
    What tim'rous worms we mortals are!
Death is the gate of endless joy,
And yet we dread to enter there.

2 The pains, the groans, and dying strife
Fright our approaching souls away;
Still we shrink back again to life,
Fond of our prison and our clay.

3 O! if my Lord would come and meet,
My soul should stretch her wings in haste,
Fly fearless through death's iron gate,
Nor feel the terrors as she pass'd.

4 Jesus can make a dying bed
Feel soft as downy pillows are,

While on his breast I lean my head,
 And breathe my life out sweetly there.

215 C. M. *Dublin.*

1 THEE we adore, Eternal Name!
 And humble own to thee,
How feeble is our mortal frame,
 What dying worms are we!

2 Our wasting lives grow shorter still,
 As months and days increase;
And every beating pulse we tell,
 Leaves but the number less.

3 The year rolls round and steals away
 The breath that first it gave;
Whate'er we do, whate'er we be,
 We're trav'ling to the grave.

4 Dangers stand thick through all the ground,
 To push us to the tomb;
And fierce diseases wait around,
 To hurry mortals home.

5 Good God! on what a slender thread
 Hang everlasting things!
Th' eternal state of all the dead
 Upon life's feeble strings!

6 Infinite joy, or endless woe,
 Attends on every breath;
And yet how unconcerned we go
 Upon the brink of death.

7 Waken, O Lord, our drowsy sense
 To walk this dang'rous road:

FUNERAL.

And if our souls are hurried hence,
May they be found with God.

216 L. M. *Supplication.*

1 REMEMBER, Lord, our mortal state,
How frail our life, how short the date!
Where is the man that draws his breath,
Safe from disease, secure from death.

2 Lord, while we see whole nations die,
Our flesh and strength repine and cry,
"Must death for ever rage and reign!
Or hast thou made mankind in vain?

3 "Where is thy promise to the just?
Are not thy servants turned to dust!"
But faith forbids these mournful sighs,
And sees the sleeping dust arise.

4 That glorious hour, that dreadful day,
Wipes the reproach of saints away,
And clears the honor of thy word;
Awake our souls and bless the Lord.

217 L. M. *Solemnity.*

1 THROUGH every age, eternal God,
Thou art our rest, our safe abode;
High was thy throne ere heaven was made,
Or earth, thy humble footstool laid.

2 Long hadst thou reigned ere time began,
Or dust was fashioned into man:
And long thy kingdom shall endure
When earth and time shall be no more.

3 But man, weak man is born to die,
   Made up of guilt and vanity:
   Thy dreadful sentence, Lord, was just,
   "Return ye sinners, to your dust."

4 A thousand years of ours amount
   Scarce to a day in thine account;
   Like yesterday's departing light,
   Or the last watch of ending night.

5 Death, like an overflowing stream,
   Sweeps us away; our life's a dream:
   An empty tale: a morning flower,
   Cut down and withered in an hour.

6 Our age to seventy years is set;
   How short the time, how frail the state
   And if to eighty we arrive,
   We rather sigh and groan, than live.

7 But oh, how oft thy wrath appears,
   And cuts off our expected years!
   Thy wrath awakes our humble dread!
   We fear the Power that strikes us dead.

8 Teach us, O Lord, how frail is man;
   And kindly lengthen out the span,
   Till a wise care of piety
   Fits us to die and dwell with thee.

218　　　C. M.　　*Youthful Piety.*

1 LORD, must I die? O let me die
      Trusting in thee alone!
   My living testimony giv'n,
      Then leave my dying one!

FUNERAL.

2 If I must die—oh let me die
   In peace with all mankind;
And change these fleeting joys below
   For pleasures all refined.

3 If I must die—as die I must—
   Let some kind seraph come,
And bear me on his friendly wing
   To my celestial home!

4 Of Canaan's land, from Pisgah's top,
   May I but have a view!
Though Jordan should o'erflow its banks,
   I'll boldly venture through.

219   C. M.   *Dublin.*

1 WHEN blooming youth is snatch'd away
   By death's resistless hand,
Our hearts the mournful tribute pay,
   Which pity must demand.

2 While pity prompts the rising sigh,
   Oh, may this truth impress'd
With awful pow'r,—"I too must die!"
   Sink deep in every breast.

3 Let this vain world engage no more:
   Behold the gaping tomb!
It bids us seize the present hour:
   To-morrow death may come.

4 The voice of this alarming scene
   May every heart obey;
Nor be the heavenly warning vain,
   Which calls to watch and pray.

5 O let us fly—to Jesus fly,
  Whose powerful arm can save;
Then shall our hopes ascend on high,
  And triumph o'er the grave.

6 Great God! thy sovereign grace impart,
  With cleansing, healing power;
This only can prepare the heart
  For Death's surprising hour.

JUDGMENT.

220   C. M.   *Awful Majesty.*

1 SING to the Lord, ye heavenly hosts,
  And thou, O earth, adore;
Let death and hell, through all their coasts
  Stand trembling at his power.

2 His sounding chariot shakes the sky,
  He makes the clouds his throne;
There all his stores of lightning lie
  Till vengeance darts them down.

3 His nostrils breathe out fiery streams,
  And from his awful tongue
A sovereign voice divides the flames,
  And thunders roar along.

4 Think, O my soul, the dreadful day
  When this incensed God
Shall rend the skies and burn the seas,
  And fling his wrath abroad.

JUDGMENT.

5 What shall the wretch, the sinner do?
  He once defied the Lord!
But he shall dread the Thund'rer now,
  And sink beneath his word.

6 Tempests of angry fire shall roll,
  To blast the rebel worm,
And beat upon his naked soul
  In one eternal storm.

221.   Metre 4.   Melody.

1 SINNERS, take the friendly warning—
  Soon that awful day shall break,
And the trumpet with its dawning,
  All the slumb'ring millions wake.

2 See assembled every nation!
  Lofty cities, temples, towers,
Wrapp'd in dreadful conflagration,
  Earth and sea the flames devours.

3 Ye who to the world dissemble,
  While you practice deeds of night,
Sinners, now behold and tremble,
  All your crimes are brought to light.

4 Lost in ease or carnal pleasure,
  Sporting on the burning brink;
Now you say you have no leisure,
  You can find no time to think.

5 Ye who now conviction stifling,
  Waste your time, the loss deplore;
Hear the angel—cease your trifling—
  "Time," he cries, "shall be no more."

JUDGMENT.

6 Pause and hear the voice of reason—
  Catch the moments as they fly
You who lose the present season,
  You must all find time to die.

222 C. M. *Suffield.*

1 AND must I be to judgment brought,
  And answer in that day,
For every vain and idle thought,
  And every word I say?

2 Yes, every secret of my heart
  Shall shortly be made known,
And I receive my just desert
  For all that I have done.

3 How careful then ought I to live!
  With what religious fear,
Who such a strict account must give
  For my behavior here!

4 Thou awful Judge of quick and dead,
  The watchful pow'r bestow;
So shall I to my ways take heed,
  To all I speak or do.

5 If now thou standest at the door,
  O let me feel thee near!
And make my peace with God, before
  I at thy bar appear.

223 METRE 7. *Judgment.*

1 DAY of Judgment! day of wonders!
  Hark! the trumpet's awful sound,

JUDGMENT.

Louder than a thousand thunders,
  Shake the vast creation round!
    How the summons
  Will the sinner's heart confound!

2 See the Judge our nature wearing,
    Cloth'd in majesty divine!
  You who long for his appearing,
    They shall say "This God is mine!"
      Gracious Savior!
    Own me in that day for thine!

3 At his call the dead awaken,
    Rise to life from earth and sea!
  All the pow'rs of nature shaken,
    By his looks, prepare to flee:
      Careless sinner!
    What will then become of thee?

4 Horrors past imagination,
    Will surprise your trembling hearts,
  When you hear your condemnation,
    "Hence accursed wretch, depart!
      Thou with Satan
    And his angels, have thy part!"

5 But to those who have confessed,
    Loved and served the Lord below,
  He will say, 'Come near, ye blessed!
    See the kingdom I bestow!
      You for ever
    Shall my love and glory know."

6 Under sorrows and reproaches,
    May this thought our courage raise;

Swiftly God's great day approaches,
 Sighs will then be changed to praise!
  May we triumph,
 When the world is in a blaze!

224 METRE 7. *Dresden.*

1 LO! he comes in clouds descending,
  Once for favor'd sinners slain!
 Thousand thousand saints attending,
  Swell the triumph of his train!
   Hallelujah!
  Jesus now shall ever reign!

2 Every eye shall now behold him
  Rob'd in dreadful majesty:
 Those who set at naught and sold him,
  Pierc'd and nail'd him to the tree,
   Deeply wailing,
  Shall the great Messiah see!

3 Every island, sea, and mountain,
  Heav'n and earth shall flee away:
 All who hate him, must, confounded,
  Hear the trump proclaim the day:
   Come to judgment!
  Come to judgment, come away!

4 Now redemption long expected,
  See in solemn pomp appear!
 All his saints, by man rejected,
  Now shall meet him in the air!
   Hallelujah,
  See the day of God appear!

5 Answer thine own Bride and Spirit,
  Hasten, Lord, the gen'ral doom!

JUDGMENT.

The new heaven and earth t' inherit
  Take thy pining exiles home:
    All creation
    Travails, groans, and bids thee come!

5 Yea, Amen! let all adore thee,
  High on thine exalted throne!
Savior, take the power and glory;
  Claim the kingdoms for thine own!
    O come quickly!
  Hallelujah! come, Lord, come.

225   METRE 7.   *Littleton.*

1 LO! he cometh! countless trumpets
    Blow to raise the sleeping dead;
  'Mid ten thousand saints and angels,
    See their great exalted Head!
      Hallelujah!
    Welcome, welcome, Son of God.

2 Now his merit, by the harpers,
    Through th' eternal deep resounds;
  Now resplendent shine his nail-prints,
    Every eye shall see his wounds:
      They who pierced him
    Shall at his appearance wail.

3 Full of joyful expectation,
    Saints, behold the Judge appear;
  Truth and justice go before him,
    Now the joyful sentence hear!
      Hallelujah!
    Welcome, welcome, Judge divine.

4 "Come, ye blessed of my Father,
    Enter into life and joy!

Banish all your fears and sorrows:
   Endless praise be your employ!"
      Hallelujah!
   Welcome, welcome, to the skies.

5 Now at once they rise to glory
      Jesus brings them to the King;
   There, with all the hosts of heaven.
      They eternal anthems sing;
         Hallelujah!
      Boundless glory to the Lamb.

VANITY OF EARTHLY THINGS.

226   C. M.   *Primrose.*

1 WHY doth the man of riches grow
      To insolence and pride,
   To see his wealth and honors flow
      With every rising tide?

2 Why doth he treat the poor with scorn,
      Made of the self-same clay;
   And boast, as though his flesh were born
      Of better dust than they?

3 Not all his treasures can procure
      His soul a short reprieve,
   Redeem from death one guilty hour,
      Or make his brother live.

4 Eternal life can ne'er be sold,
      The ransom is too high;

Justice will ne'er be bribed with gold.
   That man may never die.

5 He sees the brutish and the wise,
   The timorous and the brave,
Quit their possessions, close their eyes.
   And hasten to the grave.

6 Yet 'tis his inward thought and pride
   "My house shall ever stand;
And that my name may long abide
   I'll give it to my land."

7 Vain are his thoughts, his hopes are lost,
   How soon his mem'ry dies!
His name is buried in the dust
   Where his own body lies.

8 This is the folly of their way;
   And yet their sons, as vain,
Approve the words their fathers say,
   And act their works again.

9 Men, void of wisdom and of grace,
   Though honor raise them high,
Live like the beast, a thoughtless race,
   And like the beast they die.

10 Laid in the grave, like silly sheep,
   Death triumphs o'er them there,
Till the last trumpet breaks their sleep,
   And wakes them in despair.

227   C. M.   *Divinity.*

1 HOW vain are all things here below,
   How false and yet how fair!

Each pleasure has its poison too,
  And every sweet a snare.

2 The brightest things below the sky
  Give but a flatt'ring light;
We should suspect some danger nigh
  Where we possess delight.

3 Our dearest joys and nearest friends,
  The partners of our blood,
How they divide our wav'ring minds,
  And leave but half for God!

4 The fondness of a creature's love,
  How strong it strikes the sense!
Thither the warm affections move,
  Nor can we call them thence.

5 Dear Savior! let thy beauties be
  My soul's eternal food;
And grace command my heart away
  From all created good.

HEAVENLY JOY.

228 C. M. *Condescension.*

1 THERE is a house not made with hands,
  Eternal, and on high;
And here my spirit waiting stands,
  Till God shall bid it fly.

2 Shortly this prison of my clay
    Must be dissolved and fall;
Then, O my soul, with joy obey
    Thy heavenly Father's call.

3 'Tis he, by his Almighty grace,
    That forms thee fit for heav'n;
And as an earnest of the place,
    Has his own Spirit given.

4 We walk by faith of joys to come;
    Faith lives upon his word:
But while the body is our home,
    We're absent from the Lord.

5 'Tis pleasant to believe thy grace;
    But we had rather see;
We would be absent from the flesh,
    And present, Lord, with thee.

229   S. M.   *New Hope.*

1 COME we that love the Lord,
    And let our joys be known:
Join in a song with sweet accord,
    And thus surround the throne.

2 The sorrows of the mind,
    Be banish'd from the place!
Religion never was designed
    To make our pleasures less.

3 Let those refuse to sing
    Who never knew our God,
But favorites of the heavenly King
    May speak their joys abroad.

4 The God that rules on high,
   And thunders when he please,
Who rides upon the stormy sky,
   And manages the seas.

5 This awful God is ours,
   Our Father and our love,
He shall send down his heavenly powers
   To carry us above.

6 There shall we see his face,
   And never, never sin:
There from the rivers of his grace.
   Drink endless pleasures in.

7 Yes, and before we rise
   To that immortal state,
The thoughts of such amazing bliss
   Should constant joys create.

8 The men of grace have found
   Glory begun below,
Celestial fruits on earthly ground,
   From faith and hope may grow.

9 The hill of Zion yields
   A thousand sacred sweets,
Before we reach the heavenly fields.
   Or walk the golden streets.

10 Then let our songs abound,
   And every tear be dry;
We're marching thro' Immanuel's ground
   To fairer worlds on high.

230   C. M.   *Solon.*

1 ON Jordan's stormy banks I stand,
   And cast a wishful eye

HEAVENLY JOY. 205

To Canaan's fair and happy land,
  Where my possessions lie.

2 Oh the transporting, rapt'rous scene,
    That rises to my sight!
  Sweet fields arrayed in living green,
    And rivers of delight.

3 There gen'rous fruits that never fail,
    On trees immortal grow:
  There rocks and hills, and brooks and vales,
    With milk and honey flow.

4 All o'er those wide extended plains
    Shines one eternal day:
  There God the Son forever reigns,
    And scatters night away.

5 No chilling winds, nor poisonous breath
    Can reach that healthful shore:
  Sickness and sorrow, pain and death,
    Are felt and fear'd no more.

6 When shall I reach that happy place,
    And be for ever blest?
  When shall I see my Father's face,
    And in his bosom rest?

7 Fill'd with delight, my raptur'd soul
    Can here no longer stay;
  Though Jordan's waves around me roll,
    Fearless I'd launch away.

231   C. M.   *Felicity.*

1 EARTH has engross'd my love too long!
    'Tis time I lift mine eyes

HEAVENLY JOY.

Upward, dear Father, to thy throne,
 And to my native skies.

2 There the blest Man, my Savior, sits,
 The God! how bright he shines!
And scatters infinite delight
 On all the happy minds.

3 Seraphs with elevated strains,
 Circle the throne around;
And move and charm the starry plains
 With an immortal sound.

4 Jesus the Lord their harps employs:—
 Jesus, my love, they sing!
Jesus, the life of both our joys,
 Sounds sweet from every string.

5 Hark! how beyond the narrow bounds
 Of time and space they run;
And echo in majestic sounds
 The Godhead of the Son.

6 And now they sink the lofty tune,
 And gentler notes they play!
And bring the Father's Equal down
 To dwell in humble clay.

7 O sacred beauties of the Man!
 (The God resides within;)
His flesh all pure, without a stain,
 His soul without a sin.

8 But when to Calvary they turn,
 Silent their harps abide;
Suspended songs, a moment, mourn
 The God that loved and died.

HEAVENLY JOY.

9 Then all at once, to living strains
   They summon every chord,
 Tell how he triumphed o'er his pains,
   And chant the rising Lord.

10 Now let me mount and join their song,
   And be an angel too;
 My heart, my hand, my ear, my tongue,—
   Here's joyful work for you.

11 I would begin the music here,
   And so my soul should rise;
 O, for some heavenly notes to bear
   My passions to the skies.

12 There ye that love my Savior sit,
   There I would fain have place,
 Among your thrones, or at your feet,
   So I might see his face.

232   C. M.   *Wiltshire—Solon.*

1 FROM thee, my God, my joys shall rise,
   And run eternal rounds,
 Beyond the limits of the skies,
   And all created bounds.

2 The holy triumphs of my soul
   Shall death itself outbrave;
 Leave dull mortality behind,
   And fly beyond the grave.

3 There, where my blessed Jesus reigns,
   In heaven's unmeasured space,
 I'll spend a long eternity
   In pleasure and in praise.

HEAVENLY JOY.

4 Millions of years my wond'ring eyes
    Shall o'er thy beauties rove,
  And endless ages I'll adore
    The glories of thy love,

5 Sweet Jesus! every smile of thine
    Shall fresh endearments bring;
  And thousand tastes of new delight
    From all thy graces spring.

6 Haste, my Beloved, fetch my soul
    Up to thy bless'd abode;
  Fly, for my spirit longs to see
    My Savior and my God.

233   L. M.   Devotion.

1 O FOR a sweet, inspiring ray,
    To animate our feeble strains,
  From the bright realms of endless day,
    The blissful realms where Jesus reigns.

2 There low before his glorious throne,
    Adoring saints and angels fall;
  And, with delightful worship, own
    His smiles their bliss, their heav'n, their all.

3 Immortal glories crown his head,
    While tuneful hallelujahs rise,
  And love, and joy, and triumph spread
    Through all th' assemblies of the skies.

4 He smiles, and seraphs tune their songs
    To boundless rapture while they gaze;
  Ten thousand thousand joyful tongues
    Resound his everlasting praise.

HEAVENLY JOY.

5 There all the favorites of the Lamb,
  Shall join at last the heavenly choir;
 Oh, may the joy-inspiring theme
  Awake our faith and warm desire.

6 Dear Savior, let thy Spirit seal
  Our int'rest in that blissful place;
 Till death remove this mortal vail,
  And we behold thy lovely face.

234   METRE 20.   *New Concord.*

1 OH! how happy are they,
   Who their Savior obey,
 And have laid up their treasure above,
   Oh what tongue can express
   The sweet comfort and peace,
 Of a soul in its earliest love.

2 'T was a heaven below,
   My Redeemer to know;
 And the angels could do nothing more
   Than to fall at his feet,
   And the story repeat,
 And the Lover of sinners adore.

3 Jesus, all the day long,
   Was my joy and my song;
 Oh! that more his salvation might see:
   He hath loved me, I cried,
   He hath suffered and died,
 To redeem such a rebel as me!

4 Now my remnant of days
   Would I spend in his praise,
 Who hath died me from death to redeem

    Whether many or few,
    All my days are his due—
  May they all be devoted to him!

5 What a mercy is this!
    What a heaven of bliss!
  How unspeakably happy am I!
    Gathered into the fold,
    With believers enroll'd—
  With believers to live and to die!

6 Lo! the day's drawing nigh,
    When, my soul, thou shalt fly
  To the place thy salvation began—
    Where the Three and the One,
    Father, Spirit, and Son,
  Laid the scheme of redemption for man.

235   C. M.   *Heavenly Jerusalem.*

1 JERUSALEM! my happy home,
    Name ever dear to me!
  When shall my labors have an end,
    In joy, and peace, and thee?

2 When shall these eyes thy heav'n built walls
    And pearly gates behold?
  Thy bulwarks, with salvation strong,
    And streets of shining gold?

3 O when, thou city of my God,
    Shall I thy courts ascend,
  Where congregations ne'er break up,
    And sabbaths never end?

4 There happier bowers than Eden's bloom,
    Nor sin nor sorrow know:

HEAVENLY JOY. 211

Bless'd seats! through rude and stormy scenes
  I onward press to you.

5 Why should I shrink at pain or woe?
    Or feel at death dismay?
  I've Canaan's goodly land in view,
    And realms of endless day.

6 Apostles, martyrs, prophets, there,
    Around my Savior stand:
  And soon my friends in Christ below
    Will join the glorious band.

7 Jerusalem! my happy home!
    My soul still pants for thee;
  Then shall my labors have an end,
    When I thy joys shall see.

236   METRE 12.   *Greenfields.*

1 AWAY with our sorrow and fear,
    We soon shall recover our home;
  The city of saints shall appear;
    The day of eternity come.
  From earth we shall quickly remove,
    And mount to our native abode:
  The house of our Father above,
    The palace of angels and God.

2 Our mourning is all at an end,
    When, raised by the life-giving Word,
  We see the new city descend,
    Adorn'd as a bride for her Lord:
  The city, so holy and clean,
    No sorrow can breathe in the air;
  No gloom of affliction or sin;
    No shadow of evil is there!

14*

3 By faith we already behold
 That lovely Jerusalem here;
Her walls are of jasper and gold,
 As crystal her buildings are clear:
Immovably founded in grace,
 She stands, as she ever hath stood,
And brightly her Builder displays,
 And flames with the glory of God.

4 No need of the sun in that day,
 Which never is follow'd by night,
Where Jesus' beauties display
 A pure and a permanent light.
The Lamb is their Light and their Sun,
 And lo! by reflection they shine;
With Jesus ineffably one,
 And bright in effulgence divine!

5 The saints in his presence receive
 Their great and eternal reward;
In Jesus, in heaven they live;
 They reign in the smile of their Lord!
The flame of angelical love
 Is kindled at Jesus' face;
And all the enjoyment above
 Consists in the rapturous gaze!

237   METRE 11.   *Prescott.*

1 I WOULD not live always: I ask not to stay,
 Where storm after storm rises dark o'er the way;
The few cloudy mornings that dawn on us here,
Enough for life's woes, full enough for its cheer.

2 I would not live always thus fetter'd by sin;
 Temptation without, and corruption within;

HEAVENLY JOY. 213

Where rapture of pardon is mingled with fears;
The cup of thanksgiving with penitent tears.

3 I would not live always; no — welcome the tomb—
Since Jesus hath lain there I'll enter its gloom;
There sweet be my rest. till he bid me arise,
To hail him in triumph descending the skies.

4 Who, who would live always, away from his God :
Away from yon heaven, that blissful abode;
Where rivers of pleasure flow o'er the bright plains,
And noon-tide of glory eternally reigns:

5 Where saints of all ages in harmony meet,
Their Savior and brethren transported to greet;
While anthems of rapture unceasingly roll,
The smile of the Lord is the feast of the soul.

238   METRE 7.   *Seraph's Harp.*

1 SEE, from Zion's sacred mountain,
    Streams of living water flow:
God has open'd there a fountain:
    This supplies the plains below:
      They are blessed,
    Who its sovereign virtues know.

2 Through ten thousand channels flowing,
    Streams of mercy find their way;
Life, and health, and joy bestowing,
    Making all around look gay,
      O, ye nations!
    Hail the long expected day.

3 Gladden'd by the flowing treasure,
  All enriching as it goes:
Lo! the desert smiles with pleasure,
  Buds and blossoms as the rose,
    Ev'ry object
  Sings for joy where'er it flows.

4 Trees of life the banks adorning,
  Yield their fruit to all around:
Those who eat are saved from mourning,
  Pleasure comes and hopes abound;
    Fair their portion!
  Endless life with glory crown'd.

239   C. M.   Awful Majesty.

1 "THESE glorious minds, how bright they shine!
  Whence all their white array?
How came they to the happy seats
  Of everlasting day?"

2 From tort'ring pains to endless joys,
  On fiery wheels they rode,
And strangely wash'd their raiment white
  In Jesus' dying blood.

3 Now they approach a spotless God,
  And bow before his throne;
Their warbling harps and sacred songs,
  Adore the Holy One.

4 The unveil'd glories of his face
  Among his saints reside,
While the rich treasure of his grace
  Sees all their wants supplied.

HEAVENLY JOY.

5 Tormenting thirst shall leave their souls.
  And hunger flee as fast;
 The fruit of life's immortal tree
  Shall be their sweet repast;

6 The lamb shall lead his heavenly flock
  Where living fountains rise;
 And love divine, shall wipe away
  The sorrows of their eyes.

240   C. M.   Augusta.

1 LO, what a glorious sight appears
  To our believing eyes!
 The earth and seas are past away,
  And the old rolling skies.

2 From the third heaven, where God resides,
  That holy happy place,
 The new Jerusalem comes down,
  Adorn'd with shining grace.

3 Attending angels, shout for joy,
  And the bright armies sing,
 "Mortals, behold the sacred seat
  Of your descending King.

4 "The God of glory down to men
  Removes his blest abode;
 Men, the dear objects of his grace,
  And he, the loving God.

5 His own soft hands shall wipe the tears
  From every weeping eye;
 And pains, and groans, and griefs, and fears,
  And death itself shall die."

6 How long, dear Savior, O how long
　Shall this bright hour delay?
　Fly swiftly round, ye wheels of time,
　And bring the welcome day.

BREATHING AFTER GOD AND HOLINESS.

241　　　Metre 15.　　　*New Salem.*

1 O THOU, in whose presence my soul takes
　　delight,
　On whom in affliction I call;
　My comfort by day, and my song in the night,
　My hope, my salvation, my all!

2 Where dost thou at noon-tide resort with thy
　　sheep,
　To feed on the pastures of love?
　For why in the valley of death should I weep,
　Alone in the wilderness rove!

3 Oh! why should I wander an alien from thee,
　And cry in the desert for bread?
　My foes will rejoice when my sorrows they see,
　And smile at the tears I have shed.

4 Ye daughters of Zion, declare, have you seen
　The star that on Israel shone?
　Say, if in your tents, my Beloved has been,
　And where with his flocks he has gone?

5 This is my Beloved; his form is divine,
  His vestments shed odors around;
The locks on his head are as grapes on the vine,
  When autumn with plenty is crown'd.

6 The roses of Sharon, the lilies that grow
  In vales on the banks of the stream,
His cheeks. in the beauty of excellence glow,
  His eyes all invitingly beam.

7 His voice as the sound of a dulcimer sweet,
  Is heard through the shadows of death,
The cedars of Lebanon bow at his feet,
  The air is perfumed with his breath;

8 His lips as a fountain of righteousness flow,
  That waters the garden of grace. [know.
From which their salvation the Gentiles shall
  And bask in the smiles of his face.

9 Love sits in his eye-lids, and scatters delight
  Through all the bright mansions on high,
Their faces the cherubim vail in his sight,
  And tremble with fulness of joy:

10 He looks, and ten thousand of angels rejoice,
  And myriads wait for his word;
He speaks, and eternity fill'd with his voice,
  Re-echoes the praise of her Lord.

11 His vestment of righteousness who shall describe?
  Its purity words would defile;
The heavens from his presence fresh beauties imbibe,
  And earth is made rich by his smiles.

12 Such is my Beloved, in excellence bright,
  When pleased, he looks down from above,
 (Like th' morn, when it breathes from the
   chambers of light,)
 And comforts his people with love.

242   S. M.   *Matthias—Shirland.*

1 ALMIGHTY Maker, God!
  How wond'rous is thy name!
 Thy glories how diffused abroad
  Through the creation's frame!

2 Nature in ev'ry dress,
  Her humble homage pays,
 And finds a thousand ways t' express
  Thine undissembled praise.

3 My soul would rise and sing
  To her Creator too;
 Fain would my tongue adore my King,
  And pay the worship due.

4 But pride, that busy sin,
  Spoils all that I perform,
 Cursed pride, that creeps securely in,
  And swells a haughty worm.

5 Create my soul anew,
  Else all my worship's vain;
 This wretched heart will ne'er be true,
  Until 'tis formed again.

6 Let joy and worship spend
  The remnant of my days,
 And to my God my soul ascend,
  In sweet perfumes of praise.

243 C. M. *Balerma—Solon.*

1 WHEN I can read my title clear
  To mansions in the skies,
I'll bid farewell to every fear,
  And wipe my weeping eyes.

2 Should earth against my soul engage,
  And hellish darts be hurl'd,
Then I can smile at Satan's rage,
  And face a frowning world.

3 Let cares, like a wild deluge, come,
  And storms of sorrow fall;
May I but safely reach my home,
  My God, my heaven, my all:

4 There shall I bathe my wearied soul
  In seas of heavenly rest,
And not a wave of trouble roll
  Across my peaceful breast.

244 Metre 4. *New Monmouth.*

1 COME, thou Fount of every blessing,
  Tune my heart to sing thy grace,
Streams of mercy never ceasing,
  Call for songs of loudest praise:
Teach me some melodious sonnet,
  Sung by flaming tongues above;
Praise the mount—I'm fixed upon it;
  Mount of thy redeeming love!

2 Here, I'll raise mine Ebenezer,
  Hither by thy help I'm come;
And I hope by thy good pleasure,
  Safely to arrive at home.

Jesus sought me when a stranger,
 Wand'ring from the fold of God;
He to rescue me from danger,
 Interpos'd his precious blood!

3 O! to grace how great a debtor
 Daily I'm constrain'd to be!
Let thy goodness, like a fetter,
 Bind my wand'ring heart to thee;
Prone to wander, Lord, I feel it;
 Prone to leave the God I love—
Here's my heart, O take and seal it;
 Seal it for thy courts above.

245   L M.   *Tender Thought.*

1 ARISE, my tenderest thoughts, arise;
 To torrents melt my streaming eyes;
And thou, my heart, with anguish feel
Those evils which thou canst not heal.

2 See human nature sunk in shame;
See scandals pour'd on Jesus' name;
The Father wounded through the Son;
The world abused, the soul undone;

3 See the short course of vain delight
Closing in everlasting night—
In flames that no abatement know,
Though briny tears for ever flow.

4 My God, I fell the mournful scene;
My bowels yearn o'er dying men;
And fain my pity would reclaim,
And snatch the firebrands from the flame.

5 But feeble my compassion proves,
  And can but weep where most it loves;
  Thy own all-saving arm employ,
  And turn those drops of grief to joy.

246   METRE 5.   *Sovereign Grace.*

1 TELL me, Savior, from above,
    Dearest object of my love,
  Where thy little flock abide,
  Shelter'd near thy bleeding side?

2 Tell me, Shepherd all divine,
  Where I may my soul recline;
  Where for refuge shall I fly,
  While the burning sun is high?

3 Wilt thou let me run astray,
  Mourning, grieving all the day?
  Wilt thou bear to see me rove,
  Seeking base and mortal love?

4 Never have I sought thy name,
  Never felt the inward flame,
  Had not love first touched my heart
  With the painful, pleasing smart.

5 Didst thou leave thy glorious throne,
  Put a mortal raiment on,
  On the tree a victim die,
  For a wretch so vile as I?

247   C. M.   *Bethel.*

1 MY Savior, my Almighty Friend,
    When I begin thy praise

BREATHING AFTER GOD

Where will the growing numbers end,
　The numbers of thy grace?

2 Thou art my everlasting trust,
　Thy goodness I adore;
And since I knew thy graces first,
　I speak thy glories more.

3 My feet shall travel all the length
　Of the celestial road,
And march with courage, in thy strength,
　To see my Father, God.

4 When I am fill'd with sore distress
　For some surprising sin.
I'll plead thy perfect righteousness,
　And mention none but thine.

5 How will my lips rejoice to tell
　The victories of my King!
My soul redeem'd from sin and hell,
　Shall thy salvation sing.

6 My tongue shall all the day proclaim
　My Savior and my God,
His death has brought my foes to shame.
　And saved me by his blood.

7 Awake, awake, my tuneful powers;
　With this delightful song
I'll entertain the darkest hours,
　Nor think the seasons long.

248　　　　C. M.　　　*Consolation.*

1 OH, that I had a bosom friend,
　To tell my secrets to!

AND HOLINESS.

On whose advice I might depend,
  In every thing I do.

2 How do I wander up and down,
    And no one pities me;
  I seem a stranger quite unknown,
    A son of misery.

3 None lends an ear to my complaint,
    Nor minds my cries and tears,
  None comes to help me tho' I faint,
    Nor my vast burden bears.

4 While others live in mirth and ease,
    And feel no want nor woe;
  Through this dark howling wilderness
    I full of sorrow go.

5 O faithless soul to reason thus,
    And murmur without end!
  Did Christ expire upon the cross,
    And is not he thy friend?

6 Why dost thou envy carnal men,
    And think their state so blest!
  How great salvation hast thou seen!
    And Jesus is thy rest.

7 What can this lower world afford,
    Compared with gospel grace?
  Thy happiness is in the Lord,
    And thou shalt see his face.

8 Can present griefs be counted great,
    Compared with future woes?
  Will transient pleasure seem so sweet,
    Compared with endless joys?

BREATHING AFTER GOD

9 How soon will God withdraw the scene
  And burn the world he made;
 Then woe to carnal, careless men;
  My soul, lift up thine head.

10 Thy Savior is thy real friend,
  Constant, and true, and good;
 He will be with thee to the end,
  And bring thee safe to God.

11 What then, my soul, hast thou to fear?
  Or why shouldst thou repine,
 Look up, behold redemption's near,
  Rejoice, for heaven is thine.

12 Why, O my soul, art thou so sad?
  When will thy sighs be o'er?
 Rejoice in Jesus, and be glad,
  Rejoice, for evermore.

249.   C. M.   *Solon.*

1 MY God, the spring of all my joys,
  The life of my delights,
 The glories of my brightest days,
  And comfort of my nights;

2 In darkest shades, if he appear,
  My dawning is begun!
 He is my soul's bright morning star,
  And he my rising sun.

3 The opening heav'ns around me shine
  With beams of sacred bliss,
 While Jesus shows his heart is mine,
  And whispers "I am his."

4 My soul would leave this heavy clay
  At that transporting word,
 Run up, with joy, the shining way,
  T' embrace my dearest Lord.

5 Fearless of hell, and ghastly death,
  I'd break through every foe;
 The wings of love, and arms of faith,
  Should bear me conqueror through.

250 L. M. *Adisham—Portugal.*

1 HOW pleasant, how divinely fair,
  O Lord of hosts, thy dwellings are!
 With long desire my spirit faints,
 To meet th' assemblies of thy saints.

2 My flesh would rest in thine abode;
 My panting heart cries out for God;
 My God! my King! why should I be
 So far from all my joys and thee?

3 The sparrow chooses where to rest,
 And for her young provides her nest:
 But will my God to sparrows grant
 That pleasure which his children want!

4 Bless'd are the saints who sit on high,
 Around thy throne above the sky;
 Thy brightest glories shine above,
 And all their work is praise and love.

5 Bless'd are the souls, who find a place
 Within the temple of thy grace;
 There they behold thy gentler rays,
 And seek thy face and learn thy praise.

6 Bless'd are the men whose hearts are set
To find the way to Zion's gate;
God is their strength; and through the road
They lean upon their helper, God.

7 Cheerful they walk with growing strength,
Till all shall meet in heaven at length;
Till all before thy face appear,
And join in nobler worship there.

251 C. M. *Fidelia*

1 FATHER, I long, I faint, to see
The place of thine abode;
I'd leave these earthly courts, and flee
Up to thy seat, my God!

2 Here I behold thy distant face,
And 'tis a pleasing sight;
But to abide in thine embrace,
Is infinite delight.

3 I'd part with all the joys of sense,
To gaze upon thy throne;
Pleasure springs fresh forever thence
Unspeakable, unknown.

4 There all the heavenly hosts are seen,
In shining ranks they move,
And drink immortal vigor in,
With wonder and with love.

5 Then at thy feet, with awful fear,
Th' adoring armies fall;
With joy they shrink to nothing there
Before th' eternal All.

AND HOLINESS.

6 There I would vie with all the host,
    In duty and in bliss;
  While less than nothing I could boast.
    And vanity confess,

7 The more thy glories strike mine eyes,
    The humbler I shall lie;
  Thus, while I sink, my joy shall rise
    Unmeasurably high.

252   C. M.   *Land of Rest*

1 O LAND of rest, for thee I sigh,
    When will the moment come,
  When I shall lay my armor by,
    And dwell in peace at home!

CHORUS.

  O, this is not my home—
    No, this is not my home:
  This world's a wilderness of woe—
    This world is not my home.

2 No tranquil joys on earth I know,
    No peaceful sheltering dome:
  This world's a wilderness of woe—
    This world is not my home.
      O, this is not my home, &c.

3 To Jesus Christ I sought for rest,
    He bid me cease to roam,
  And fly for refuge to his breast
    And He'd conduct me home.
      O, this is not my home, &c.

4 I would at once have quit the field.
    Where foes with fury roam,

15*

But O, my passport was not sealed,—
I could not yet go home,
O, this is not my home, &c.

5 When by affliction sharply tried,
I view the gaping tomb;
Although I dread death's chilling tide,
Yet still I sigh for home,
O, this is not my home, &c.

6 Weary of wand'ring round and round,
This vale of sin and gloom,
I long to quit th' unhallowed ground.
And dwell with Christ at home,
O, this is not my home, &c.

253. METRE 36. *Home.*

1 'MID scenes of confusion and creature complaints,
How sweet to my soul is communion with saints:
To find at the banquet of mercy there's room.
And feel, in the presence of Jesus, at home.
Home, home, sweet, sweet home,
Receive me, dear Savior, in glory, my home.

2 Sweet bonds that unite all the children of peace,
And thrice, precious Jesus, whose love cannot cease :
Though oft from thy presence in sadness I roam.
I long to behold thee, in glory, at home.
Home, home, sweet, sweet home,
Receive me, dear Savior, in glory, my home.

3 I sigh from this body of sin to be free,
Which hinders my joy and communion with thee:

AND HOLINESS.

Though now my temptations like billows may foam,
All, all will be peace when I'm with thee at home.
   Home, home, sweet, sweet home,
Receive me, dear Savior, in glory, my home.

4 While here in the valley of conflict I stay,
O give me submission and strength as my day:
In all my afflictions to thee would I come,
Rejoicing in hope of my glorious home.
   Home, home, sweet, sweet home,
Receive me, dear Savior, in glory, my home.

5 Whate'er thou deniest, O give me thy grace!
The Spirit's sure witness, and smiles of thy face:
Indulge me with patience to wait till thou come,
And find even now a sweet foretaste of home.
   Home, home, sweet, sweet home,
Receive me, dear Savior, in glory, my home.

6 I long, dearest Lord, in thy beauties to shine,
No more, as an exile, in sorrow to pine,
And in thy fair image, arise from the tomb,
With glorified millions, to praise thee at home.
   Home, home, sweet, sweet home,
Receive me, dear Savior, in glory, my home.

7 The days of my exile are passing away,
The time is approaching when Jesus will say:
Well done, faithful servant, sit down on my throne,
And dwell in my presence forever at home.
   Home, home, sweet, sweet home,
O, there I shall rest with the Savior at home.

BREATHING AFTER GOD

254   C. M.   *Salvation.*

1 HEAR, gracious God, my humble moan.
   To thee I breathe my sighs:
When will the mournful night be gone?
   And when my joys arise?

2 My God—O could I make the claim—
   My Father and my Friend—
And call thee mine by ev'ry name,
   On which thy saints depend!

3 By ev'ry name of power and love,
   I would thy grace entreat:
Nor should my humble hopes remove,
   Nor leave thy sacred seat.

4 Yet though my soul in darkness mourns,
   Thy word is all my stay;
Here I would rest till light returns,
   Thy presence makes my day.

5 Speak, Lord, and bid celestial peace
   Relieve my aching heart;
O smile and bid my sorrows cease,
   And all the gloom depart.

6 Then shall my drooping spirits rise,
   And bless the healing rays,
And change these deep complaining sighs
   For songs of sacred praise.

255   METRE 13.   *Warning Voice.*

1 RISE, my soul! and stretch thy wings,
   Thy better portion trace;

Rise, from transitory things,
  Tow'rds heav'n, thy native place!
Sun, and moon, and stars decay;
  Time shall this earth remove.
Rise, my soul, and haste away
  To seats prepared above.

2 Rivers to the ocean run,
  Nor stay in all their course:
Fire, ascending, seeks the sun;
  Both speed them to their source;
Thus a soul new-born of God,
  Pants to view his glorious face,
Upward tends to his abode,
  To rest in his embrace.

3 Cease, ye pilgrims! cease to mourn;
  Press onward to the prize;
Soon the Savior will return
  Triumphant in the skies;
Yet a season, and you know
  Happy entrance will be giv'n,—
All your sorrows left below,
  And earth exchanged for heav'n.

256   METRE 4.   *Charleston.*

1 HAIL, my ever blessed Jesus,
  Only thee I wish to sing;
To my soul thy name is precious,
  Thou my Prophet, Priest, and King.

2 Oh, what mercy flows from heaven,
  Oh, what joy and happiness!
Love I much?—I've much forgiven—
  I'm a miracle of grace.

3 Once, with Adam's race in ruin,
  Unconcern'd in sin I lay;
  Swift destruction still pursuing,
  Till my Savior passed that way.

4 Witness all ye hosts of heaven,
  My Redeemer's tenderness!
  Love I much?—I've much forgiven—
  I'm a miracle of grace.

5 Should ye bright angelic choir;
  Praise the Lamb enthroned above;
  While astonish'd, I admire
  God's free grace, and boundless love.

6 That blest moment I received him,
  Fill'd my soul with joy and peace;
  Love I much?—I've much forgiven—
  I'm a miracle of grace.

257   C. M.   Warwick—Dublin.

1 HOW sweet the name of Jesus sounds
  In a believer's ear!
  It soothes his sorrows, heals his wounds,
  And drives away his fear.

2 It makes the wounded spirit whole,
  And calms the troubled breast;
  'Tis manna to the hungry soul,
  And to the weary rest.

3 Dear Name! the Rock on which I build,
  My shield and hiding place;
  My never-failing treasury, fill'd
  With boundless stores of grace.

4 Jesus! my Shepherd, Husband, Friend,
  My Prophet, Priest and King;
My Lord, my Life, my Way, my End,
  Accept the praise I bring.

5 Weak is the effort of my heart,
  And cold my warmest thought;
But when I see thee as thou art,
  I'll praise thee as I ought.

6 Till then I would thy love proclaim
  With every fleeting breath;
And may the music of thy name
  Refresh my soul in death.

258 L. M. *Kingsbridge.*

1 LORD, I am thine; but thou wilt prove
  My faith, my patience, and my love;
When men of spite against me join,
They are the sword—the hand is thine.

2 Their hope and portion lie below;
'Tis all the happiness they know,
'Tis all they seek; they take their shares,
And leave the rest among their heirs.

3 What sinners value, I resign;
Lord, 'tis enough that thou art mine:
I shall behold thy blissful face,
And stand complete in righteousness.

4 This life's a dream, an empty show;
But the bright world, to which I go,
Hath joys substantial and sincere;
When shall I wake and find me there?

5 O glorious hour! O blest abode!
I shall be near, and like my God;
And flesh and sin no more control
The sacred pleasures of the soul.

6 My flesh shall slumber in the ground,
Till the last trumpet's joyful sound;
Then burst the chains with sweet surprise,
And in my Savior's image rise.

259   Metre 12.   *New Jerusalem.*

1 THOU Shepherd of Israel and mine,
  The joy and desire of my heart,
For closer communion I pine,
  I long to reside where thou art;
The pasture I languish to find,
  Where all who their Shepherd obey,
Are fed, on thy bosom reclin'd,
  And screened from the heat of the day.

2 Ah! show me that happiest place,
  The place of thy people's abode:
Where saints in an ecstasy gaze,
  And hang on a crucified God:
Thy love for a sinner declare;
  Thy passion and death on the tree:
My spirit to Calvary bear,
  To suffer and triumph with thee.

3 'Tis there with the lambs of thy flock,
  There only I covet to rest;
To lie at the foot of the rock,
  Or rise to be hid in thy breast;
'Tis there I would always abide,
  And never a moment depart;

Conceal'd in the cleft of thy side,
Eternally held in thy heart.

260 L. M. *Windham.*

1 O COULD I find some peaceful bow'r,
Where sin hath neither place nor pow'r;
This traitor vile, I fain would shun,
But cannot from his presence run.

2 When to the throne of grace I flee,
He stands between my God and me,
Where'er I rove, where'er I rest,
I feel him working in my breast.

3 When I attempt to soar above,
To view the heights of Jesus' love;
This monster seems to mount the skies,
And veils his glory from mine eyes.

4 Lord, free me from this deadly foe,
Which keeps my faith and hope so low;
I long to dwell in heaven, my home,
Where not one sinful thought can come.

261 C. M. *Augusta.*

1 RELIGION in the chief concern
Of mortals here below;
May I its great importance learn,
Its sovereign virtue know.

2 More needful this than glitt'ring wealth,
Or aught the world bestows;
Not reputation, food or health,
Can give us such repose.

3 Religion should our thoughts engage
    Amidst our youthful bloom;
'Twill fit us for declining age,
    And for the awful tomb.

4 Oh, may my heart, by grace renew'd,
    Be my Redeemer's throne
And be my stubborn will subdued,
    His government to own!

5 Let deep repentance, faith and love,
    Be join'd with godly fear;
And all my conservation prove
    My heart to be sincere.

6 Preserve me from the snares of sin,
    Through my remaining days:
And in me let each virtue shine,
    To my Redeemer's praise.

7 Let lively hope my soul inspire;
    Let warm affections rise;
And may I wait with strong desire
    To mount above the skies.

262   L. M.   *Hebron.*

1 UP to the fields where angels lie,
    And living waters gently roll,
Fain would my thoughts leap out and fly,
But sin hangs heavy on my soul.

2 Thy wondrous blood, dear dying Christ,
    Can make this world of guilt remove;
And thou canst bear me where thou fly'st.
On thy kind wings, celestial Dove.

3 O might I once mount up and see
　The glories of th' eternal skies;
　What little things these worlds would be!
　How despicable to my eyes!

4 Had I a glance of thee, my God,
　Kingdoms and men would vanish soon:
　Vanish, as though I saw them not,
　As a dim candle dies at noon.

5 Then they might fight, and rage, and rave,
　I should perceive the noise no more
　Than we can hear a shaking leaf,
　When rattling thunders round us roar.

6 Great All in All, eternal King!
　Let me but view thy lovely face,
　And all my powers shall bow, and sing
　Thine endless grandeur and thy grace.

263　　　　L. M.　　　　*Armley.*

1 THOU, whom my soul admires above
　All earthly joy and earthly love,
　Tell me, dear Shepherd, let me know
　Where doth thy sweetest pastures grow?

2 Where is the shadow of that Rock,
　That from the sun defends thy flock?
　Fain would I feed among thy sheep,
　Among them rest, among them sleep.

3 Why should thy bride appear like one
　That turns aside to paths unknown?
　My constant feet would never rove,
　Would never seek another love.

4 The footsteps of thy flock I see;
Thy sweetest pastures here they be;
A wondrous feast thy love prepares,
Bought with thy wounds, and groans and tears

5 His dearest flesh he makes my food,
And bids me drink his richest blood;
Here, to these hills my soul will come,
Till my Beloved leads me home.

264   L. M.   *Rockbridge,*

1 OFTEN I seek my Lord by night,
Jesus, my love, my soul's delight:
With warm desire and restless thought
I seek him oft but find him not.

2 Then I arise and search the street,
Till I my Lord, my Savior meet;
I ask the watchmen of the night,
"Where did you see my soul's delight?"

3 Sometimes I find him in my way,
Directed by a heavenly ray;
I leap for joy to see his face,
And hold him fast in my embrace.

4 I bring him to my mother's home;
Nor does my Lord refuse to come
To Zion's sacred chambers, where
My soul first drew the vital air.

5 He gives me there his bleeding heart,
Pierc'd for my sake with deadly smart:
I give me soul to him, and there
Our loves their mutual tokens share.

6 I charge you all, ye earthly toys,
   Approach not to disturb my joys;
   Nor sin, nor hell, come near my heart,
   Nor cause my Savior to depart.

265   C. M.   *Solon.*

1 THERE is a land of pure delight,
   Where saints immortal reign;
   Infinite day excludes the night
   And pleasures banish pain.

2 There everlasting spring abides,
   And never-with'ring flowers;
   Death, like a narrow sea divides
   This heavenly land from ours.

3 Sweet fields beyond the swelling flood
   Stand dress'd in living green:
   So to the Jews old Canaan stood,
   While Jordan roll'd between.

4 But tim'rous mortals start and shrink,
   To cross this narrow sea,
   And linger, shiv'ring on the brink,
   And fear to launch away.

5 O, could we make our doubts remove,
   Those gloomy doubts that rise,
   And see the Canaan that we love,
   With unbeclouded eyes!

6 Could we but climb where Moses stood,
   And view the landscape o'er,
   Not Jordan's stream, nor death's cold flood,
   Should fright us from the shore.

BREATHING AFTER GOD

266   L. M.   *Devotion.*

1 DESCEND from heaven, immortal Dove,
  Stoop down and take us on thy wings,
And mount and bear us far above
The reach of these inferior things:

2 Beyond, beyond this lower sky,
Up where eternal ages roll,
Where solid pleasures never die,
And fruits immortal feast the soul.

3 O for a sight—a pleasing sight
Of our Almighty Father's throne!
There sits our Savior crown'd with light,
Cloth'd in a body like our own.

4 Adoring saints around him stand,
And thrones and powers before him fall:
The God shines gracious through the Man,
And sheds sweet glories on them all.

5 O what amazing joys they feel,
While to their golden harps they sing,
And sit on every heavenly hill,
And spread the triumphs of their King!

6 When shall the day, dear Lord, appear,
That I shall mount to dwell above,
And stand and bow among them there,
And view thy face, and sing, and love!

267   C. M.   *Liberty Hall.*

1 GOD of my life, look gently down,
  Behold the pains I feel:

But I am dumb before thy throne,
  Nor dare dispute thy will.

2 Diseases are thy servants, Lord,
  They come at thy command;
I'll not attempt a murmuring word,
  Against thy chastening hand.

3 Yet I may plead with humble cries,
  Remove thy sharp rebukes;
My strength consumes, my spirit dies,
  Through thy repeated strokes.

4 Crush'd as a moth beneath thy hand,
  We moulder in the dust;
Our feeble powers can ne'er withstand,
  And all our beauty's lost.

5 I'm but a stranger here below,
  As all my fathers were:
May I be well prepared to go,
  When I thy summons hear!

6 But if my life be spared awhile
  Before my last remove,
Thy praise shall be my business still,
  And I'll declare thy love.

268 L. M. *Portugal*.

1 AND is the Gospel peace and love!
  Such let our conversation be:
The serpent blended with the dove,
Wisdom and meek simplicity.

2 Whene'er the angry passions rise,
  And tempt our thoughts or tongues to strife,

242 BREATHING AFTER GOD

To Jesus let us lift our eyes,
Bright pattern of the Christian life!

3 Oh, how benevolent and kind!
How mild! how ready to forgive!
Be this the temper of our mind.
And these the rules by which we live.

4 To do his heavenly Father's will,
Was his employment and delight;
Humility and holy zeal
Shone through his life divinely bright!

5 Dispensing good where'er he came,
The labors of his life were love;
Oh, if we love the Savior's name,
Let his divine example move.

6 But ah! how blind! how weak we are!
How frail! how apt to turn aside!
Lord, we depend upon thy care,
And ask thy Spirit for our guide.

7 Thy fair example may we trace,
To teach us what we ought to be!
Make us by thy transforming grace,
Dear Savior, daily more like thee!

269   L. M.   *Gravity.*

1 THOU art, O God! a Spirit pure,
Invisible to mortal eyes;
Th' immortal, and th' eternal King,
The Great, the Good, the only wise.

2 Whilst nature changes, and her works
Corrupt, decay, dissolve, and die,

Thy essence pure no change shall see,
Secure of immortality.

3 Thou great Invisible! what hand
Can draw thine image spotless fair?
To what in heaven, to what on earth,
Can men th' immortal King compare?

4 Let stupid heathens frame their gods
Of gold and silver, wood and stone;
Our's is the God that made the heav'ns:
Jehovah he, and God alone.

5 My soul the purest homage pay,
In truth and spirit him adore;
More shall this please then sacrifice,
Than outward forms delight him more.

270   C. M.   *Augusta.*

1 THERE is a voice of sovereign grace
Sounds from the sacred word;
"Ho! ye despairing sinners, come,
And trust upon the Lord."

2 My soul obeys th' Almighty call,
And runs to this relief;
I would believe thy promise, Lord,
Oh! help my unbelief.

3 To the dear fountain of thy blood,
Incarnate God, I fly;
Here let me wash my spotted soul
From crimes of deepest dye.

4 Stretch out thine arm, victorious King.
My reigning sin subdue;

BREATHING AFTER GOD &c.

Drive the old dragon from his seat
With his apostate crew.

5 A guilty, weak, and helpless worm
On thy kind arms I fall;
Be thou my strength and righteousness,
My Jesus, and my all!

271　　　　　C. M.　　　　　*Mear.*

1 O THAT the Lord would guide my ways,
To keep his statutes still!
O that my God would grant me grace
To know and do his will!

2 O send thy Spirit down, to write
Thy law upon my heart.
Nor let my tongue indulge deceit,
Nor act the liar's part.

3 From vanity turn off my eyes:
Let no corrupt design,
Nor covetous desire, arise
Within this soul of mine.

4 Order my footsteps by thy word,
And make my heart sincere;
Let sin have no dominion, Lord,
But keep my conscience clear.

5 My soul hath gone too far astray,
My feet too often slip;
Yet since I've not forgot thy way,
Restore thy wand'ring sheep.

6 Make me to walk in thy commands,
'Tis a delightful road;
Nor let my head, nor heart, nor hands
Offend against my God.

ADORATION AND PRAISE.

272 C. M. *Bethel.*

1 THE Savior! Oh, what endless charms
  Dwell in the blissful sound!
  Its influence every fear disarms,
  And spreads sweet peace around.

2 Here pardon, life, and joys divine,
  In rich effusion flow,
  For guilty rebels, lost in sin,
  And doomed to endless woe.

3 Oh, the rich depths of love divine,
  Of bliss! a boundless store!
  Dear Savior, let me call the mine;
  I cannot wish for more.

4 On thee alone my hope relies,
  Beneath thy cross I fall;
  My Lord, my life, my sacrifice,
  My Savior and my all.

273 C. M. *Solon.*

1 ETERNAL Wisdom, thee we praise!
  Thee the creation sings!
  With thy lov'd name, rocks, hills, and seas,
  And heaven's high palace rings.

2 Thy hand, how wide it spread the sky!
  How glorious to behold!
  Ting'd with the blue of heavenly dye,
  And star'd with sparkling gold.

3 Thy glories blaze all nature round
   And strike the gazing sight,
Through skies, and seas, and solid ground,
   With terror and delight.

4 Infinite strength, and equal skill,
   Shine through the worlds abroad,
Our souls with vast amazement fill,
   And speak the builder, God.

5 But still the wonders of thy grace
   Our softer passions move;
Pity divine in Jesus' face
   We see, adore, and love.

274   C. M.   *Balerma.*

1 LET Zion and her sons rejoice,
   Behold the promised hour:
Her God hath heard her mourning voice,
   And comes t' exalt her power.

2 Her dust and ruins that remain,
   Are precious in our eyes:
Those ruins shall be built again,
   And all that dust shall rise.

3 The Lord will raise Jerusalem,
   And stand in glory there;
Nations shall bow before his name,
   And kings attend with fear.

4 He sits a Sovereign on his throne,
   With pity in his eyes;
He hears the dying prisoner's groan,
   And sees their sighs arise.

ADORATION AND PRAISE.

5 He frees the souls condemned to death,
   And when his saints complain,
It sha'n't be said, "that praying breath
   Was ever spent in vain."

6 This shall be known when we are dead,
   And left on long record;
That ages yet unborn may read,
   And trust, and praise the Lord.

275   C. M.   *Augusta.*

1 AMID the splendors of thy state,
   My God, thy love appears,
With the soft radiance of the moon,
   Among a thousand stars.

2 Nature through all her ample round
   Thy boundless power proclaims,
And, in melodious accents, speaks
   The goodness, of thy names.

3 Thy justice, holiness, and truth,
   Our solemn awe excite;
But the sweet charms of sovereign grace
   O'erwhelm us with delight.

4 Sinai, in clouds, and smoke. and fire,
   Thunders thy dreadful name;
But Zion sings, in melting notes,
   The honors of the Lamb.

5 In all thy doctrines and commands,
   Thy counsels and designs—
In ev'ry work thy hands have fram'd,
   Thy love supremely shines.

5 Angels and men the news proclaim
  Through earth and heav'n above—
The joyful and transporting news,
  That God the Lord is Love.

276   L. M.   *Rockbridge.*

1 ETERNAL power! whose high abode
  Becomes the grandeur of a God:
Infinite lengths, beyond the bounds
Where stars revolve their little rounds.

2 The lowest step around thy seat
Rises too high for Gabriel's feet;
In vain the tall archangel tries
To reach thine height with wond'ring eyes.

3 Lord, what shall earth and ashes do?
We would adore our Maker too;
From sin and dust to thee we cry,
The Great, the Holy, and the High!

4 Earth from afar has heard thy fame,
And worms have learn'd to lisp thy name;
But O, the glories of thy mind
Leave all our soaring thoughts behind.

5 God is in heav'n, but man below;
Be short our tunes; our words be few:
A sacred rev'rence checks our songs,
And praise sits silent on our tongues.

277   C. M.   *Divinity.*

1 COME, let us join our cheerful songs,
  With angels round the throne;
Ten thousand thousand are their tongues,
  But all their joys are one.

ADORATION AND PRAISE.

2 "Worthy the Lamb that died," they cry,
   "To be exalted thus;"
 "Worthy the Lamb," our lips reply,
   For he was slain for us.

3 Jesus is worthy to receive
   Honor and power divine;
 And blessings more than we can give,
   Be, Lord, forever thine.

4 Let all that dwell above the sky,
   And air, and earth, and seas,
 Conspire to raise thy glories high,
   And speak thine endless praise!

278   L. M.   *Portugal.*

1 PRAISE ye the Lord, who reigns above,
   Fix'd on his throne of truth and love;
 Behold the finger of his power
 Contemplate, wonder, and adore.

2 When man, debased, and guilty man,
 From crime to crime with madness ran;
 Well might His arm its thunders launch,
 And blast th' ungrateful root and branch.

3 But clemency with justice strove,
 To save the people of his love.
 "Go, my beloved Son!" He cried,
 "Be thou their Savior, thou their guide."

4 The eastern star with glory streams;
 It comes, with healing on its beams,
 Dark mists of error flee away,
 And Judah hails the rising day.

5 His sacred memory we bless,
  Whose holy gospel we profess;
  And praise that great Almighty name,
  From whom such light and favor came.

279   L. M.   *Wells.*

1 YE nations round the earth, rejoice
    Before the Lord, your sovereign King,
  Serve him with cheerful heart and voice,
    With all your tongues his glory sing.

2 The Lord is God; 'tis he alone
    Doth life, and breath, and being give;
  We are his work, and not our own;
    The sheep that on his pastures live.

3 Enter his gates with songs of joy,
    With praises to his courts repair;
  And make it your divine employ,
    To pay your thanks and honors there.

4 The Lord is good, the Lord is kind;
    Great is his grace, his mercy sure;
  And the whole race of man shall find
    His truth from age to age endure.

280   Metre 10.   *Unitia.*

1 O WHAT shall I do my Savior to praise!
    So faithful and true, so plenteous in grace;
  So strong to deliver, so good to redeem,
    The weakest believer that hangs upon him.

2 How happy the man whose heart is set free!
    The people that can be joyful in thee;

ADORATION AND PRAISE.

Their joy is to walk in the light of thy face,
And still they are talking of Jesus' grace.

3 Their daily delight shall be in thy name;
They shall as their right thy righteousness claim
Thy righteousness wearing, and cleansed by
thy blood,
Bold shall they appear in the presence of God.

4 For thou art their boast, their glory and power,
And I also trust to see the glad hour,
My soul's new creation a life from the dead,
The day of salvation that lifts up my head.

5 For Jesus, my Lord, is now my defence,
I trust in his word, none plucks me from thence;
Since I have found favor, he all things will do;
My King and my Savior shall make me anew.

6 Yes, Lord, I shall see the bliss of thine own;
Thy secret to me shall soon be made known:
For sorrow and sadness I joy shall receive,
And share in the gladness of all that believe.

281 Metre 16. *Mendon.*

1 GOD of my salvation, hear,
 And help me to believe,
Simply do I now draw near,
 Thy blessing to receive;
Full of guilt, alas! I am,
 But to thy wounds for refuge flee;
Friend of sinners, spotless Lamb,
 Thy blood was shed for me.

2 Standing now as newly slain,
 To thee I lift mine eyes,

Balm of all my grief and pain,
  Thy blood is always nigh.
Now as yesterday the same
  Thou art and wilt forever be:
Friend of sinners, spotless Lamb;
  Thy blood was shed for me.

3 Nothing have I, Lord, to pay,
  Nor can thy grace procure;
Empty send me not away,
  For I, thou knowest, am poor;
Dust and ashes is my name;
  My all is sin and misery;
Friend of sinners, spotless Lamb,
  Thy blood was shed for me.

4 No good word, or work, or thought,
  Bring I to buy thy grace;
Pardon I accept, unbought,
  Thy proffer I embrace.
Coming as at first I came,
  To take, and not bestow on thee:
Friend of sinners, spotless Lamb,
  Thy blood was shed for me.

5 Savior, from thy wounded side
  I never will depart;
Here will I my spirit hide,
  When I am pure in heart;
Till my place above I claim,
  This only shall be all my plea,
Friend of sinners, spotless Lamb,
  Thy blood was shed for me.

RESIGNATION TO GOD.

282　　　METRE 5.　　　*Ebenezer.*

1 MY Ebenezer raise
   To my kind Redeemer's praise
   With a grateful heart I own
   Hitherto thy help I've known.

2 What may be my future lot,
   Well I know concerns me not;
   This should set my heart at rest,
   What thy will ordains is best.

3 I may all to thee resign:
   Father, let thy will be mine;
   May but all thy dealings prove
   Fruits of thy paternal love.

4 Guard me, Savior, by thy power!
   Guard me in the trying hour:
   Let thy unremitting care
   Save me from the lurking snare.

5 Let my few remaining days
   Be directed to thy praise;
   So the last, the closing scene,
   Shall be tranquil and serene.

6 To thy will I leave the rest,
   Grant me but this one request,
   Both in life and death to prove
   Tokens of thy special love.

RESIGNATION TO GOD.

283   Metre 8.   *Vernon.*

1 WHEN gathering clouds around I view
And days are dark, and friends are few,
On him I lean, who, not in vain,
Experienced every human pain;
He sees my wants, allays my fears,
And counts and treasures up my tears.

2 If aught should tempt my soul to stray
From heavenly virtue's narrow way,
To fly the good I would pursue
Or do the sin I would not do,
Still he who felt temptation's power
Shall guard me in that dang'rous hour.

3 When vexing thoughts within me rise,
And sore dismay'd my spirit dies,
Yet he who once vouchsafed to bear
The sickening anguish of despair,
Shall sweetly soothe, shall gently dry,
The trobbing heart, the streaming eye.

4 When sorrowing, o'er some stone I bend,
Which covers all that was a friend:
And from his voice, his hand, his smile,
Divides me—for a little while,—
Thou, Savior, seest the tears I shed,
For thou didst weep o'er Lazarus dead.

5 And O, when I have safely past
Through every conflict but the last,
Still, still unchanging, watch beside
My painful bed,—for thou hast died;
Then point to realms of cloudless day,
And wipe the latest tear away.

RESIGNATION TO GOD.

284   L. M.   *Windham.*

1 WHILE I keep silence, and conceal
   My heavy guilt within my heart,
What torments doth my conscience feel
   What agonies of inward smart!

2 I spread my sins before the Lord,
   And all my secret faults confess;
Thy gospel speaks a pardoning word,
   Thine Holy Spirit seals the grace.

3 For this shall every humble soul
   Make swift addresses to thy seat:
When floods of huge temptations roll,
   There shall they find a bless'd retreat:

4 How safe beneath thy wings I lie,
   When days grow dark, and storms appear,
And when I walk, thy watchful eye
   Shall guide me safe from every snare.

285   L. M.   *Wells.*

1 I SEND the joys of earth away;
   Away, ye tempters of the mind,
False as the smooth deceitful sea,
   And empty as the whistling wind.

2 Your streams were floating me along,
   Down to the gulf of black despair,
And whilst I listen'd to your song,
   Your streams had e'en convey'd me there.

3 Lord I adore thy matchless grace,
   That warn'd me of that dark abyss;

That drew me from those treach'rous seas,
And bid me seek superior bliss.

4 Now to the shining realms above
I stretch my hands and glance mine eyes:
O for the pinions of a dove,
To bear me to the upper skies!

5 There from the bosom of my God,
Oceans of endless pleasures roll;
There would I fix my last abode,
And drown the sorrows of my soul.

TRUSTING IN GOD.

286   Metre 14.   *Brandenburg.*

1 AH! I shall soon be dying,
Time swiftly glides away;
But on my Lord relying,
I hail the happy day—

2 The day when I must enter
Upon a world unknown;
My helpless soul I venture
On Jesus Christ alone.

3 He once a spotless victim,
Upon Mount Calv'ry bled:
Jehovah did afflict him,
And bruise him in my stead.

TRUSTING IN GOD.

4 Hence all my hope arises,
  Unworthy as I am :
My soul most surely prizes
  The sin-atoning Lamb.

5 To him by grace united,
  I joy in him alone ;
And now, by faith delighted,
  Behold him on his throne.

6 There he is interceding
  For all who on him rest :
The grace from him proceeding
  Shall waft me to his breast.

7 Then with the saints in glory
  The grateful song I'll raise,
And chant my blissful story
  In high seraphic lays.

8 Free grace, redeeming merit,
  And sanctifying love,
Of Father, Son and Spirit,
  Shall charm the courts above.

287   L. M.   *Social Band.*

1 SAY now, ye lovely social band,
  Who walk the way to Canaan's land ;
Ye who have fled from Sodom's plain,
Say, would you now return again?

2 Have you just ventured to the field,
  Well armed with helmet, sword and shield,
And shall the world with dread alarms,
Compel you now to ground your arms?

3 Beware of pleasure's siren song;
  Alas! it cannot soothe you long;
  It cannot quiet Jordan's wave,
  Nor cheer the dark and silent grave.

4 O let your thoughts delight to soar,
  Where earth and time shall be no more;
  Explore by faith the heavenly fields,
  And pluck the fruit that Canaan yields

5 There see the glorious hosts on wing,
  And hear the heavenly seraphs sing!
  The shining ranks in order stand,
  Or move like lightning at command.

6 Jehovah there reigns not alone,
  The Savior shares his Father's throne;
  While angels circle round his seat,
  And worship prostrate at his feet.

7 Behold! I see, among the rest,
  A host in richer garments dress'd;
  A host that near his presence stands,
  And palms of victory grace their hands.

8 Say, who are these I now behold,
  With blood-wash'd robes and crowns of gold?
  This glorious host is not unknown
  To him who sits upon the throne.

9 These are the followers of the Lamb;
  From tribulation great they came;
  And on the hill of sweet repose,
  They bid adieu to all their woes.

10 Soon on the wings of love you'll fly,
   To join them in that world on high.

O make it now your chiefest care,
The image of your Lord to bear.

288   METRE 9.   *Carmarthan—Lenox.*

1 ARISE, my soul, arise,
   Shake off thy guilty fears,
The bleeding Sacrifice
   In my behalf appears;
Before the throne my Surety stands,
My name is written on his hands.

2 He ever lives above,
   For me to intercede;
His all-redeeming love,
   His precious blood to plead;
His blood aton'd for all our race,
And sprinkles now the throne of grace.

3 Five bleeding wounds he bears,
   Received on Calvary;
They pour effectual prayers,
   They strongly speak for me:
Forgive him, O forgive, they cry,
Nor let the ransom'd sinner die!

4 The Father hears him pray,
   His dear anointed One:
He cannot turn away
   The presence of his Son:
His Spirit answers to the blood,
And tells me I am born of God.

5 My God is reconciled,
   His pard'ning voice I hear;
He owns me for his child,
   I can no longer fear;

TRUSTING IN GOD.

With confidence I now draw nigh,
And Father, Abba Father, cry.

289.   S. M.   Idumea.

1 I LIFT my soul to God,
   My trust is in his name;
  Let not my foes, that seek my blood,
   Still triumph in my shame.

2 Sin and the powers of hell
   Persuade me to despair:
  Lord, make me know thy cov'nant well,
   That I may 'scape the snare.

3 From gleams of dawning light
   Till evening shades arise,
  For thy salvation, Lord, I wait,
   With ever longing eyes.

4 Remember all thy grace,
   And lead me in thy truth;
  Forgive the sins of riper days,
   And follies of my youth.

5 The Lord is just and kind,
   The meek shall learn his ways,
  And every humble sinner find
   The methods of his grace.

6 For his own goodness' sake
   He saves my soul from shame,
  He pardons (though my guilt be great)
   Through my Redeemer's name.

WARNING HYMNS.

290 S. M. *Watchman*

1 TO GOD in whom I trust,
 I lift my heart and voice:
Oh! let me not be put to shame,
 Nor let my foes rejoice.

2 Thy mercies, and thy love,
 O Lord, recall to mind;
And graciously continue still,
 As thou wert ever kind.

3 Let all my youthful crimes
 Be blotted out by thee;
And for thy wondrous goodness' sake,
 In mercy think on me.

4 His mercy and his truth,
 The righteous Lord displays,
In bringing wandering sinners home,
 And teaching them his ways.

WARNING HYMNS.

291. L. M. *Windham.*

1 BROAD is the road that leads to death,
 And thousands walk together there;
But wisdom shows a narrow path,
With here and there a traveler.

2 "Deny thyself and take thy cross,"
Is the Redeemer's great command!

Nature must count her gold but dross,
If she would gain this heavenly land.

3 The fearful soul that tires and faints,
And walks the ways of God no more,
Is but esteem'd almost a saint,
And makes his own destruction sure.

4 Lord, let not all my hopes be vain,
Create my heart entirely new;
Which hypocrites could ne'er attain,
Which false apostates never knew.

292   S. M.   *Strait Gate—Idumea.*

1 DESTRUCTION'S dangerous road
   What multitudes pursue!
While that which leads the soul to God,
   Is known or sought by few.

2 Believers find the way
   Through Christ the living Gate;
But those who hate this holy way,
   Complain it is too strait.

3 If self must be denied,
   And sin no more caress'd,
They rather choose the way that's wide,
   And strive to think it best.

4 Encompass'd by a throng,
   On numbers they depend;
They say so many can't be wrong,
   And miss a happy end.

5 But hear the Savior's word,
   "Strive for the heav'nly gate,

Many will call upon the Lord,
  And find their cries too late."

2 Obey the gospel call,
  And enter while you may;
The flock of Christ is always small,
  And none are safe but they.

3 Lord, open sinners' eyes,
  Their awful state to see:
And make them, ere the storm arise,
  To thee for safety flee.

293. Metre 5. *Alarming Voice.*

1 SINNER, art thou still secure?
  Wilt thou still refuse to pray?
Can thy heart or hands endure
  In the Lord's avenging day?

2 See, his mighty arm is bared!
  Awful terrors clothe his brow!
For his judgment stand prepared,
  Thou must either break or bow.

3 At his presence nature shakes,
  Earth affrighted hastes to flee:
Solid mountains melt like wax,
  What will then become of thee?

4 Who his advent may abide?
  You that glory in your shame,
Will you find a place to hide,
  When the world is wrapt in flame?

5 Lord, prepare us by thy grace!
  Soon we must resign our breath,

And our souls be call'd to pass
  Through the iron gate of death.

6 Let us now our day improve,
  Listen to the gospel voice:
Seek the things that are above;
  Scorn the world's pretended joys.

294   S. M.   *Shirland.*

1 IS this the kind return,
    And these the thanks we owe,
  Thus to abuse eternal love,
    Whence all our blessings flow!

2 To what a stubborn frame
    Hath sin reduced our mind!
  What strange rebellious, wretches we,
    And God as strangely kind!

3 On us he bids the sun
    Shed his reviving rays;
  For us the skies their circles run,
    To lengthen out our days.

4 The brutes obey their God,
    And bow their necks to men;
  But, we more base, more brutish things,
    Reject his easy reign.

5 Turn, turn, us mighty God,
    And mould our souls afresh;
  Break sovereign grace, these hearts of stone,
    And give us hearts of flesh.

6 Let past ingratitude
    Provoke our weeping eyes,

And hourly as new mercies fall,
Let hourly thanks arise.

295   C. M.   *Dublin.*

1 THE time is short!—sinners beware,
    Nor trifle time away,
The word of great salvation hear,
    While yet 'tis called to-day.

2 The time is short!—O sinners, now,
    To Christ, the Lord, submit;
To mercy's golden scepter bow,
    And fall at Jesus' feet.

3 The time is short!—ye saints, rejoice,
    The Lord will quickly come;
Soon shall you hear the Savior's voice,
    To call you to your home.

4 The time is short!—it swiftly flies—
    The hour is just at hand,
When we shall mount above the skies,
    And reach the wished-for land.

5 The time is short!—The moment near,
    When we shall dwell above;
And be forever happy there,
    With Jesus, whom we love.

296   C. M.   *Mear.*

1 THAT awful day will surely come,
    Th' appointed hour makes haste,
When I must stand before my Judge
    And pass the solemn test.

2 Thou lovely Chief of all my joys,
  Thou Sovereign of my heart,
 How could I bear to hear thy voice
  Pronounce the sound, "Depart."

3 The thunder of that dismal word
  Would so torment my ear,
 'Twould tear my soul asunder, Lord,
  With most tormenting fear.

4 What, to be banish'd for my life,
  And yet forbid to die!
 To linger in eternal pain,
  Yet death forever fly!

5 Oh, wretched state of deep despair,
  To see my God remove,
 And fix my doleful station where
  I must not taste his love!

6 Jesus, I throw my arms around
  And hang upon thy breast;
 Without a gracious smile from thee
  My spirit cannot rest.

7 O! tell me that my worthless name
  Is graven on thy hands,
 Show me some promise in thy book,
  Where my salvation stands.

8 Give me one kind, assuring word,
  To sink my fears again,
 And, cheerfully, my soul shall wait
  Her threescore years and ten.

WARNING HYMNS.

297 L. M. *Retirement.*

1 HASTEN, O sinner, to be wise,
  And stay not for the morrow's sun;
  The longer wisdom you despise,
  The harder is she to be won.

2 O hasten mercy to implore,
  And stay not for the morrow's sun;
  For fear thy season should be o'er,
  Before this ev'ning stage be run.

3 O hasten, sinner, to return,
  And stay not for the morrow's sun,
  For fear thy lamp should fail to burn,
  Before the needful work is done.

4 O hasten, sinner, to be blest,
  And stay not for the morrow's sun,
  For fear the curse should thee arrest,
  Before the morrow is begun.

5 O Lord, do thou the sinner turn!
  Now rouse him from his senseless state!
  O let him not thy counsel spurn,
  Nor rue his fatal choice too late.

298 METRE 13. *Warning Voice.*

1 STOP, poor sinners, stop and think,
    Before you farther go;
  Will you sport upon the brink
    Of everlasting woe?
  On the verge of ruin stop—
    Now the friendly warning take—
  Stay your footsteps—e'er you drop
    Into the burning lake.

2 Say, have you an arm like God,
  That you his will oppose?
Fear ye not that iron rod
  With which he breaks his foes?
Can you stand in that dread day,
  Which his justice shall proclaim
When the earth shall melt away
  Like wax before the flame?

3 Ghastly death will quickly come,
  And drag you to his bar;
Then to hear your awful doom,
  Will fill you with despair!
All your sins will round you crowd;
  You shall mark their crimson dye:
Each for vengeance crying loud,
  And what can you reply?

4 Though your heart were made of steel,
  Your forehead lined with brass;
God at length will make you feel,
  He will not let you pass;
Sinners then in vain will call,
  Those who now despise his grace,
"Rocks and mountains on us fall,
  And hide us from his face."

299 Metre 54. *Voice of Warning.*

1 AH guilty sinner, ruin'd by transgression,
  What shall thy doom be, when arrayed in terror,
God shall command thee, cover'd with pollution.
    Up to the judgement?

WARNING HYMNS.

2 Wilt thou escape from his omniscient notice,
  Fly to the caverns, court annihilation?
  Vain thy presumption, justice still shall triumph
      In thy destruction.

3 Stop, thoughtless sinner, stop awhile and ponder,
  Ere death arrest thee, and the Judge in vengeance,
  Hurl from his presence thine affrighted spirit,
      Swift to perdition.

4 Oft has he call'd thee, but thou wouldst not hear him,
  Mercies and judgments have alike been slighted
  Yet he is gracious and with arms unfolded,
      Waits to embrace thee.

5 Come, then, poor sinner, come away this moment,
  Just as you are, come, filthy and polluted,
  Come to the fountain open for uncleanness;
      Jesus invites you.

6 But if you trifle with his gracious message,
  Cleave to the world and love its guilty pleasures,
  Mercy grown weary, shall in righteous judgment
      Quit you forever.

7 Where the worm dies not, and the fire eternal,
  Fills the lost soul with anguish and with terror,
  There shall the sinner spend a long forever.
      Dying unpardon'd.

8 Oh! guilty sinner, hear the voice of warning;
Fly to the Savior, and embrace his pardon;
So shall your spirit meet with joy triumphant
　　　　　　　Death and the judgment.

PENITENTIAL.

300　　　　L. M.　　　　*Munich.*

1 BEHOLD a stranger at the door!
　He gently knocks, has knock'd before;
　Hath waited long—is waiting still;
　You treat no other friend so ill.

2 Oh, lovely attitude, he stands
　With melting heart and loaded hands!
　Oh, matchless, kindness and he shows
　This matchless kindness to his foes!

3 But will he prove a friend indeed?
　He will; the very Friend you need;
　The Friend of sinners—yes, 'tis He,
　With garments dyed on Calvary.

4 Rise, touch'd with gratitude divine;
　Turn out his enemy and thine,
　That soul-destroying monster, sin,
　And let the heavenly stranger in.

5 Admit him e'er his anger burn,
　His feet departed, ne'er return;
　Admit him, or the hour's at hand,
　You'll at his door rejected stand.

PENITENTIAL.

301   C. M.   *Youthful Piety*

1 HOW oft, alas! this wretched heart
    Has wander'd from the Lord!
How oft my roving thoughts depart,
    Forgetful of his word.

2 Yet sovereign mercy calls, "Return;"
    Dear Lord, and may I come?
My vile ingratitude I mourn;
    Oh, take the wand'rer home.

3 And canst thou, wilt thou yet forgive,
    And bid my crimes remove?
And shall a pardon'd rebel live
    To speak thy wondrous love?

4 Almighty grace, thy healing power,
    How glorious, how divine!
That can to life and bliss restore
    So vile a heart as mine.

5 Thy pard'ning love, so free, so sweet,
    Dear Savior I adore;
Oh keep me at thy sacred feet,
    And let me rove no more.

302   METRE 8.   *Vernon*

1 COME, O thou Traveler unknown,
    Whom still I hold, but cannot see;
My company before is gone,
    And I am left alone with thee:
With thee all night I mean to stay,
And wrestle till the break of day.

PENITENTIAL.

2 I need not tell thee who I am;
  My misery and sin declare;
Thyself hast call'd me by my name,
  Look on thy hands and read it there;
But who, I ask thee, who art thou?
Tell me thy name, and tell me now.

3 In vain thou strugglest to get free,
  I never will unloose my hold;
Art thou the Man that died for me?
  The secret of thy love unfold;
Wrestling, I will not let thee go,
Till I thy name, thy nature know.

4 Wilt thou not yet to me reveal
  Thy new, unutterable name?
Tell me, I still beseech thee, tell;
  To know it now resolv'd I am:
Wrestling, I will not let thee go,
Till I thy name, thy nature know.

5 What though my shrinking flesh complain
  And murmur to contend so long:
I rise superior to my pain:
  When I am weak, then I am strong!
And when my all of strength shall fail,
I shall with thee, God-Man, prevail.

303   S. M.   *Aylesbury.*

1 HAVE mercy, Lord, on me,
    As thou wert ever kind:
  Let me, oppress'd with loads of guilt,
    The wonted pardon find.

2 Against thee, Lord, alone,
    And only in thy sight,

PRODIGAL SON.

Have I transgress'd; and tho' condemn'd,
  Must own thy judgments right.

3 Blot out my crying sins,
    Nor me in anger view;
  Create in me a heart that's clean,
    An upright mind renew.

4 Withdraw not thou thy help,
    Nor cast me from thy sight,
  Nor let thy Holy Spirit take
    Its everlasting flight.

5 The joy thy favor gives,
    Let me again obtain;
  And thy free Spirit's firm support
    My fainting soul sustain.

PRODIGAL SON.

304   C. M.   *Awful Majesty*.

1 BEHOLD the wretch whose lust and wine
    Have wasted his estate;
  He begs a share among the swine
    To taste the husks they eat.

2 "I die with hunger here," he cries,
    "I starve in foreign lands;
  My Father's house hath large supplies,
    And bounteous are his hands."

PRODIGAL SON.

3 "I'll go, and with a mournful tongue,
　Fall down before his face;
Father, I've done thy justice wrong,
　Nor can deserve thy grace."

4 He said and hasten'd to his home,
　To seek his father's love;
The father saw the rebel come,
　And all his bowels move.

5 He ran and fell upon his neck,
　Embraced and kiss'd his son;
The rebel's heart with sorrow brake
　For follies he had done.

6 "Take off his clothes of shame and sin,"
　(The father gives command,)
"Dress him in garments white and clean,
　With rings adorn his hand.

7 "A day of fasting I ordain,
　Let mirth and joy abound:
My son was dead, and lives again,
　Was lost, and now is found.

305 　　C. M. 　　*Communion.*

1 AFFLICTIONS, tho' they seem severe,
　In mercy oft are sent,
They stopp'd the prodigal's career,
　And caused him to repent.

2 Although he no relentings felt,
　Till he had spent his store,
His stubborn heart began to melt,
　When famine pinch'd him sore.

PRODIGAL SON.

3 "What have I gain'd by sin," he said,
  "But hunger, shame, and fear?
My father's house abounds with bread,
  While I am starving here.

4 "I'll go and tell him all I've done,
  Fall down before his face,
Unworthy to be call'd his son,
  I'll seek a servant's place."

5 His father saw him coming back,
  He saw, and ran, and smiled;
Then drew his arms around the neck
  Of his rebellious child.

6 "Father, I've sinn'd, but O! forgive,"—
  "Enough," the father said,
"Rejoice, my house, my son's alive,
  For whom I mourn'd as dead.

7 "Now let the fatted calf be slain,
  Go spread the news around,
My son was dead, but lives again;
  Was lost, but now is found."

8 'Tis thus the Lord his love reveals,
  To call poor sinners home!
More then a father's love he feels,
  And welcomes all that come.

MARRIAGE HYMNS.

306   C. M.   *Solon.*

1 SINCE Jesus freely did appear
   To grace a marriage feast;
O Lord, we ask thy presence here,
   To make a wedding guest.

2 Upon the bridal pair look down,
   Who now have plighted hands;
Their union with thy favor crown,
   And bless the nuptial bands.

3 In purest love these souls unite,
   That they with Christian care,
May make domestic burdens light,
   By taking mutual share.

4 And when that solemn hour shall come,
   And life's short space be o'er;
May they in triumph reach that home,
   Where they shall part no more.

307   L. M.   *Hebron.*

1 WITH grateful hearts and tuneful lays,
   We bow before th' Eternal throne,
And offer up our humble praise,
   To him whose name is God alone.

2 On this auspicious eve draw near,
   And shed thy richest blessings down;
Fill every heart with love sincere,
   And all thy faithful mercies crown.

3 Grant now thy presence, gracious Lord.
 And hearken to our fervent pray'r;
The nuptial vow in heaven record,
 And bless the newly married pair.

4 Oh! guide them safe, this desert through,
 Mid all the cares of life and love;
At length with joy thy face to view,
 In fairer, better worlds above.

308 L. M. *Abingdon.*

1 WITH cheerful voices rise and sing
 The praises of our God and King:
For he alone can minds unite,
And bless with conjugal delight.

2 Oh, may this pair increasing find,
Substantial pleasures of the mind;
Happy together may they be,
And both united, Lord, to thee.

3 So may they live as truly one;
And when their work on earth is done,
Rise, hand in hand, to heaven, and share
The joys of love forever there.

COMMUNION.

309 L. M. *Kedron.*

1 YE that pass by, behold the Man!
 The Man of grief condemned for you!

COMMUNION.

The Lamb of God for sinners slain!
  Weeping, to Calvary pursue.

2 His sacred limbs, they stretch, they tear,
  With nails they fasten to the wood—
His sacred limbs—exposed and bare,
  Or only cover'd with his blood.

3 See there! his temples crown'd with thorns,
  His bleeding hands extended wide,
His streaming feet transfixed and torn,
  The fountain gushing from his side.

4 Thou dear, thou suff'ring Son of God,
  How doth thy heart to sinners move!
Sprinkle on us thy precious blood,
  And melt us with thy dying love!

5 The earth could to her centre quake,
  Convulsed, when her Creator died;
Or, may our inmost nature shake,
  And bow with Jesus crucified!

6 At thy last gasp, the graves displayed
  Their horrors to the upper skies;
Oh, that our souls might burst the shades,
  And quicken'd by thy death, arise!

7 The rocks could feel thy powerful death,
  And tremble, and asunder part;
Oh, rend, with thy expiring breath,
  The harder marble of our heart!

310   Metre 7.   *Seraph's Harp.*

1 HARK! the voice of love and mercy!
  Sounds aloud from Calvary;

COMMUNION.

   See, it rends the rocks asunder—
     Shakes the earth and vails the sky!
      "It is finished!"—
   Hear the dying Savior cry.

2 It is finished? Oh, what pleasure
    Do these precious words afford!
  Heavenly blessings without measure,
    Flow to us from Christ the Lord:
      It is finished!—
  Saints, the dying words record.

3 Finished—all the types and shadows
    Of the ceremonial law;
  Finished—all that God had promised;
    Death and hell no more shall awe:
      It is finished!—
  Saints, from hence your comforts draw.

4 Tune your harps anew, ye seraphs,—
    Join to sing the pleasing theme;
  All on earth and all in heaven,
    Join to praise Immanuel's name:
      Hallelujah!
  Glory to the bleeding Lamb!

311   C. M.   *Mear.*

1 LET us adore th' Eternal Word;
    'Tis he our souls hath fed;
  Thou art our living stream, O Lord,
    And thou th' immortal bread.

2 The manna came from lower skies,
    But Jesus from above,
  Where the fresh springs of pleasure rise,
    And rivers flow with love.

3 The Jews, the fathers, died at last,
　　Who ate that heavenly bread;
　But these provisions which we taste,
　　Can raise us from the dead.

4 Bless'd be the Lord that gives his flesh
　　To nourish dying men,
　And often spreads his table fresh,
　　Lest we should faint again.

5 Our souls shall draw their heavenly breath,
　　While Jesus finds supplies;
　Nor shall our graces sink to death,
　　For Jesus never dies.

6 Daily our mortal flesh decays,
　　But Christ our life shall come;
　His unresisted power shall raise
　　Our bodies from the tomb.

312　　　　C. M.　　　　　　*Solor.*

1 LORD, how divine thy comforts are:
　　How heavenly is the place,
　Where Jesus spreads the sacred feast
　　Of his redeeming grace!

2 Our humble faith here takes her rise,
　　While sitting round his board;
　And back to Calvary she flies
　　To view her groaning Lord.

3 His soul, what agonies it felt,
　　When his own God withdrew!
　And the large loads of all our guilt
　　Lay heavy on him too.

COMMUNION. 281

4 "Here," (says the kind, redeeming Lord,
   And shows his wounded side,)
"See, here the spring of all your joys,
   That opened when I died.

5 He smiles and cheers my mournful heart
   And tells of all his pain;
"All this," says he, "I bore for thee"—
   And then he smiles again.

6 Shout and proclaim the Savior's love,
   Ye saints that taste his wine:
Join with your kindred saints above,
   In loud hosannahs join!

7 A thousand glories to the God
   That gives such joy as this;
Hosannah! let it sound abroad,
   And reach where Jesus is.

313   L. M.   *Kedron.*

1 'TIS midnight—and on Olave's brow,
   The star is dimm'd that lately shone;
'Tis midnight—in the garden now,
   The suffering Savior prays alone.

2 'Tis midnight—and from all removed,
   Immanuel wrestles 'lone with fears;
E'en the disciple that he loved
   Heeds not his Master's grief and tears.

3 'Tis midnight—and for others' guilt
   The Man of sorrows weeps in blood:
Yet he that hath in anguish knelt,
   Is not forsaken by his God.

COMMUNION.

4 'Tis midnight—and from ether plains,
  Is borne the song that angels know;
Unheard by mortals are the strains
  That sweetly soothe the Savior's woe.

314   C. M.   *Communion.*

1 HOW sweet and awful is the place
    With Christ within the doors,
  While everlasting love displays
    The choicest of her stores.

2 Here every bowel of our God
    With soft compassion rolls;
  Here peace and pardon bought with blood,
    Is food for dying souls.

3 While all our hearts and all our songs
    Join to admire the feast,
  Each of us cry, with thankful tongues,
    "Lord, why was I a guest?

4 "Why was I made to hear thy voice,
    And enter while there's room;
  When thousands make a wretched choice,
    And rather starve than come?"

5 'Twas the same love that spread the feast
    That sweetly forced us in;
  Else we had still refused to taste,
    And perish'd in our sin.

6 Pity the nations, O our God,
    Constrain the earth to come;
  Send thy victorious word abroad,
    And bring the strangers home.

COMMUNION.

7 We long so see thy churches full,
   That all the chosen race
May with one voice, and heart, and soul,
   Sing thy redeeming grace.

315   C. M.   *Rockingham.*

1 THAT doleful night before his death,
   The Lamb, for sinners slain,
Did, almost with his latest breath,
   This solemn feast ordain.

2 To keep the feast, Lord, we are met,
   And to remember thee:
Help each poor trembler to repeat,
   "The Savior died for me."

3 Thy sufferings, Lord, each sacred sign
   To our remembrance brings;
We eat the bread and drink the wine,
   But think on nobler things.

4 O, tune our tongues, and put in frame
   Each heart that pants for thee,
To sing, "Hosannah to the Lamb,
   The Lamb that died for me."

316   S. M.   *Idumea.*

1 JESUS invites his saints
   To meet around his board;
Here pardon'd rebels sit and hold
   Communion with their Lord.

2 For food he gives his flesh,
   He bids us drink his blood;
Amazing favor! matchless grace
   Of our descending God.

3 This holy bread and wine
   Maintains our fainting breath,
By union with our living Lord
   And interest in his death.

4 Our heavenly Father calls
   Christ and his members one;
We the young children of his love,
   And he the first-born Son.

5 We are but several parts
   Of the same broken bread;
One body hath its several limbs,
   But Jesus is the Head.

6 Let all our powers be join'd
   His glorious name to raise
Pleasure and love fill every mind,
   And every voice be praise.

317   S. M.   *Little Malborough.*

1 LET all our tongues be one,
   To praise our God on high,
Who from his bosom sent his Son,
   To fetch us strangers nigh.

2 Nor let our voices cease,
   To sing the Savior's name;
Jesus, th' embassador of peace,
   How cheerfully he came.

3 It cost him cries and tears
   To bring us near to God;
Great was our debt, and he appears
   To make the payment good.

COMMUNION.

4 Infinite was our guilt,
  But he our Priest atones;
On the cold ground his life was spilt,
  And offered with his groans.

5 Look up my soul, to him
  Whose death was thy desert,
And humbly view the living stream
  Flow from his breaking heart.

6 While the eternal Three
  Bear their record above,
Here I believe he died for me,
  And seal my Savior's love.

318 C. M. *Resignation.*

1 JESUS, at whose supreme command,
  We now approach to God,
Before us in thy vesture stand,
  Thy vesture dipp'd in blood.
Obedient to thy gracious word,
  We break the hallowed bread,
Commem'rate thee, our dying Lord,
  And trust on thee to feed.

2 Now, Savior, now thyself reveal,
  And make thy nature known,
Affix thy blessed Spirit's seal,
  And stamp us for thine own.
The tokens of thy dying love
  O let us all receive,
And feel the quickening Spirit move,
  And sensibly believe!

3 The cup of blessing, blest by thee,
  Let it thy blood impart;

The bread thy mystic body be,
  And cheer each languid heart.
The grace which sure salvation brings,
  Let us herewith receive;
Satiate the hungry with good things,
  The hidden manna give.

4 The living bread sent down from heaven,
  In us vouchsafe to be;
Thy flesh for all the world is given.
  And all may live by thee.
Now, Lord, on us thy flesh bestow,
  And let us drink thy blood,
Till all our souls are filled below,
  With all the life of God.

319   METRE 16.   *Warning Voice.*

1 LAMB of God, whose dying love
    We now recall to mind,
  Send the answer from above,
    And let us mercy find;
  Think on us who think on thee,
    And every struggling soul release!
  O remember Calvary,
    And bid us go in peace!

2 By thine agonizing pain,
    And bloody sweat we pray,
  By thy dying love to man,
    Take all our sins away;
  Burst our bonds and set us free,
    From all iniquity release:
  O, remember Calvary,
    And bid us go in peace.

COMMUNION.

3 Let thy blood by faith applied,
 The sinner's pardon seal,
Speak us freely justified,
 And all our sickness heal:
By thy passion on the tree,
 Let all our griefs and troubles cease;
O remember Calvary,
 And bid us go in peace.

4 Never will we hence depart,
 Till thou our wants relieve:
Write forgiveness on our heart,
 And all thy image give:
Still our souls shall cry to thee,
 Till perfected in holiness,
O remember Calvary,
 And bid us go in peace.

320   METRE 4.   *Disciple.*

1 COME, thou everlasting Spirit,
 Bring to every thankful mind,
All the Savior's dying merit,
 All his suff'rings for mankind:
True recorder of his passion,
 Now the living fire impart,
Now reveal his great salvation,
 Preach his gospel to our heart.

2 Come, thou Witness of his dying,
 Come, Remembrancer divine,
Let us feel thy power applying
 Christ to every soul and mine:
Let us groan thine inward groaning,
 Look on him we pierced, and grieved,

All receive the grace atoning,
  All the sprinkled blood receive.

FEET-WASHING.

321 C. M. *Mear.*

1 TO show how humble Christians ought
    To one another be,
  Christ with his own example taught,
    As plainly we may see.

2 Though he was Lord and Master great,
    Who giveth all commands,
  He wash'd his own disciples' feet,
    With his own blessed hands.

3 When thus their Master with them dealt,
    And proved his love to them,
  How must their drooping hearts have felt,
    To meet with such esteem.

4 May they who worldly honor seek,
    Learn what it is to be
  Like Jesus, humble, truly meek,
    From self-applauses free.

5 Such facts as these should have effect,
    To bring the haughty low;
  The proudest heart should feel a check,
    And deeply humbled too.

6 Thus Peter's mind was much impress'd
    He thought himself too mean;
  But also felt himself distress'd,
    To have no part with him.

7 "Till thou art wash'd, thou hast no part
   With me," the Savior said;
Then Peter cried, "with all my heart!
   Wash thou my hands and head."

322   L. M.   *Rockbridge.*

1 THE night in which Christ was betrayed,
   For us a plain example laid,
He to a private room retired,
With those he afterward inspired.

2 There the Lord's Supper was prepared,
And Christ the Lord had with them shared,
Of which th' apostles did partake,
He thus an ordinance did make.

3 He rose and laid his garments by,
When tow'l and water were brought nigh,
To prove his love divinely sweet,
Proceeds to wash his servants' feet.

4 So after he had washed their feet,
Resumed his garments, took his seat:
So we should love and kindness show,
To all our brethren here below.

5 Ye call me Master and your Lord,
Which is according to my word,
If I have done this unto you,
Ye ought to serve each other too.

6 Example give I unto you,
As I have done so ye should do,
And if ye then my servants be,
Obey my word and follow me.

7 The Lord who did from heaven descend,
Bids us his doctrine to defend;
If we in all things faithful prove,
We shall obtain redeeming love.

323 L. M. *Devotion*

1 WHEN Jesus Christ was here below,
He taught his people what to do:
And if we would his precepts keep,
We must descend to washing feet.

2 For in that night he was betray'd,
He for us all a pattern laid;
So let our works and virtues shine,
To prove his patterns all divine.

3 The Lord who made the earth and sky,
Arose and laid his garments by,
And wash'd their feet to show that we
Should always kind and humble be.

4 He wash'd them all to make them clean.
But Judas still was full of sin;
May none of us like Judas sell
The Lord for gold and go to hell.

5 Peter said, "Lord, it shall not be,
Thou shalt not stoop to washing me."
O that no Christians here may say,
I'm too unworthy to obey.

6 You call me Lord and Master, too,
Then do as I have done to you;
All my commands and counsels keep,
And show your love by washing feet.

7 Ye shall be happy if you know,
　And do these things by faith below,
　And I'll protect you till you die,
　And then remove you up on high.

PARTING HYMNS.

324　　　L. M.　　　*Social Band.*

1 MY dearest friends, in bonds of love,
　Our hearts in sweetest union prove,
　Your friendship 's like a drawing band,
　Yet we must take the parting hand.
　Your presence sweet, your union dear,
　Your words delightful to my ear;
　And when I see that we must part,
　You draw like chords around my heart.

2 How sweet the hours have pass'd away,
　When we have met to sing and pray,
　How loathe I've been to leave the place
　Where Jesus shows his smiling face.
　O could I stay with friends so kind,
　How would it cheer my struggling mind!
　But duty makes me understand,
　That we must take the parting hand.

3 And since it is God's holy will,
　We must be parted for a while.
　In sweet submission all in one,
　We'll say, our Father's will be done.
　Dear fellow-youth in Christian ties,
　Who seek for mansions in the skies:

19*

Fight on, you'll win the happy shore.
Where parting hands are known no more.

4 How oft I've seen the flowing tears.
And heard you tell your hopes and fears;
Your hearts with love have seem'd to flame,
Which makes me hope we'll meet again.
Ye mourning souls, in sad surprise,
Jesus remembers all your cries;
O taste his grace, in all that land
We'll no more take the parting hand.

325   METRE 11. *Christian Farewell.*

1 FAREWELL, my dear brethren, the time is at hand.
That we must be parted from this social band;
Our sev'ral engagements now call us away;
Our parting is needful, and we must obey.

2 Farewell, my dear brethren, farewell for a while,
We'll soon meet again, if kind Providence smile:
And while we are parted and scattered abroad
We'll pray for each other and trust in the Lord

3 Farewell, faithful soldiers, you'll soon be discharged,
The war will be ended, your bounty enlarged:
With shouting and singing, though Jordan may roar,
We'll enter fair Canaan, and rest an the shore

4 Farewell, younger brethren, just listed for war
Sore trials await you, but Jesus is near;
Although you must travel the dark wilderness,
Your Captain's before you, he'll lead you in peace.

5 The world, and the devil, and sin, all unite,
With bold opposition, your souls to affright:
But Jesus, your leader, is stronger than they:
Let this animate you to march on your way.

6 Farewell, trembling mourner, with sad broken heart,
O, hasten to Jesus and choose the good part:
He's full of compassion, and mighty to save,
His arms are extended your soul to receive.

7 Farewell, careless sinners! for you I must grieve
To think of your danger while careless you live;
The judgment approaches — O think of your doom.
And turn to the Savior, while yet there is room.

326   C. M.   *Salvation.*

1 DEAR friends, farewell, I do you tell,
   Since you and I must part:
I go away, and here you stay,
   But still we're join'd in heart.
Your love to me has been most free,
   Your conversation sweet;
How can I bear to journey where
   With you I cannot meet?

2 Yet do I find my heart inclined
   To do my work below;
When Christ doth call, I trust I shall
   Be ready then to go.
I leave you all, both great and small,
   In Christ's encircling arms,
Who can you save from the cold grave,
   And shield you from all harm.

3 I trust you'll pray, both night and day.
 And keep your garments white,
For you and me, that we may be
 The children of the light.
If you die first, anon you must,
 The will of God be done,
I hope the Lord will you reward,
 With an immortal crown.

4 If I'm call'd home whilst I am gone,
 Indulge no tears for me;
I hope to sing and praise my King.
 To all eternity.
Millions of years over the spheres
 Shall pass in sweet repose,
While beauty bright unto my sight.
 Thy sacred sweets disclose.

5 I long to go, then farewell woe,
 My soul will be at rest;
No more shall I complain or sigh,
 But taste the heavenly feast.
O may we meet, and be complete,
 And long together dwell,
And serve the Lord with one accord;
 And so, dear friends, farewell.

327   METRE 8. *Missionary Farewell.*

1 FAREWELL, my brethren in the Lord!
 The gospel sounds the Jubilee;
My tongue shall bear the news abroad,
 From land to land, from sea to sea;
And as I preach from place to place,
I'll trust alone in God's free grace.

PARTING HYMNS.

2 Farewell! in bonds of union dear,
  Like strings you twine about my heart:
I humbly beg your earnest prayer,
  Till we shall meet no more to part;
Till we shall meet in worlds above,
Encircled in eternal love.

3 Farewell, my earthly friends below!
  Though all so kind and dear to me;
My Jesus calls, and I must go,
  To sound the gospel-jubilee:
To bear the joy-inspiring news
To Gentile worlds, and blinded Jews.

4 Farewell, dear people, one and all!
  While God the breath of life shall give,
I hope on him in prayer to call,
  That your dear souls in Christ may live:
That your dear souls prepar'd may be,
To reign in bliss eternally.

5 Farewell to all below the sun!
  And as I journey here below,
The path is strait my feet must run,
  And God will keep me as I go;
Will guard me by his powerful hand,
And bring me to the promis'd land.

6 Farewell! farewell!—I look above;
  Jesus, my Friend, to thee I call!
Be thou my joy, my crown, my love,
  My safeguard and my heavenly all;
My theme till life shall close, and then
My only hope in death—Amen!

PARTING HYMNS.

328 L. M. *Hebron—Devotion.*

1 O HAPPY day! when saints shall meet
To part no more—the thought is sweet;
No more to feel the rending smart,
Oft felt below, when Christians part.

2 O happy place! I still must say,
Where all but love is done away;
All cause of parting there is past;
There social feast will ever last.

3 Such union here is sought in vain,
As there, in every heart will reign,
There separation can't compel
The saints to bid the sad farewell.

4 On earth when friends together meet,
And find the passing moments sweet,
Time's rapid motions soon compel,
With grief to say—dear friends, farewell.

5 The shepherd feels the smarting shock,
Of parting from his weeping flock;
His feelings for them, none can tell,
When forc'd to say—my friends, farewell.

6 The happy season soon will come,
When saints shall meet in heav'n their home;
Eternally with Christ to dwell,
Nor ever hear the sound: farewell.

329 C. M. *Mear.*

1 BLEST be the dear, uniting love,
That will not let us part;

Our bodies may far off remove—
We still are one in heart.

2 Join'd in one Spirit to our Head,
Where he appoints we go;
And still in Jesus' footsteps tread,
And show his praise below.

3 Partakers of the Savior's grace,
The same in mind and heart,
Nor joy, nor grief, nor time, nor place,
Nor life, nor death can part.

4 But let us hasten to the day,
Which shall our flesh restore;
When death shall all be done away,
And Christians part no more!

VARIOUS SUBJECTS.

330　　　Metre 12.　　　*Greenfields.*

1 HOW tedious and tasteless the hours,
When Jesus no longer I see! [flowers,
Sweet prospects, sweet birds, and sweet
Have all lost their sweetness to me:
The midsummer sun shines but dim.
The fields strive in vain to look gay;
But when I am happy in him,
December's as pleasant as May.

2 His name yields the richest perfume,
And sweeter than music his voice;

His presence disperses my gloom,
  And makes all within me rejoice;
I should were he always thus nigh,
  Have nothing to wish or to fear,
No mortal so happy as I,
  My summer would last all the year.

3 Content with beholding his face,
  My all to his pleasure resign'd;
No changes of season or place
  Would make any change in my mind:
While bless'd with a sense of his love,
  A palace a toy would appear;
And prisons would palaces prove,
  If Jesus would dwell with me there.

4 Dear Lord, if indeed I am thine,
  If thou art my sun and my song,
Say, why do I languish and pine?
  And why are my winters so long?
O drive these dark clouds from my sky,
  Thy soul-cheering presence restore;
Or take me to thee up on high,
  Where winter and clouds are no more.

331   Metre 12.   *Greenfields*

1 WHEN Joseph his brethren beheld;
    Afflicted and trembling with fear,
His heart with compassion was fill'd,
  From weeping he could not forbear;
Awhile his behavior was rough,
  To bring their past sin to their mind;
But when they were humbled enough,
  He hasted to show himself kind.

2 How little they thought it was he,
   Whom they had ill-treated and sold!
How great their confusion must be,
   As soon as his name he had told!
"I'm Joseph, your brother!" he said,
   "And still to my heart you are dear;
You sold me, and thought I was dead,
   But God, for your sakes, sent me here."

3 Though greatly distressed before,
   When charg'd with purloining the cup:
They now were confounded much more,
   Not one of them durst to look up:
'Can Joseph, whom we would have slain.
   Forgive us the evil we did?
And will he our household maintain?
   O! this is a brother indeed!"

4 Thus dragg'd by my conscience, I came,
   And laden with guilt to the Lord;
Surrounded with terror and shame,
   Unable to utter a word.
At first, he look'd stern and severe,
   What anguish then pierced my heart,
Expecting each moment to hear,
   The sentence, "Thou cursed, depart!"

5 But O! what surprise when he spoke!
   While tenderness beam'd in his face;
My heart then to pieces was broke,
   O'erwhelm'd and confounded by grace.
"Poor sinner, I know thee full well;
   By thee I was sold and was slain;
But died to redeem thee from hell,
   And raise thee in glory to reign.

6 "I'm Jesus whom thou hast blasphemed,
   And crucified often afresh;
But let me henceforth be esteem'd,
   Thy brother, thy bone and thy flesh.
My pardon I freely bestow,
   Thy wants will I fully supply;
I'll guide thee, and guard thee below,
   And soon will remove thee on high.

7 "Go, publish to sinners around,
   That they may be willing to come,
The mercy which now you have found,
   And tell them that yet there is room."
O sinners! the message obey:
   No more vain excuses pretend;
But come without further delay,
   To Jesus, our brother and friend.

332   METRE 7.   *Greenwood.*
1 SAVIOR, visit thy plantation,
   Grant us, Lord, a gracious rain!
All will come to desolation,
   Unless thou return again.
          CHORUS.
       Lord, revive us!
All our help must come from thee.

2 Keep no longer at a distance,
   Shine upon us from on high,
Lest, for want of thy assistance,
   Every plant should droop and die.
       Lord, revive us, &c.

3 Surely, once thy garden flourish'd,
   Every plant look'd gay and green;

Then thy word our spirits nourish'd,—
　Happy seasons we have seen.
　　Lord, revive us, &c.

4 But a drought has since succeeded,
　And a sad decline we see;
Lord, thy help is greatly needed,
　Help can only come from thee.
　　Lord, revive us, &c.

5 Where are those we counted leaders?
　Fill'd with zeal, and love, and truth;
Old professors, tall as cedars,
　Bright examples to our youth.
　　Lord, revive us, &c.

6 Some in whom we once delighted,
　We shall meet no more below:
Some alas! we fear are blighted,
　Scarce a single leaf they show.
　　Lord, revive us, &c.

7 Younger plants—the sight how pleasant!
　Cover'd thick with blossoms stood;
But they cause us grief at present;
　Frosts have nipp'd them in the bud.
　　Lord, revive us, &c.

8 Dearest Savior, hasten hither;
　Thou canst make them bloom again;
Oh! permit them not to wither,
　Let not all our hopes be vain.
　　Lord, revive us, &c.

9 Let our mutual love be fervent.
　Make us prevalent in prayers;

Let each one, esteem'd thy servant,
  Shun the world's bewitching snares.
    Lord, revive us, &c.

10 Break the tempter's fatal power,
  Turn the stony heart to flesh:
And begin from this good hour,
  To revive thy work afresh.
    Lord, revive us, &c.

333   METRE 4.   *Advocate*

1 SAVIOR, I do feel thy merit,
    Sprinkled with redeeming blood;
  And my weary, troubled spirit,
    Now finds rest with thee, my God;
  I am safe, and I am happy,
    While in thy dear arms I lie,
  Sin and Satan cannot hurt me,
    While my Savior is so nigh.

2 Now I'll sing a Savior's merit,
    Tell the world of his dear name;
  That if any want his Spirit,
    He is still the very same:
  He that asketh soon receiveth,
    He that seeks is sure to find;
  Whomso'er on him believeth,
    He will never cast behind.

3 Now our Advocate is pleading
    With his Father and our God;
  Now for us is interceding
    As the purchase of his blood:
  Now methinks I hear him praying,
    Father, save them, I have died;

And the Father answers, saying,
They are freely justified.

334 METRE 7. *Tamworth.*

1 OH thou God of my salvation,
My Redeemer from all sin,
Moved by thy divine compassion,
Who hast died my heart to win;
I will praise thee,
Where shall I thy praise begin?

2 While the angel choirs are crying,
Glory to the great I AM,
I with them would still be vicing,
Glory, glory to the Lamb!
O how precious
Is the sound of Jesus' name.

3 Now I see with joy and wonder,
Whence the healing streams arose;
Angel minds are lost to ponder
Dying love's mysterious cause;
Yet the blessing
Down to all, to me it flows,

4 Though unseen, I love the Savior—
He hath brought salvation near;
Manifests his pard'ning favor,
And when Jesus doth appear,
Soul and body
Shall his glorious image wear.

5 Angels now are hov'ring round us,
Unperceived they mix the throng,

Wond'ring at the love that crowned us,
　Glad to join the holy song;
　　Hallelujah!
　Love and praise to Christ belong.

335　　　Metre 4.　　　*Conquest.*

1 DARK and thorny is the desert
　Thro' which pilgrims make their way:
But beyond this vale of sorrows,
　Lie the fields of endless day;
Fiends loud howling through the desert,
　Make them tremble as they go;
And the fiery darts of Satan
　Often bring their courage low.

2 O young soldiers, are you weary
　Of the troubles of the way?
Does your strength begin to fail you,
　And your vigor to decay?
Jesus, Jesus will go with you—
　He will lead you to his throne;
He who dyed his garments for you,
　And the wine-press trod alone;

3 He whose thunder shakes creation,
　He who bids the planets roll;
He who rides upon the tempest,
　And whose sceptre sways the whole—
Round him are ten thousand angels,
　Ready to obey command;
They are always hov'ring round you,
　Till you reach the heav'nly land.

4 There, on flow'ry hills of pleasure,
　In the fields of endless rest,

Love and joy, and peace, shall ever
Reign and triumph in your breast.
Who can paint those scenes of glory,
Where the ransom'd dwell on high?
Where the golded harps forever
Sound redemption through the sky!

5 Millions there of flaming seraphs
Fly across the heavenly plain;
There they sing immortal praises —
Glory! glory! is their strain;
But methinks a sweeter concert
Makes the heav'nly arches ring,
And a song is heard in Zion
Which the angels cannot sing.

6 See the heav'nly host in rapture
Gaze upon this shining band,
Wond'ring at their costly garment,
And their laurels in their hands;
There, upon the golden pavement,
See the ransom'd march along,
While the splendid courts of glory
Sweetly echo to their song.

7 O their crowns! how bright they sparkle,
Such as monarchs never wore;
They have gone to heavenly pastures —
Jesus is their Shepherd there.
Hail, ye happy, happy spirits!
Welcome to the blissful plain;
Glory, honor, and salvation! —
Reign, sweet Shepherd! ever reign!

336   METRE 16.   *Mendon.*
1 VAIN, delusive world, adieu!
With all thy creature good,

Only Jesus I pursue,
 Who bought me with his blood!
All thy pleasures I forego,
 I trample on thy wealth and pride,
Only Jesus will I know,
 And Jesus crucified.

2 Other knowledge I disdain,
 Tis all but vanity:
Christ the Lamb of God was slain,
 He tasted death for me!
Me to save from endless woe
 The sin-atoning Victim died!
Only Jesus will I know,
 And Jesus crucified!

3 Here will I set up my rest;
 My fluctuating heart
From the haven of his breast
 Shall never more depart:
Whither should a sinner go?
 His wounds for me stand open wide;
Only Jesus will I know
 And Jesus crucified.

4 Him to know is life and peace,
 And pleasure without end;
This is all my happiness,
 On Jesus to depend:
Daily in his grace to grow,
 And ever in his faith abide,
Only Jesus will I know,
 And Jesus crucified.

5 O that I could all invite,
 This saving truth to prove:

Show the length, the breadth, the height
  And depth of Jesus' love!
Fain I would to sinners show
  The blood by faith alone applied!
Only Jesus will I know,
  And Jesus crucified.

337   METRE 25.   *Redeeming Grace.*

1 COME, all who love my Lord and Master,
    And like old David I will tell,
  Though chief of sinners, I've found favor,
    By grace redeemed from death and hell:
  Far as the east from west is parted,
    So far my sins by dying love
  From me by faith are separated,
    Blest antepast of joys above.

2 I late estranged from Jesus wandered,
    And thought each dangerous poison good;
  But he in mercy long pursued me,
    With cries of his redeeming blood;
  Though like Bartimeus I was blinded
    In nature's darkest night conceal'd,
  But Jesus' love removed my blindness,
    And he his pard'ning grace reveal'd.

3 Now I will serve Him while He spares me,
    And with His people sing aloud;
  Though hell oppose, and sinners mock me,
    In rapt'rous songs I'll praise my God;
  By faith I view the heavenly concert,
    They sing high strains of Jesus' love;
  Oh! with desire my soul is longing,
    And fain would be with Christ above.

4 That blessed day is fast approaching,
   When Christ in glorious clouds will come,
With sounding trumps and shouts of angels.
   To call each faithful spirit home:
There's Abra'm, Isaac, holy prophets,
   And all the saints at God's right hand;
There hosts of angels join in concert —
   Shout as they reach the promised land.

338   Metre 4.   *Disciple.*

1 JESUS, I my cross have taken,
   All to leave and follow thee;
Naked, poor despised, forsaken,
   Thou, from hence my all shalt be;
Perish, ev'ry fond ambition,
   All I've sought, or hoped or known,
Yet, how rich is my condition,
   God and heaven are still my own!

2 Let the world despise and leave me —
   They have left my Savior too:
Human hearts and looks deceive me —
   Thou art not like them untrue;
And whilst thou shalt smile upon me,
   God of wisdom, love and might,
Foes may hate and friends disown me —
   Show thy face and all is bright.

3 Go, then, earthly fame and treasure,
   Come disaster, scorn, and pain;
In thy service pain is pleasure,
   With thy favor loss is gain;
I have call'd thee Abba, Father,
   I have set my heart on thee;
Storms may howl, and clouds may gather —
   All must work for good to me.

4 Man may trouble and distress me,
 'T will but drive me to thy breast;
Life with trials hard may press me,
 Heaven will give me sweeter rest;
Oh! 'tis not in grief to harm me,
 While thy love is left to me;
Oh! 'twere not in joy to charm me,
 Were that joy unmix'd with thee.

5 Soul then know thy full salvation —
 Rise o'er sin, and fear, and care;
Joy to find in every station,
 Something still to do or bear;
Think what Spirit dwells within thee —
 Think what Father's smiles are thine;
Think that Jesus died to win thee,
 Child of heaven, canst thou repine?

6 Haste thee on from grace to glory,
 Armed by faith and winged by prayer —
Heaven's eternal day's before thee,
 God's own hand shall guide thee there;
Soon shall close thy earthly mission,
 Soon shall pass thy pilgrim days;
Hope shall change to glad fruition,
 Faith to sight and prayer to praise.

339 C. M. *Rockingham.*

1 FATHER, how wide thy glories shine!
 How high thy wonders rise!
Known through the earth by thousand signs,
 By thousands through the skies:
Those mighty orbs proclaim thy power;
 Their motions speak thy skill:
And on the wings of every hour
 We read thy patience still.

2 Part of thy name divinely stands
  On all thy creatures writ,
 They show the labor of thy hands,
  Or impress of thy feet;
 But when we view thy strange design
  To save rebellious worms,
 Where vengeance and compassion join
  In their divinest forms:

3 Here the whole Deity is known,
  Nor dares a creature guess
 Which of the glories brightest shone,
  The justice or the grace;
 Now the full glories of the Lamb
  Adorn the heavenly plains:
 Bright seraphs learn Immanuel's name,
  And try their choicest strains.

4 O may I bear some humble part
  In that immortal song!
 Wonder and joy shall tune my heart,
  And love command my tongue.
 To Father, Son and Holy Ghost,
  Who sweetly all agree
 To save a world of sinners lost —
  Eternal glory be.

340   METRE 53.   *Heavenly Treasure.*

1 RELIGION! 'tis a glorious treasure,
  The purchase of a Savior's blood,
 It fills the soul with consolation,
  It lifts the thoughts to things above.
 It calms our fears, it soothes our sorrows,
  It smoothes our way o'er life's rough sea,
 'Tis mix'd with goodness, meek humble patience
  This heavenly portion mine shall be.

2 While journeying here through tribulation,
   In Christian love we'll march along;
And while strife severs the ambitious —
   In Jesus Christ we'll all be one:
Religion pure unites together
   In bonds of love and makes us free:
While endless ages are onward rolling,
   This heavenly portion mine shall be.

3 How fleeting — vain — how transitory,
   This world with all its pomp and show;
Its vain delights, and short-lived pleasure —
   I'll gladly leave them all below.
But love and grace shall be my story,
   While I in Christ such beauties see;
While endless ages are onward rolling,
   This heavenly portion mine shall be.

4 This earthly house must be dissolved,
   And mortal life will soon be o'er;
All earthly care, and earthly sorrow
   Shall pain my eyes and heart no more;
Religion pure will stand forever,
   And my glad heart shall strengthen'd be,
While endless ages are onward rolling,
   This heavenly portion mine shall be.

341   C. M.   *St. Stephens.*

1 WHEN languor and disease invade
   This trembling house of clay,
'Tis sweet to look beyond my pains,
   And long to fly away.

2 Sweet to look inward and attend
   The whispers of his love;

Sweet to look upward to the place
Where Jesus pleads above.

3 Sweet to look back and see my name
In life's fair book set down;
Sweet to look forward and behold
Eternal joys my own.

4 Sweet to reflect how grace divine
My sins on Jesus laid:
Sweet to remember that his blood
My debt of suffering paid.

5 Sweet in his righteousness to stand,
Which saves from second death;
Sweet to experience, day by day,
His Spirit's quick'ning breath.

342 C. M. *Youthful Piety.*

1 COME, let us now forget our mirth,
And think that we must die;
What are our best delights on earth,
Compared with those on high!

2 Our pleasures here will soon be past—
Our brightest joys decay;
But pleasures there forever last,
And cannot fade away.

3 Here sins and sorrows we deplore,
With many cares distress'd;
But there the mourners weep no more,
And there the weary rest.

4 Our dearest friends, when death shall call,
At once must hence depart;

But there we hope to meet them all,
  And never, never part.

5 Then let us love and serve the Lord,
  With all our youthful pow'rs
And we shall gain this great reward,
  This glory shall be ours.

343   METRE 12.   *Solemn Summons.*

1 HOW solemn the signal I hear!
  The summons that calls me away,
In regions unknown to appear.
  How shall I the summons obey?
What scenes in that world shall arise,
  When life's latest sigh shall be fled,
And darkness has seal'd up mine eyes;
  And deep in the dust I am laid.

2 No longer the world can I view,
  The scenes which so long I have known:
My friends, I must bid you adieu,
  For here I travel alone;
Yet here my Redeemer has trod,
  His hallowed footsteps I know;
I'll trust for defence to his rod,
  And lean on his staff as I go.

3 Dear Shepherd of Israel, lead on,
  My soul follows hard after thee;
The phantoms of death are all down,
  When Jesus my Shepherd I see,
Dear brethren and sisters, I go
  To wait your arrival above;
Be faithful, and soon you shall know
  The triumphs and joys of his love.

344   C. M.   *Rochester.*

1 WHAT poor despised company
    Of travelers are these,
That walk in yonder narrow way,
    Along that rugged maze?

2 Why, they are of a royal line,
    All children of a King:
Heirs of immortal crowns divine,
    And loud for joy they sing.

3 Why do they then appear so mean,
    And why so much despis'd?
Because of their rich robes unseen,
    The world is not appriz'd.

4 But some of them seem poor distress'd,
    And lacking daily bread!
Ah! they're of wealth divine possess'd,
    With hidden manna fed.

Why do they keep that narrow road,
    That rugged, thorny maze?
Because, that way their Leader trod,
    They love and keep his ways.

Why do they shun the pleasing path,
    That worldings love so well?
Because it is the road of death,
    The open way to hell.

7 What! is there then no other road,
    To Canaan's happy ground?
Christ is the only way to God,
    No other can be found.

345   C. M.   *Resignation.*

1 YE weary, heavy laden souls,
    Who are oppressed sore,
  Ye trav'lers through the wilderness,
    To Canaan's peaceful shore:
  Through chilling winds, and beating rain,
    The waters deep and cold,
  And enemies surrounding you,
    Take courage, and be bold.

2 Though storms and hurricanes arise
    The desert all around,
  And fiery serpents oft appear
    Through the enchanted ground,
  Dark nights, and clouds, and gloomy fear,
    And dragons often roar;
  But while the gospel trump we hear,
    We'll press for Canaan's shore.

3 We're often like the lonesome dove,
    Who mourns her absent mate;
  From hill to hill, from vale to vale,
    Her sorrows to relate;
  But Canaan's land is just before,
    Sweet spring is coming on,
  A few more beating winds and rains,
    And winter will be gone.

4 Sometimes like mountains to the sky,
    Black Jordan's billows roar,
  Which often makes the pilgrims fear,
    They never will get o'er:
  But let us gain Mount Pisgah's top,
    And view the vernal plain.
  To fright our souls may Jordan roar,
    And hell may rage in vain.

5 Methinks I now begin to see
　　The borders of that land;
　The trees of life, with heav'nly fruit,
　　In beauteous order stand:
　The wint'ry time is past and gone,
　　Sweet flowers now appear,
　The fiftieth year hath now rolled round,
　　The great Sabbatic year.

6 O, what a glorious sight appears,
　　To my believing eyes;
　Methinks I see Jerusalem,
　　A city in the skies:
　Bright angels whisp'ring me away,
　　"O come, my brother, come,"
　And I am willing to be gone
　　To my eternal home.

7 Farewell, my brethren in the Lord,
　　We are to Canaan bound;
　And should we never meet again
　　'Till the last trump shall sound,
　I hope that I shall meet you there,
　　On that delightful shore;
　In oceans of eternal bliss,
　　Where parting is no more.

346　　　Metre 8.　　*Mysterious Love.*

1 AND can it be that I should gain
　　An interest in the Savior's blood?
　Died he for me, who caused his pain?
　　For me, who him to death pursued?
　Amazing love! and can it be,
　　That thou, my Lord, shouldst die for me!

2 'T is myst'ry all, th' Immortal dies!
  Who can explore his strange design!
In vain the first-born seraph tries
  To sound the depths of love divine!
'T is mercy all! let earth adore:
Let angel minds inquire no more.

3 He left his Father's throne above;
  (So free, so infinite his grace!)
Emptied himself of all but love,
  And bled for Adam's helpless race;
'T is mercy all, immense and free,
For, O my God, it found out me!

4 Long my imprison'd spirit lay,
  Fast bound in sin and nature's night:
Thine eye diffused a quick'ning ray;
  I woke: The dungeon flamed with light!
My chains fell off, my heart was free,
I rose, went forth, and followed thee.

5 No condemnation now I dread,
  Jesus, and all in him is mine!
Alive in him, my living Head,
  And cloth'd in righteousness divine,
Bold I approach th' eternal throne,
And claim the crown, thro' Christ, my own.

347 METRE 6. *Chapel.*

1 AND am I only born to die?
    And must I suddenly comply
      With nature's stern decree?
  What after death for me remains?
  Celestial joys or hellish pains,
      To all eternity.

2 How then ought I on earth to live,
While God prolongs the kind reprieve,
   And props the house of clay:
My sole concern, my single care
To watch, and tremble, and prepare
   Against that fatal day.

3 No room for mirth or trifling here,
For worldly hope or worldly fear,
   If life so soon is gone:
If now the Judge is at the door,
And all mankind must stand before
   Th' inexorable throne!

4 No matter which my thoughts employ;
A moment's misery or joy;
   But O! when both shall end,
Where shall I find my destined place?
Shall I my everlasting days,
   With fiends or angels spend?

5 Nothing is worth a thought beneath,
But how I may escape the death
   That never, never dies!
How make my own election sure;
And when I fail on earth, secure
   A mansion in the skies.

6 Jesus, vouchsafe a pitying ray,
Be thou my Guide, be thou my Way
   To glorious happiness!
Ah! write the pardon on my heart!
And whensoe'er I hence depart,
   Let me depart in peace!

348   S. M.   *Aylesbury.*

1 AND let our bodies part,
   To different climes repair;
Inseparably join'd in heart,
   The friends of Jesus are.

2 Jesus the Corner-Stone,
   Did first our hearts unite;
And still he keeps our spirits one,
   We walk with him in white.

3 O let us still proceed
   In Jesus' work below;
And following our triumphant Head,
   To farther conquests go.

4 The vineyard of the Lord
   Before his laborers lies:
And lo! we see the vast reward
   Which 'waits us in the skies.

5 O let our heart and mind
   Continually ascend,
That haven of repose to find,
   Where all our labors end!

6 Where all our toils are o'er,
   Our suff'ring and our pain;
We meet on that eternal shore,
   Shall never part again.

7 O happy, happy place,
   Where saints and angels meet!
There we shall see each others' face,
   And all our brethren greet.

8 The church of the first-born,
  We shall with them be blest,
And crowned with endless joy, return
  To our eternal rest.

9 With joy we shall behold,
  In yonder blest abode,
The patriarchs and prophets old,
  And all the saints of God.

10 Abra'm and Isaac, there,
  And Jacob shall receive,
The followers of their faith and prayer.
  Who now in bodies live.

11 We shall our time beneath,
  Live out in cheerful hope,
And fearless pass the vale of death,
  And gain the mountain top.

12 To gather home his own
  God shall his angels send,
And bid our bliss on earth begun,
  In deathless triumphs end.

349   L. M.   *Abingdon.*

1 THE wond'ring world inquires to know
  Why I should love my Jesus so;
"What are his charms," say they, "above
The objects of a mortal love?

2 Yes, my Beloved, to my sight,
Shows a sweet mixture, red and white:
All human beauties, all divine,
In my Beloved meet and shine.

3 White is his soul, from blemish free;
  Red with the blood he shed for me:
  The fairest of ten thousand fairs;
  A sun among ten thousand stars.

4 His head the finest gold excels;
  There wisdom in perfection dwells;
  And glory, like a crown, adorns
  Those temples once beset with thorns.

5 Compassions in his heart are found,
  Near to the signals of his wound:
  His sacred side no more shall bear
  The cruel scourge, the piercing spear.

6 His hands are fairer to behold
  Than diamonds set in rings of gold;
  Those heavenly hands, that on the tree
  Were nail'd and torn, and bled for me.

7 Though once he bowed his feeble knees,
  Loaded with sins and agonies.
  Now on the throne of his command,
  His legs, like marble pillars stand.

8 His eyes are majesty and love,
  The eagle temper'd with the dove;
  No more shall trickling sorrow roll
  Through those dear windows of his soul.

9 His mouth, that pour'd out long complaints,
  Now smiles and cheers his fainting saints;
  His countenance more graceful is
  Than Lebanon with all its trees.

10 All over glorious is my Lord,
   Must be beloved and yet adored!

His worth if all the nations knew,
Sure the whole earth would love him too!

350 C. M. *St. Martin's.*

1 BEHOLD the glories of the Lamb,
    Amidst his Father's throne:
  Prepare new honors for his name,
    And songs before unknown.

2 Let elders worship at his feet,
    The church adore around;
  With vials full of odors sweet,
    And harps of sweeter sound.

3 Those are the prayers of all the saints,
    And these the hymns they raise:
  Jesus is kind to our complaints,
    He loves to hear our praise.

4 Eternal Father, who shall look
    Into thy secret will?
  Who but the Son shall take that book,
    And open every seal.

5 He shall fulfil thy great decrees,
    The Son deserves it well;
  Lo! in his hand, the sovereign keys
    Of heav'n, and death, and hell!

6 Now to the Lamb that once was slain,
    Be endless blessings paid;
  Salvation, glory, joy, remain
    Forever on thy head.

7 Thou hast redeem'd our souls with blood,
    Hast set the pris'ners free,

Hast made us kings and priests to God,
And we shall reign with thee.

 The worlds of nature and of grace
Are put beneath thy power;
Then shorten these delaying days,
And bring the promised hour.

351   L. M.   *Wells.*

1 LIFE is the time to serve the Lord,
The time t' insure the great reward,
And while the lamp holds out to burn,
The vilest sinner may return.

2 Life is the hour that God hath given
To 'scape from hell and fly to heav'n!
The day of grace, and mortals may
Secure the blessings of the day.

3 The living know that they must die,
But all the dead forgotten lie;
Their memory and their sense is gone,
Alike unknowing and unknown.

4 Their hatred and their love is lost,
Their envy buried in the dust;
They have no share in all that's done
Beneath the circuit of the sun.

5 Then what my thoughts design to do,
My hands with all your might pursue,
Since no device nor work is found,
Nor faith, nor hope, beneath the ground.

6 There are no acts of pardon past
In the cold grave to which we haste;

But darkness, death, and long despair
Reign in eternal silence there.

352   METRE 9.   Lenox.

1 BLOW ye the trumpet, blow,
    The gladly solemn sound;
Let all the nations know,
    To earth's remotest bound:
The year of Jubilee is come;
Return, ye ransom'd sinners, home.

2 Jesus our Great High Priest,
    Hath full atonement made:
Ye weary spirits, rest,
    Ye mournful souls, be glad;
The year of Jubilee is come;
Return, ye ransom'd sinners, home.

3 Extol the Lamb of God,
    The all-atoning Lamb;
Redemption in his blood
    Throughout the world proclaim:
The year of Jubilee is come;
Return, ye ransom'd sinners, home.

4 Ye slaves of sin and hell,
    Your liberty receive,
And safe in Jesus dwell;
    And blest in Jesus live;
The year of Jubilee is come;
Return, ye ransom'd sinners, home.

5 Ye who have sold for nought
    Your heritage above,
Shall have it back unbought,
    The gift of Jesus' love;

The year of Jubilee is come;
Return, ye ransom'd sinners, home.

6 The Gospel trumpet hear,
  The news of heavenly grace;
And, sav'd from earth, appear
  Before your Savior's face;
The year of Jubilee is come,
Return, ye ransom'd sinners, home.

353   L. M.   *Portugal.*

1 FAR from my thoughts, vain world, be gone,
    Let my religious hours alone:
  Fain would my eyes my Savior see;
  I wait a visit, Lord, from thee.

2 My heart grows warm with holy fire
  And kindles with a pure desire:
  Come, my dear Jesus, from above,
  And feed my soul with heavenly love.

3 The trees of life immortal stand
  In fragrant rows at thy right hand,
  And in sweet murmurs by their side
  Rivers of bliss perpetual glide.

4 Haste then, but with a smiling face,
  And spread the table of thy grace:
  Bring down a taste of truth divine,
  And cheer my heart with sacred wine.

5 Bless'd Jesus! what delicious fare,
  How sweet thy entertainments are!
  Never did angels taste above,
  Redeeming grace, and dying love.

6 Hail, great Immanuel, all divine!
In thee thy Father's glories shine:
Thou brightest, sweetest, fairest One,
That eyes have seen or angels known.

354   L. M.   *Windham.*

1 NOW, in the heat of youthful blood,
Remember your Creator, God;
Behold the months come hast'ning on,
When you shall say,—"My joys are gone."

2 Behold the aged sinner goes,
Laden with guilt and heavy woes,
Down to the regions of the dead,
With endless curses on his head.

3 The dust returns to dust again;
The soul in agonies of pain
Ascends to God; not there to dwell,
But hears her doom and sinks to hell.

4 Eternal King! I fear thy name;
Teach me to know how frail I am;
And when my soul must hence remove,
Give me a mansion in thy love.

355   L. M.   *Old Hundred.*

1 FIRM was my health, my day was bright,
And I presumed 't would ne'er be night;
Fondly I said within my heart,
"Pleasure and peace shall ne'er depart."

2 But I forgot thine arm was strong,
Which made my mountain stand so long:

Soon as thy face began to hide,
My health was gone, my comforts died.

3 I cried aloud to thee, my God,
"What canst thou profit by my blood?
Deep in the dust can I declare
Thy truth, or sing thy goodness there?

4 "Hear me, O God of grace," I said,
"And bring me from among the dead;"
Thy words rebuked the pains I felt,
Thy pard'ning love remov'd my guilt.

5 My groans, and tears, and forms of woe,
Are turn'd to joy and praises now;
I throw my sackcloth on the ground,
And ease and gladness gird me round.

6 My tongue, the glory of my frame,
Shall ne'er be silent of thy name;
Thy praise shall sound thro' earth and heav'n,
For sickness heal'd, and sins forgiven.

356   C. M.   *Divinity.*

1 O ALL ye nations, praise the Lord,
   Each with a diff'rent tongue!
In every language learn his word,
   And let his name be sung.

2 His mercy reigns through every land:
   Proclaim his grace abroad:
Forever firm his truth shall stand;
   Praise ye the faithful God.

357 S. M. *St. Thomas.*

1 THE God Jehovah reigns,
    Let all the nations fear:
  Let sinners tremble at his throne,
    And saints be humble there.

2 Jesus the Savior reigns,
    Let earth adore its Lord;
  Bright cherubs his attendants stand,
    Swift to fulfil his word.

3 In Zion stands his throne,
    His honors are divine;
  His church shall make his wonders known,
    For there his glories shine.

4 How holy is his name!
    How terrible his praise!
  Justice and truth, and judgement join
    In all his works of grace.

358 Metre 4. *Charleston.*

1 HAPPY soul, thy days are ended,
    All thy mourning days below;
  Go, by angel-guards attended,
    To the sight of Jesus, go!

2 Waiting to receive thy spirit,
    Lo! the Savior stands above,
  Shows the glory of his merit,
    Reaches out the crown of love.

3 Struggle through thy latest passion
    To thy dear Redeemer's breast,

> To his uttermost salvation,
> To his everlasting rest.

4 For the joy he sets before thee,
Bear a momentary pain:
Die, to live the life of glory —
Suffer, with thy Lord to reign.

359   C. M.   *Dublin.*

1 WHEN rising from the bed of death,
O'erwhelm'd with guilt and fear,
I see my Maker face to face,
O how shall I appear!

2 If yet while pardon may be found,
And mercy may be sought,
My heart with inward horror shrinks,
And trembles at the thought!

3 When thou, O Lord, shalt stand disclosed,
In majesty severe,
And sit in judgment on my soul,
Oh how shall I appear!

4 But thou hast told the troubled mind,
Who does her sins lament,
The timely tribute of her tears
Shall endless woe prevent.

5 Then see the sorrows of my heart,
Ere yet it be too late;
And hear my Savior's dying groans,
To give these sorrows weight.

6 For never shall my soul despair
Her pardon to procure,

Who knows thine only Son has died,
  To make her pardon sure.

360   L. M.   *Solemnity.*

1 IN glory bright the Savior reigns,
    And endless grandeur there sustains;
  We view his beams, and from afar
  Hail him the bright, the Morning-Star.

2 Blest Star! where'er his lustre shines,
  He all the soul with grace refines;
  And makes each happy saint declare,
  He is the bright, the Morning-Star.

3 Sweet Star! his influence is divine:
  Life, peace, and joy, attending shine;
  Death, hell, and sin, before him flee;
  The bright, the Morning-Star is he.

4 Great Star! in whom salvation dwells,
  His beam the thickest cloud dispels;
  The grossest darkness flies afar,
  Before this bright, this Morning-Star.

5 Eternal Star! our songs shall rise,
  When we shall meet thee in the skies;
  And, in eternal anthems, there
  Praise thee, the bright, the Morning-Star.

361   C. M.   *Mear.*

1 MY drowsy powers, why sleep ye so?
    Awake, my sluggish soul!
  Nothing has half thy work to do,
    Yet nothing's half so dull.

2 The little ants, for one poor grain
    Labor, and tug, and strive:
Yet we, who have a heaven t' obtain.
    How negligent we live!

3 We, for whose sake all nature stands,
    And stars their courses move;
We, for whose guard the angel-bands
    Come flying from above.

4 We, for whom God the Son, came down,
    And labor'd for our good;
How careless to secure that crown
    He purchased with his blood!

5 Lord, shall we lie so sluggish still
    And never act our parts?
Come, holy Dove, from th' heavenly hill,
    And sit and warm our hearts.

6 Then shall our active spirits move,
    Upward our souls shall rise;
With hands of faith, and wings of love,
    We'll fly and take the prize.

362   S. M.   *St. Thomas.*

1 SHALL Wisdom cry aloud,
    And not her speech be heard?
The voice of God's eternal Word,
    Deserves it no regard?

2 "I was his chief delight,
    His everlasting Son,
Before the first of all his works,
    Creation, was begun.

3 "Before the flying clouds,
  Before the solid land,
Before the fields, before the floods,
  I dwelt at his right hand.

4 "When he adorn'd the skies,
  And built them, I was there,
To order when the sun should rise,
  And marshal every star.

5 "When he pour'd out the sea,
  And spread the flowing deep;
I gave the flood a firm decree,
  In its own bounds to keep.

6 "Upon the empty air
  The earth was balanced well:
With joy I saw the mansion, where
  The sons of men should dwell.

7 "My busy thoughts at first
  On their salvation ran,
Ere sin was born, or Adam's dust
  Was fashion'd into man.

8 "Then come, receive my grace,
  Ye children, and be wise;
Happy the man that keeps my ways;
  The man that shuns them dies."

363   METRE 5.   *Cookham.*
1 WHEN on Sinai's top I see
    God descend in Majesty
  To proclaim his holy law,
  All my spirit sinks with awe.

2 When in ecstacy sublime,
    Tabor's glorious steep I climb,
    At the too transporting light,
    Darkness rushes o'er my sight.

3 When on Calvary I rest,
    God in flesh made manifest,
    Shines in my Redeemer's face,
    Full of beauty, truth, and grace.

4 Here I would forever stay,
    Weep and gaze my soul away:
    Thou art heaven on earth to me,
    Lovely, mournful, Calvary.

364   C. M.   *Rockingham.*

1 AWAKE, my soul, to sound his praise,
    Awake, my harp, to sing;
  Join, all my powers, the song to raise,
    And morning incense bring.

2 Among the people of his care,
    And through the nations round,
  Glad songs of praise will I prepare,
    And there his name resound.

3 Be thou exalted, O my God,
    Above the starry frame;
  Diffuse thy heavenly grace abroad,
    And teach the world thy name.

4 So shall thy chosen sons rejoice,
    And throng thy courts above;
  While sinners hear thy pard'ning voice,
    And taste Redeeming love.

VARIOUS SUBJECTS.

365 C. M. *Liberty Hall.*

1 DEAR Refuge of my weary soul,
  On thee, when sorrows rise,
On thee, when waves of trouble roll,
  My fainting hope relies.

2 To thee I tell each rising grief,
  For thou alone canst heal;
Thy word can bring a sweet relief,
  For every pain I feel.

3 Hast thou not bid me seek thy face?
  And shall I seek in vain?
And can the ear of sovereign grace
  Be deaf when I complain?

4 No — still the ear of sovereign grace
  Attends the mourner's pray'r;
Oh may I ever find access
  To breathe my sorrows there!

5 Thy mercy-seat is open still;
  Here let my soul retreat,
With humble hope attend thy will,
  And wait beneath thy feet.

366 METRE 26. *Trinity.*

1 GLORY to God on high!
  Let heaven and earth reply,
    "Praise ye his name!
Angels, his love adore,
Who all our sorrows bore;
Saints, sing for evermore,
    "Worthy the Lamb."

2 Ye, who surround the throne,
Cheerfully join in one,
Praising his name:
Ye, who have felt his blood
Sealing your peace with God,
Sound through the earth abroad,
"Worthy the Lamb!"

3 Join all the ransom'd race,
Our Lord and God to bless:
Praise ye his name!
In him we will rejoice,
Making a cheerful noise,
Shouting with heart and voice,
"Worthy the Lamb!"

4 Soon must we change our place,
Yet we will never cease
Praising his name:
Still we will tribute bring,
Hail him our gracious King;
And through all ages sing,
"Worthy the Lamb!"

367   C. M.   *Dublin.*

1 VAIN Man, thy fond pursuits forbear;
Repent! — thy end is nigh!
Death at the farthest, can't be far —
Oh, think before thou die!

2 Reflect, thou hast a soul to save:
Thy sins — how high they mount!
What are thy hopes beyond the grave?
How stands that dread account?

3 Death enters — and there's no defence —
   His time there's none can tell:
   He'll in a moment call thee hence,
   To heaven — or to hell!

4 Thy flesh, perhaps thy chiefest care,
   Shall crawling worms consume:
   But, ah! destruction stops not there —
   Sin kills beyond the tomb.

5 To-day the gospel calls: to-day,
   Sinners, it speaks to you;
   Let every one forsake his way,
   And mercy will ensue.

368   C. M.   *Peterborough.*

1 BLESS'D is the man who shuns the place,
   Where sinners love to meet;
   Who fears to tread their wicked ways,
   And hates the scoffer's seat:

2 But in the statutes of the Lord,
   Has plac'd his chief delight;
   By day he reads or hears the word,
   And meditates by night.

3 (He like a plant of generous kind
   By living waters set,
   Safe from the storms and blasting wind,
   Enjoys a peaceful state.)

4 Green as the leaf, and ever fair
   Shall his professions shine;
   While fruits of holiness appear
   Like clusters on the vine.

5 Not so the impious and unjust:
   What vain designs they form!
 Their hopes are blown away like dust,
   Or chaff before the storm.

6 Sinners in judgment shall not stand
      Among the sons of grace,
 When Christ, the Judge, at his right hand
      Appoints his saints a place.

7 His eye beholds the path they tread,
   His heart approves it well;
 But crooked ways of sinners lead
   Down to the gates of hell.

369   L. M.   *Portugal.*

1 HOW lovely, how divinely sweet,
    O Lord, thy sacred courts appear!
  Fain would my longing passions meet
    The glories of thy presence there.

2 O, blest the men, blest their employ,
  Whom thy indulgent favors raise
  To dwell in those abodes of joy,
  And sing thy never-ceasing praise.

3 Happy the men whom strength divine
  With ardent love and zeal inspires;
  Whose steps to thy blest way incline,
  With willing hearts and warm desires.

4 One day within thy sacred gate
  Affords more real joy to me,
  Than thousands in the tents of state;
  The meanest place is bliss with thee.

5 God is a sun—our brightest day
From his reviving presence flows;
God is a shield, through all the way,
To guard us from surrounding foes.

6 He pours his kindest blessings down,
Profusely down on souls sincere;
And grace shall guide, and glory crown,
The happy fav'rites of his care.

7 O Lord of hosts, thou God of grace,
How blest, divinely blest is he
Who trusts thy love, and seeks thy face,
And fixes all his hopes on thee.

370   Metre 5.   *Frankfort.*

1 COME, my soul! thy suit prepare,
  Jesus loves to answer prayer;
He himself has bid thee pray;
Rise and ask without delay.

2 With my burden I begin;
Lord! remove this load of sin;
Let thy blood, for sinners spilt,
Set my conscience free from guilt.

3 Lord! I come to thee for rest,
Take possession of my breast;
There, thy sovereign right maintain,
And without a rival reign.

4 While I am a pilgrim here,
Let thy love my spirit cheer;
By my Guide, my Guard, my Friend;
Lead me to my journey's end.

5 Show me what I have to do,
   Every hour my strength renew;
   Let me live a life of faith,
   Let me die thy people's death.

371   C. M.   *Bangor—Walsall.*

1 LORD, I approach thy mercy-seat,
   Where thou dost answer prayer;
   There humbly fall before thy feet,
   For none can perish there.

2 Thy promise is my only plea;
   With this I venture nigh;
   Thou callest burden'd souls to thee,
   And such, O Lord, am I.

3 Bow'd down beneath a load of sin,
   By Satan sorely press'd,
   By war without and fear within,
   I come to thee for rest.

4 Be thou my Shield and Hiding-place;
   That, sheltered near thy side,
   I may my fierce accuser face,
   And tell him—thou hast died.

5 Oh wondrous love!—To bleed and die,
   To bear the cross and shame
   That guilty sinners, such as I,
   Might plead thy gracious name.

372   METRE 4.   *Disciple.*

1 SWEET the moments, rich in blessing,
   Which before the cross I spend;

Life, and health, and peace possessing
  From the sinner's dying Friend;
Here I'll sit forever viewing.
  Mercy's streams in streams of blood:
Precious drops my soul bedewing,
  Plead and claim my peace with God.

2 Truly blessed is this station
  Low before his cross to lie;
While I see divine compassion
  Floating in his languid eye:
Here it is I find my heaven,
  While upon the Lamb I gaze:
Love I much? I've much forgiven,
  I'm a miracle of grace.

3 Love and grief my heart dividing,
  With my tears his feet I'll bathe;
Constant still in faith abiding,
  Life deriving from his death.
May I still enjoy this feeling,
  In all need to Jesus go;
Prove his wounds each day more healing,
  And himself more deeply know.

373   METRE 24.   *Gospel Trumpet.*

1 HARK! how the gospel trumpet sounds!
  Thro' all the earth the echo bounds;
And Jesus by redeeming blood,
Is bringing sinners back to God,
And guides them safely by his word,
  To endless day.

2 Hail! all-victorious, conq'ring Lord!
  Be thou by all thy works ador'd,

Who undertook for sinful man,
And brought salvation through thy name,
That we with thee may ever reign
  In endless day.

3 Fight on, ye conq'ring souls, fight on,
And when the conquest you have won,
Then palms of vict'ry you shall bear,
And in his kingdom have a share,
And crowns of glory ever wear
  In endless day.

4 There we shall in full chorus join,
With saints and angels all combine,
To sing of his redeeming love,
When rolling years shall cease to move,
And this shall be our theme above
  In endless day.

374   C. M.   *Rockingham.*

1 O HOW I love thy holy law!
    "Tis daily my delight;
  And thence my meditations draw
    Divine advice by night.

2 My waking eyes prevent the day
    To meditate thy word;
  My soul with longing melts away
    To hear thy gospel, Lord.

3 How doth thy word my heart engage!
    How well employ my tongue!
  And in my tiresome pilgrimage,
    Yields me a heavenly song.

4 Am I a stranger, or at home,
  "Tis my perpetual feast;
Not honey dropping from the comb,
  So much allures my taste.

5 No treasures so enrich the mind;
  Nor shall thy word be sold
For loads of silver well refined,
  Or heaps of choicest gold.

6 When nature sinks and spirits droop,
  Thy promises of grace
Are pillars to support my hope,—
  And there I write thy praise.

375   METRE 5.   *Sovereign Grace.*

1 TO thy pastures, fair and large,
    Heavenly Shepherd, lead thy charge;
  And my couch with tenderest care,
  Midst the springing grass prepare.

2 When I faint, with summer's heat,
  Thou shalt guide my weary feet
  To the streams, that still and slow,
  Through the verdant meadows flow.

3 Safe the dreary vale I tread,
  By the shades of death o'erspread;
  With thy rod and staff supplied
  This my guard—and that my guide.

4 Constant to my latest end,
  Thou my footsteps shalt attend;
  And shalt bid thy hallowed dome
  Yield me an eternal home.

VARIOUS SUBJECTS.

376   Metre 5.   *Divine Inquiry.*

1 SEEK, my soul, the narrow gate,
   Enter ere it be too late;
Many ask to enter there,
When too late to offer prayer.

2 God from mercy's seat shall rise,
And forever bar the skies;
Then, though sinners cry without,
He will say, "I know you not."

3 Mournfully will they exclaim,
"Lord, we have profess'd thy name;
We have ate with thee, and heard,
Heavenly teaching in thy word."

4 Vain, alas! will be their plea,
Workers of iniquity;
Sad their everlasting lot—
Christ will say "I know you not."

377   L. M.   *Portugal.*

1 BLESS'D Redeemer, how divine—
   How righteous is this rule of thine,
"Never to deal with others worse
Than we would have them deal with us.

2 This golden lesson, short and plain,
Gives not the mind nor mem'ry pain;
And every conscience must approve
This universal law of love.

3 "Tis written in each mortal breast,
Where all our tend'rest wishes rest;

We draw it from our inmost veins,
When love to self resides and reigns.

4 Is reason ever at a loss?
Call in self-love to judge the cause;
Let our own fondest passion show
How we should treat our neighbor too.

5 How bless'd would every nation prove,
Thus ruled by equity and love!
All would be friends without a foe,
And form a paradise below.

378 C. M. *Brunswick.*

1 YE mourning saints whose streaming tears
   Flow o'er your children dead,
Say not in transports of despair,
   That all your hopes are fled.

2 While cleaving to that darling dust,
   In fond distress ye lie,
Rise, and with joy and rev'rence view
   A heavenly Parent nigh.

3 Though your young branches torn away,
   Like withered trunks ye stand!
With fairer verdure shall ye bloom,
   Touch'd by th' Almighty's hand.

4 "I'll give the mourner," saith the Lord.
   "In my own house a place;
No names of daughters and of sons
   Could yield so high a grace.

5 "Transient and vain is every hope
   A rising race can give;

VARIOUS SUBJECTS. 345

 In endless honor and delight,
  My children all shall live.

6 We welcome, Lord, those rising tears,
 Through which thy face we see,
And bless those wounds which thro' our hearts
 Prepare a way for thee.

379 Metre 41. *Evening Thought.*

1 ERE I sleep, for every favor,
  This day shown
   By my God,
 I do bless my Savior.

2 Leave me not, but ever love me;
  Let thy peace
   Be my bliss,
 Till thou hence remove me.

3 Thou my Rock, my Guard, my Tower,
  Safely keep
   While I sleep,
 Me with all thy power.

4 And when e'er in death I slumber,
  Let me rise
   With the wise,
 Counted in their number.

380 C. M. *Balerma.*

1 IN evil long I took delight,
 Unawed by shame or fear,
Till a new object struck my sight,
 And stopp'd my wild career.

2 I saw One hanging on a tree,
　In agonies and blood:
He fixed his languid eyes on me,
　As near his cross I stood.

3 Oh! never, till my latest breath,
　Shall I forget that look;
It seemed to charge me with his death,
　Though not a word he spoke.

4 My conscience felt and own'd the guilt,
　It plunged me in despair;
I saw my sins his blood had spilt,
　And helped to nail him there.

5 A second look he gave, which said,
　"I freely all forgive;
This blood is for thy ransom paid;
　I die that thou may'st live."

6 Thus while his death my sin displays
　In all its darkest hue,
Such is the mystery of grace,
　It seals my pardon too.

381　　　　C. M.　　　　*Augusta.*

1 MAJESTIC sweetness sits enthroned
　Upon the Savior's brow;
His head with radiant glories crown'd,
　His lips with grace o'erflow.

2 No mortal can with him compare,
　Among the sons of men;
Fairer is he than all the fair
　Who fill the heavenly train.

3 He saw me plunged in deep distress,
  And flew to my relief;
For me he bore the shameful cross,
  And carried all my grief.

4 To him I owe my life and breath,
  An all the joys I have:
He makes me triumph over death,
  An saves me from the grave.

5 To heaven, the place of his abode,
  He brings my weary feet,
Shows me the glories of my God,
  And makes my joys complete,

6 Since from his bounty I receive
  Such proofs of love divine,
Had I a thousand hearts to give,
  Lord, they should all be thine.

382   L. M.   *Gravity.*

1 THE heav'ns declare thy glory, Lord;
    In every star thy wisdom shines;
  But when our eyes behold thy word,
    We read thy name in fairer lines.

2 The rolling sun, the changing light,
    And nights and days thy power confess;
  But that blest volume thou hast writ,
    Reveals thy justice and thy grace.

3 Sun, moon, and stars convey thy praise
    Around the earth, and never stand;
  So, when thy truth began its race,
    It touched and glanced on every land.

4 Nor shall thy spreading gospel rest
   Till through the world thy truth has run,
 Till Christ has all the nations blest
   That see the light or feel the sun.

5 Great Sun of Righteousness, arise;
   O, bless the world with heavenly light;
 Thy gospel makes the simple wise;
   Thy laws are pure, thy judgments right.

6 Thy noblest wonders here we view,
   In souls renew'd and sins forgiven;
 Lord cleanse my sins, my soul renew,
   And make thy word my guide to heaven.

383   METRE 5.   *Divine Inquiry.*

1 MARY to the Savior's tomb,
   Hasted at the early dawn;
 Spice she brought, and sweet perfume,
   But the Lord she lov'd had gone:
 For a while she ling'ring stood,
   Fill'd with sorrow and surprise;
 Trembling while a crystal flood
   Issued from her weeping eyes.

2 But her sorrows quickly fled,
   When she heard his welcome voice;
 Christ had risen from the dead;
   Now he bids her heart rejoice;
 What a change his word can make,
   Turning darkness into day;
 Ye who weep for Jesus' sake,
   He will wipe your tears away.

384   METRE 14.   *Brandenburg.*

1 Go when the morning shineth,
     Go when the noon is bright,
  Go when the eve declineth,
     Go in the hush of night;
  Go with pure mind and feeling,
     Fling earthly thought away,
  And in thy closet kneeling,
     Do thou in secret pray.

2 Remember all who love thee,
     All who are lov'd by thee;
  Pray, too, for those who hate thee,
     If any such there be;
  Then for thyself, in meekness,
     A blessing humbly claim,
  And blend with each petition
     Thy great Redeemer's name.

3 Or if 't is e'er denied thee
     In solitude to pray,
  Should holy thoughts come o'er thee
     When friends are round thy way,
  E'en then the silent breathing,
     Thy spirit raised above,
  Will reach his throne of glory,
     Where dwells eternal love.

4 O, not a joy or blessing
     With this can we compare —
  The grace our Father gave us
     To pour our souls in prayer:
  Whenc'er thou pin'st in sadness,
     Before his footstool fall;

Remember in thy gladness,
His love who gave thee all.

385 L. M. *Gravity.*

1 LO! round the throne at God's right hand,
The saints, in countless myriads stand,
Of every tongue redeemed to God,
Arrayed in garments wash'd in blood.

2 Through tribulation great they came:
They bore the cross, despised the shame:
From all their labors, now they rest,
In God's eternal glory blest.

3 Hunger and thirst they feel no more;
Nor sin, nor pain, nor death deplore:
The tears are wiped from every eye,
And sorrow yields to endless joy.

4 They see their Savior face to face,
And sing the triumphs of his grace:
Him day and night they ceaseless praise:
To him their loud hosannas raise.

5 Worthy the Lamb, for sinners slain,
Through endless years to live and reign:
Thou hast redeem'd us by thy blood,
And made us kings and priests to God.

386 C. M. *Dublin—Walsal.*

1 HAVE mercy, gracious Lord, forgive,
Are not thy mercies free?
May not a dying sinner live,
Who truly turns to thee?

2 My sins are great, I must confess,
    Far more than I can know;
  But O, thy love and pard'ning grace!
    Are great and boundless too.

3 O, cleanse me from my sin and guilt,
    And make my conscience clean:
  My heart with godly sorrow melt,
    To mourn for ev'ry sin.

4 Great God, I must confess with shame,
    I can't deny, but own,
  Corrupted, vile, and base I am,
    As I to thee am known.

5 Yet save my soul from deep despair,
    According to thy word;
  To thee, I make my feeble prayer:
    To thee my gracious Lord.

387   METRE 5.   *Bozrah.*

1 WHO is this that comes from far,
    Clad in garments dipp'd in blood?
  Strong triumphant traveler,
    Is he man or is he God?
  I that speak in righteousness,
    Son of God and Man I am,
  Mighty to redeem your race,
    Jesus is your Savior's name.

2 Wherefore are thy garments red,
    Dy'd as in a crimson sea?
  They that in the wine-vat tread,
    Are not stain'd so much as thee.

"I the Father's favorite Son,
  Have the dreadful wine-press trod,
Borne the vengeful wrath alone,
  All the fiercest wrath of God."

3 Kind thou art, and full of love,
  Savior God, to suffer thus;
Rich the grace thy people prove —
  Thou hast shed thy blood for us.
May thy love's constraining power
  Tune our hearts and tongues to sing —
May we in this favor'd hour
  To the cross our trophies bring.

388   METRE 9.   *Carmarthen.*

1 WELCOME — delightful morn
    Thou day of sacred rest!
  I hail thy kind return; —
    Lord! make these moments blest;
  From the low train of mortal toys,
  I soar to reach immortal joys.

2 Now may the King descend
    And fill his throne of grace;
  Thy sceptre, Lord! extend,
    While saints address thy face;
  Let sinners feel thy quick'ning word,
  And learn to know and fear the Lord.

3 Descend, celestial Dove!
    With all thy quick'ning powers;
  Disclose a Savior's love,
    And bless the sacred hours;
  Then shall my soul new life obtain,
  Nor Sabbaths be bestowed in vain.

VARIOUS SUBJECTS.

389   L. M.   *Uxbridge.*

1 FROM every stormy wind that blows,
   From every swelling tide of woes,
There is a calm, a sure retreat;
'Tis found before the mercy-seat.

2 There is a place where Jesus sheds
   The oil of gladness on our heads —
A place of all on earth most sweet;
It is the blood-bought mercy seat.

3 There is a scene where spirits blend,
   Where friend holds fellowship with friend:
Though sundered far, by faith they meet
Around one common mercy-seat.

4 There, there, on eagle wings we soar,
   And sin and sense molest no more;
And heaven comes down our souls to greet,
And glory crowns the mercy-seat.

390   METRE 13.   *Amsterdam.*

1 SINNER, hear the Savior's call,
   He now is passing by;
He has seen thy grievous thrall,
   And heard thy mournful cry;
He has pardons to impart,
   Grace to save thee from thy fears;
See the love that fills his heart,
   And wipes away thy tears.

2 Why art thou afraid to come,
   And tell him all thy case?

He will not pronounce thy doom,
　Nor frown thee from his face;
Wilt thou fear Immanuel?
　Wilt thou fear the Lamb of God,
Who, to save thy soul from hell,
　Has shed his precious blood?

3 Think how on the cross he hung,
　　Pierc'd with a thousand wounds!
　Hark, from each, as with a tongue,
　　The voice of pardon sounds!
　See from all his bursting veins,
　　Blood of wondrous virtue flow!
　Sheds to wash away thy stains,
　　And ransom thee from woe.

4 Though his majesty be great,
　　His mercy is no less;
　Though he thy transgressions hate,
　　He feels for thy distress:
　By himself the Lord has sworn,
　　He delights not in thy death;
　But invites thee to return,
　　That thou mayest live by faith.

5 Raise thy downcast eyes, and see
　　What throngs his throne surround!
　These though sinners once like thee,
　　Have full salvation found.
　Yield not then to unbelief,
　　While he says, "There yet is room;"
　Though of sinners thou art chief,
　　Since Jesus calls thee, come.

391 S. M. *Watchman.*

1 BLEST are the sons of peace,
  Whose hearts and hopes are one:
 Whose kind designs to serve and please
  Through all their actions run.

2 Blest is the pious house,
  Where zeal and friendship meet,
 Their songs of praise, their mingled vows,
  Make their communion sweet.

3 Thus when on Aaron's head
  They pour'd the rich perfume,
 The oil through all his raiment spread,
  And pleasure fill'd the room.

4 Thus on the heavenly hills,
  The saints are bless'd above,
 Where joy, like morning dew, distills,
  And all the air is love.

392 METRE 4. *Disciple.*

1 MIGHTY God, while angels bless thee,
  May a mortal lisp thy name?
 Lord of men as well as angels,
  Thou art every creature's theme:
 Lord of every land and nation,
  Ancient of eternal days.
 Sounded through the wide creation
  Be thy just and lawful praise.

2 For the grandeur of thy nature,—
  Grand beyond a seraph's thought,

For the wonders of creation,—
  Works with skill and kindness wrought,—
For thy providence, that governs
  Through thine empire's wide domain,
Wings an angel, guides a sparrow,—
  Blessed be thy gentle reign.

For thy rich, thy free redemption,—
  Bright, though vail'd in darkness long,—
Thought is poor, and poor expression;
  Who can sing that wondrous song?
Brightness of the Father's glory,
  Shall thy praise unuttered lie?
Break, my tongue, such guilty silence;
  Sing the Lord who came to die!—

4 From the highest throne of glory,
  To the cross of deepest woe,
Came to ransom guilty captives;—
  Flow, my praise, forever flow:
Re-ascend, immortal Savior;
  Leave thy footstool, take thy throne;
Thence return and reign forever;
  Be the kingdom all thy own.

Metre 5. *Bozrah.*

1 WHILE with ceaseless course the sun
    Hasted through the former year,
  Many souls their race have run,
    Never more to meet us here:
  Fixed in an eternal state,
    They have done with all below;
  We a little longer wait;
    But how little—none can know.

2 Spared to see another year,
　　Let thy blessing meet us here;
Come, thy dying work revive,
　　Bid thy drooping garden thrive:
Sun of righteousness, arise!
　　Warm our hearts, and bless our eyes:
Let our prayer thy pity move;
　　Make this year a time of love.

3 Thanks for mercies past receive,
　　Pardon of our sins renew;
Teach us henceforth how to live
　　With eternity in view;
Bless thy word to old and young,
　　Fill us with a Savior's love,
When our life's short race is run,
　　May we dwell with thee above.

394　　　　C. M.　　　　*Balerma.*

1 SHEPHERD divine, our wants relieve,
　　In this our evil day;
To all thy tempted foll'wers give
　　The power to watch and pray.

2 Long as our fiery trials last,
　　Long as the cross we bear;
O let our souls on thee be cast
　　In never-ceasing prayer!

3 The spirit of redeeming grace,
　　Give us in faith to claim;
To wrestle till we see thy face,
　　And know thy hidden name.

4 Till thou thy perfect love impart,
   Till thou thyself bestow;
 Be this the cry of every heart,
   "I will not let thee go."

5 Then let me on the mountain top,
   Behold thy open face;
 Where faith in sight is swallowed up,
   And prayer in endless praise.

395   C. M.   *Arlington.*

1 DAUGHTER of Zion, from the dust
   Exalt thy fallen head;
 Again in thy Redeemer trust;
   He calls thee from the dead.

2 Awake!—Awake!—put on thy strength,
   Thy beautiful array;
 The day of freedom dawns at length,
   The Lord's appointed day.

3 Rebuild thy walls—thy bounds enlarge,
   And send thy heralds forth;
 Say to the South—"Give up thy charge,
   And keep not back, O North!"

4 They come! they come!—thine exile bands,
   Where'er they rest or roam,
 Have heard thy voice in distant lands,
   And hasten to their home.

5 Thus, though the world at last shall burn,
   And God his works destroy,
 With songs thy ransom'd shall return,
   And everlasting joy.

VARIOUS SUBJECTS.

396   L. M.   *Abingdon.*

1 ANOTHER day has passed along
   And we are nearer to the tomb,—
Nearer to join the heavenly song,
Or hear the last eternal doom.

2 Sweet is the light of Sabbath-eve,
And soft the sunbeams ling'ring there;
For these bless'd hours, the world I leave,
Wafted on wings of faith and prayer.

3 The time how lovely and how still;
Peace shines and smiles on all below,—
The plain, the stream, the wood, the hill,—
All fair with evening's setting glow.

4 Season of rest! the tranquil soul
Feels the sweet calm, and melts to love,—
And while these sacred moments roll,
Faith sees a smiling heaven above.

5 Nor will our days of toil be long,
Our pilgrimage will soon be trod;
And we shall join the ceaseless song,—
The endless Sabbath of our God.

397   L. M.   *Gravity.*

1 O HAPPY day that fix'd my choice
   On thee, my Savior and my God:
Well may this glowing heart rejoice,
And tell its raptures all abroad.

2 O happy bond, that seals my vows,
To him who merits all my love;

Let cheerful anthems fill his house,
While to that sacred shrine I move.

3 'Tis done—the great transaction's done;
I am my Lord's and he is mine;
He drew me and I followed on,
Charm'd to confess the voice divine.

4 Now rest, my long divided heart,
Fix'd on this blissful centre rest;
With ashes who would grudge to part,
When call'd on angels' bread to feast?

398   S. M.   *Aylesbury.*

1 OH! where shall rest be found,
    Rest for the weary soul?
'Twere vain the ocean-depths to sound,
    Or pierce to either pole.

2 The world can never give,
    The bliss for which we sigh;
'Tis not the whole of life to live,
    Nor all of death to die.

3 Beyond this vale of tears,
    There is a life above,
Unmeasured by the flight of years;
    And all that life is love.

4 There is a death, whose pang
    Outlasts the fleeting breath;
Oh! what eternal horrors hang
    Around the second death!

5 Lord God of truth and grace!
    Teach us that death to shun;

Lest we be banished from thy face,
And evermore undone.

399   Metre 2.   *Lenox.*

1 YES, the Redeemer rose;
   The Savior left the dead;
And o'er our hellish foes
   High raised his conquering head:
In wild dismay
   The guards around
   Fall to the ground,
And sink away.

2 Lo! the angelic bands,
   In full assembly meet,
To wait his high commands,
   And worship at his feet:
Joyful they come,
   And wing their way,
   From realms of day,
To Jesus' tomb.

3 Then back to heaven they fly,
   The joyful news to bear:
Hark! as they soar on high,
   What music fills the air!
Their anthems say,—
   "Jesus, who bled,
   Hath left the dead;—
He rose to-day."

4 Ye mortals! catch the sound,—
   Redeemed by him from hell;
And send the echo round
   The globe, on which you dwell;

Transported, cry,—
"Jesus, who bled,
Hath left the dead,
No more to die."

5 All hail! triumphant Lord!
Who sav'st us with thy blood:
Wide be thy name adored,
Thou rising reigning God!
With thee we rise,
With thee we reign,
And empires gain,
Beyond the skies.

400   Metre 14.   *Illumination.*

1 THE morning light is breaking;
The darkness disappears;
The sons of earth are waking
To penitential tears;
Each breeze that sweeps the ocean
Brings tidings from afar
Of nations in commotion,
Prepared for Zion's war.

2 Rich dews of grace come o'er us;
In many a gentle shower,
And brighter scenes before us,
Are opening every hour:
Each cry to heaven going,
Abundant answers brings,
And heavenly gales are blowing,
With peace upon their wings.

3 See heathen nations bending
Before the God we love,

And thousand hearts ascending
  In gratitude above;
While sinners, now confessing,
  The gospel call obey,
And seek the Savior's blessing, —
  A nation in a day.

4 Blest river of salvation,
  Pursue thy onward way;
Flow thou to every nation,
  Nor in thy richness stay:
Stay not till all the lowly
  Triumphant reach their home;
Stay not till all the holy
  Proclaim, "The Lord is come."

401   Metre 11.   *Hinton.*

1 O ZION, afflicted with wave upon wave,
  Whom no man can comfort, whom no man can save;
With darkness surrounded, by terror dismayed,
In toiling and rowing thy strength is decayed.

2 Loud roaring the billows now nigh overwhelm,
But skilful's the Pilot that sits at the helm,
His wisdom conducts thee, his pow'r thee defends:
In safety and quiet the warfare he ends.

3 "O fearful! O faithless!" in mercy he cries,
"My promise, my truth, are they light in thine eyes?
Still, still I am with thee, my promise shall stand
Through tempest and tossing I'll bring thee to land.

4 Then trust me and fear not; thy life is secure;
My wisdom is perfect, supreme is my pow'r;
In love I correct thee, thy soul to refine,
To make thee at length in my likeness to shine."

402   C. M.   *Balerma.*

1 BY cool Siloam's shady rill
   How fair the lily grows!
How sweet the breath beneath the hill,
   Of Sharon's dewy rose!

2 Lo! such the child whose early feet
   The paths of peace have trod,
Whose secret heart, with influence sweet,
   Is upward drawn to God.

3 By cool Siloam's shady rill
   The lily must decay;
The rose, that blooms beneath the hill,
   Must shortly fade away.

4 And soon, too soon, the wint'ry hour
   Of man's maturer age
Will shake the soul with sorrow's power
   And stormy passion's rage.

5 O Thou who givest life and breath,
   We seek thy grace alone,
In childhood, manhood, age and death,
   To keep us still thine own.

CONTENTS.

PUBLIC Worship..........From page	1 to 53
Nativity of Christ	54—63
New-Year...	64—68
Crucifixion...	69—83
Resurrection...	84—86
The Word of God	87—91
Faith and Repentance...........................	91—93
Baptism	94—101
Prayer and Supplication.......................	101—130
Invitation..	131—150
Comfort in Tribulation.........................	150—153
Infinite Mercy.......................................	154—158
The Love of God...................................	159—164
Morning Hymns....................................	165—171
Evening Hymns.....................................	172—177
Frailty of Man......................................	178—180
Funeral..	181—194
Judgment..	194—200
Vanity of Earthly Things.....................	200—202
Heavenly Joy..	202—215
Breathing after God and Holiness	216—244
Adoration and Praise...........................	245—252
Resignation to God...............................	253—255
Trusting in God	256—261
Warning Hymns	261—269
Penitential..	270—272
Prodigal Son	273—275
Marriage Hymns....................................	276—277
Communion...	277—287
Feet-Washing..	288—291
Parting Hymns.....................................	291—297
Various Subjects....................................	297—364

METRICAL INDEX.

This Index shows which hymns will be sung to the same Metre. The first three — Long, Common and Short — are here omitted. These Metres correspond with the Metrical Index of the Fourth Edition of the Music Book entitled "Genuine Church Music," or Harmonia Sacra."

METRE 4.

8's & 7's.

COME thou everlasting Spirit............Page...287
Come thou Fount of every blessing...............219
Dark and thorny is the desert.......................304
God is love, his mercy brightens 163
Great High Priest, we view thee stooping...... 82
Hail my ever-blessed Jesus 231
Hail thou once despised Jesus....................... 72
Happy soul thy days are ended.....................328
Hark what mean those holy voices............... 62
Jesus I my cross have taken.........................308
Mighty God, while angels bless thee.............355
Prince of peace be ever near us..................... 52
Savior I do feel thy merit. 302
Sinners, take the friendly warning........ 195

METRICAL INDEX.

METRE 5.
4 lines 7's & 8 lines 7's.

ANGELS roll the rock away..........PAGE......	86
Depth of mercy can there be.......................	154
Hark my soul it is the Lord........................	19
Hark the herald, angels sing......................	61
Holy Jesus, lovely Lamb...........................	122
I mine Ebenezer raise...............................	253
Jesus lover of my soul..............................	113
Jesus' precious name excels......................	131
Lord I cannot let thee go...........................	112
Lord we come before thee now..................	116
Mary to the Savior's tomb........................	348
Now the shades of night are gone..............	169
Seek my soul the narrow gate....................	343
Sinner art thou still secure.......................	263
Sinners turn, why will ye die....................	14
Softly now the light of day.......................	177
To thy pastures fair and large	342
Tell me Savior from above.......................	221
When on Sinai's top I see........................	332
Who is this that comes from far................	351

METRE 6.
8, 8, 6, 8, 8, 6.

AND am I only born to die,......................	317
My God, thy boundless love we praise........	157

METRE 7.
8, 7, 8, 7, 4, 7.

ANGELS from the realms of glory........... 63

Come ye sinners, come to Jesus........ PAGE... 38
Come ye sinners poor and needy....................148
Day of Judgment, day of wonder...................196
Hark the voice of love and mercy.................278
Lo he cometh, countless trumpets.................199
Lo he comes with clouds descending..............198
Lord, dismiss us with thy blessing............... 50
O thou God of my salvation........................303
On the mountain's top appearing.................. 42
Savior, visit thy plantation.......................300
See from Zion's sacred mountain..................213

METRE 8.
6 lines 8's.

AND can it be that I should gain.................316
Farewell my brethren in the Lord................294
Go watch and pray, thou canst not tell.........115
Jesus, thy boundless love to me..................110
My Savior thou thy love to me....................111
When gathering clouds around I view..........254
Would Jesus have the sinner die.................152

METRE 9.
6, 6, 6, 6, 8, 8.

ARISE, my soul, arise..............................259
Blow ye the trumpet, blow........................324
Come every pious heart............................140
The Lord of earth and sky......................... 66
Welcome, delightful morn.........................352
Yes, the Redeemer rose............................361

METRICAL INDEX.

METRE 10.
10, 10, 11, 11

PAGE.
BEGONE, unbelief, my Savior is near.........162
Come Lord from above the mountains.........126
O all that pass by to Jesus draw near............137
O tell me no more of this world's vain..........161
O what shall I do my Savior to praise..........250
Ye thirsty for God to Jesus give ear.............137

METRE 11.
4 lines 11's.

COME children of Zion and help us to sing... 29
Farewell, my dear brethren, the time is at....292
How firm a foundation ye saints of the Lord..155
I would not live always, I ask not to stay......212
O Zion afflicted with wave upon wave...........363
Thy mercy, my God, is the theme of my.......164
Why sleep ye my brethren, come let us.........136

METRE 12.
8 lines 8's.

AWAY with our sorrow and fear...................211
How blest is our brother bereft......................188
How solemn the signal I hear......................313
How shall a lost sinner in pain.....................123
How tedious and tasteless the hours.............297
Inspirer and hearer of prayer......................176
Thou Shepherd of Israel and mine................234
When sinners awake and perceive................100
When Joseph his brethren beheld................298

METRICAL INDEX.

METRE 13.
7, 6, 7, 6, 7, 7, 7, 6.

PAGE.

HELP thy servant, gracious Lord............... 39
Rise my soul and stretch thy wings.........230
Sinners, hear the Savior's call....................353
Stop poor sinners, stop and think..............267

METRE 14.
7, 6, 7, 6.

AH I shall soon be dying........................256
Go when the morning shineth...................349
The morning light is breaking..................362

METRE 15.
11, 8, 11, 8.

O THOU, in whose presence my soul takes....216

METRE 16.
7, 6, 7, 6, 7, 8, 7, 6.

GOD of my salvation hear........................251
Lamb of God for sinners slain...................122
Lamb of God whose dying love..................286
Vain delusive world, adieu........................305

METRE 17.
6 line's 7's.

HEARTS of stone, relent, relent.................. 74
Safely through another week..................... 49

METRE 20.
6, 6, 9, 6, 6, 9.

O HOW happy are they............................209

METRE 21.
12, 11, 12, 11, 12, 12, 12, 11.

HOW sweet to reflect on those joys that........16

METRE 24.
8, 8, 8, 8, 4.

HARK how the gospel trumpet sounds.........340

METRE 26.
6, 6, 4, 6, 6, 6, 4.

GLORY to God on high............................234

METRE 29.
8, 8, 7, 8, 8, 7.

SEE the Lord of glory dying.................... 77

METRE 32.
5, 5, 5, 11.

COME let us anew our journey pursue.......... 64

METRE 33.
11, 10, 11, 10.

HAIL the blest morn when the great Med......5˙
Restless thy spirit poor wandering sinner......13˙

METRE 36.
11, 11, 11, 11, 5, 11.

'MID scenes of confusion and creature.........225

METRE 40.
7, 6, 7, 6, 7, 6, 7, 6.

PAGE.
DROOPING souls no longer grieve................145

METRE 41.
8, 3, 3, 6.

ERE I sleep for every favor........................345

METRE 52.
9, 8, 9, 8, 9, 8, 9, 8.

COME all who love my Lord and Master......307

METRE 53.
9, 8, 9, 8, 9, 8, 10, 8.

RELIGION 'tis a glorious treasure...............310

METRE 54.
11, 11, 11, 5.

All guilty sinner ruined by transgression.....268

METRE 55.
10, 10, 10, 10.

AGAIN the day returns of holy rest..............167

METRE 56.
8, 8, 8, 8, 8, 8, 3.

HEAR the royal proclamation.....................147

METRE 60.
7, 7, 7, 7, 6, 6, 7, 7.

SEE the fountain opened wide....................134

INDEX OF FIRST LINES.

AFFLICTIONS though they seem.....PAGE.	274
Again the day returns of holy rest	167
Again our earthly cares we leave	33
Ah guilty sinner ruin'd by transgression	268
Ah I shall soon be dying	256
Alas and did my Savior bleed	70
All hail the pow'r of Jesus' name	23
All praise to him who dwells in bliss	175
Almighty Father bless the word	53
Almighty Maker God	218
Amazing sight the Savior stands	132
Am I a soldier of the cross	27
Amid the splendors of thy state	247
And am I only born to die	317
And can it be that I should gain	316
And is the gospel peace and love	241
And let our bodies part	319
And let this feeble body fail	187
And must this body die	181
And must I be to judgment brought	196
And now my soul another year	63
Angels from the realms of glory	63
Angels roll the rock away	86
Angels in shining order stand	77
Another day has passed along	359
Approach my soul the mercy seat	118
Arise my soul arise	259
Arise my tend'rest thoughts arise	220
As on the cross the Savior hung	73
As the apostles sat at meat	101
Assist thy servant Lord	35

INDEX OF FIRST LINES.

Attend young friends while I relate...PAGE...185
Awake, awake, the sacred song...................... 5
Awake my soul in joyful lays....................... 16
Awake my soul to sound his praise...............333
Awake my heart arise my tongue................. 24
Away with our sorrow and fear....................211
BEFORE Jehovah's awful throne............... 24
Begone unbelief my Savior is near... 162
Behold a stranger at the door....................270
Behold the lofty sky............................ 20
Behold the glories of the Lamb....................322
Behold the Savior of mankind...................... 83
Behold the wretch whose lust and wine.........273
Bless'd are the sons of peace....................255
Bless'd is the man who shuns the place.........336
Bless'd Redeemer how divine....................343
Bless O my soul the living God................... 17
Bless'd are the humble souls that see............ 91
Blest be the dear uniting love....................296
Bestow dear Lord upon our youth.................108
Blow ye the trumpet blow........................324
Broad is the road that leads to death............261
By cool Siloam's shady rill......................364
COME all who love my Lord and Master.....307
Come children learn to fear the Lord.......... 15
Come children of Zion and help us to sing..... 29
Come every pious heart................. 140
Come gracious Spirit heavenly Dove............130
Come Holy Spirit heavenly Dove................101
Come happy souls approach your God.......... 10
Come hither all ye weary souls....................146
Come humble sinner in whose breast............107
Come in ye blessed of the Lord.... 95
Come Lord from above the mountains...........126
Come let us all unite to praise...................... 8

INDEX OF FIRST LINES. 375

Come let us now forget our mirth ......Page...312
Come let us join our cheerful songs...............248
Come let us anew our journey pursue............ 64
Come let our voices join to raise................... 44
Come my soul thy suit prepare.....................338
Come O thou traveller unknown...................271
Come sound his praise abroad....................... 7
Come thou desire of all thy saints................. 32
Come thou fount of every blessing................219
Come thou everlasting Spirit........................287
Come we that love the Lord.........................203
Come weary souls with sins distress'd........... 48
Come ye that love the Savior's name............ 47
Come ye sinners come to Jesus..................... 38
Come ye sinners poor and needy..................148
Comfort ye ministers of grace...................... 43
DAY of Judgment day of wonders...............196
Daughter of Zion from the dust.................358
Dark and thorny is the desert......................304
Dear friends farewell I do you tell...............293
Dear refuge of my weary soul......................334
Death 'tis a melancholy day........................186
Depth of mercy can there be.......................354
Descend from heaven immortal Dove............240
Dismiss us with thy blessing Lord................ 50
Destruction's dangerous road......................262
Dread Sovereign let my evening song...........174
Drooping souls no longer grieve...................145
EARTH hath engross'd my love too long.....205
Ere I sleep for every favor.......................345
Eternal power whose high abode...................248
Eternal Wisdom thee we praise....................245
FAREWELL my brethren in the Lord........294
Farewell my dear brethren the time is at..292
Far from my thoughts vain world begone......325

INDEX OF FIRST LINES.

Father how wide thy glories shine......Page..309
Father I long I faint to see..........................226
Father I stretch my hands to thee................103
Father of mercies in thy word..................... 87
Firm was my health my day was................326
From all that dwell below the skies............. 31
From every stormy wind that blows............253
From thee my God my joys shall rise...........207
GLORY to thee my God this night............172
Glory to God on high..............................334
Go watch and pray thou canst not tell.........115
Go when the morning shineth.....................349
God is love his mercy brightens..................163
God of my life look gently down.................240
God of my life my morning song................171
God of my salvation hear..........................251
Great God indulge my humble claim...........109
Great God preserved by thine arm..............170
Great High Priest we view thee stooping...... 82
HAIL my ever blessed Jesus.....................231
Hail thou once despised Jesus................ 72
Hail the blest morn when the great Mediator 58
Hark from on high those blissful strains....... 60
Hark from the tombs a doleful sound...........182
Hark how the gospel trumpet sounds............340
Hark my soul it is the Lord......................... 19
Hark the herald angels sing....................... 61
Hark the glad sound the Savior comes.......... 55
Hark the Redeemer from on high.................138
Hark the voice of love and mercy.................278
Hark what mean those holy voices............... 62
Happy soul thy days are ended..................328
Hasten O sinner to be wise........................267
Have mercy Lord on me............................272
Have mercy gracious Lord forgive...............350

INDEX OF FIRST LINES.

He dies the Friend of sinners dies......PAGE.... 69
Hear gracious God my humble moan............230
Hear the royal proclamation........................147
Hearts of stone relent.................................. 74
Help thy servant gracious Lord..................... 39
High on his everlasting throne...................... 45
Holy Jesus lovely Lamb...............................122
Hosanna to the prince of light...................... 84
How beauteous are their feet........................ 22
How blest is our brother bereft.....................188
How condescending and how kind...............156
How did my heart rejoice to hear.................. 9
How firm a foundation ye saints of the Lord...155
How long O Lord shall I complain...............118
How lovely how divinely sweet....................337
How oft alas this wretched heart..................271
How pleasant how divinely fair....................225
How shall the young secure their hearts....... 88
How shall a lost sinner in pain....................123
How shall we praise th' Eternal God............ 6
How solemn the signal I hear......................313
How sweet and awful is the place................282
How sweet the name of Jesus sounds............232
How tedious and tasteless the hours.............297
How sweet to reflect on those joys that.........162
How vain are all things here below..............201
I'M not ashamed to own my Lord................ 37
If glorious angels do rejoice........................ 94
If Paul in Cæsar's court must stand..............150
I mine Ebenezer raise.................................253
Indulgent Father by whose care...................175
In evil long I took delight...........................3 5
In glory bright the Savior reigns..................330
Inspirer and hearer of prayer.......................176
I lift my soul to God..................................260

I'll bless the Lord from day to day.....PAGE...106
I love to steal awhile away............................177
I send the joys of earth away........................255
Is this the kind return..................................264
I would not live always I ask not to stay......212
JESUS and shall it ever be............................ 30
J JESUS at whose supreme command.........285
Jesus grant us all a blessing...................... 53
Jesus I my cross have taken........................308
Jesus invites his saints...............................283
Jesus lover of my soul................................113
Jesus my Savior, Brother, Friend.................129
Jesus my Savior let me be..........................114
Jesus' precious name excels......................131
Jesus thy boundless love, to me..................110
Jesus thou art the sinner's Friend..................124
Jesus the spring of joys divine....................129
Jesus thy blessings are not few..................... 37
Jerusalem my happy home........................210
LAMB of God for sinners slain..................122
L Lamb of God whose dying love................286
Let all our tongues be one.........................284
Let every mortal ear attend......................... 18
Let me but hear my Savior say.................... 36
Let sinners take their course....................... 89
Let the whole race of creation lie................. 90
Let us adore th' Eternal Word....................279
Let Zion and her sons rejoice....................246
Life is the time to serve the Lord................323
Lo he cometh! countless trumpets..............199
Lo he comes with clouds descending............198
Lo round the throne at God's right hand.......350
Lo what a glorious sight appears................215
Lord at thy temple we appear..................... 28
Lord if thine eyes survey our faults.............183

Lord I approach thy mercy-seat.........PAGE...339
Lord in the morning thou shalt hear............168
Lord I cannot let thee go....................112
Lord I am thine but thou wilt prove............233
Lord dismiss us with thy blessing............... 50
Lord at thy sacred feet....................... 40
Lord how divine thy comforts are................280
Lord thou wilt hear me when I pray............173
Lord must I die O let me die.................192
Lord teach thy servants how to pray............125
Lord what a feeble piece.....................180
Lord we come before thee now....................116
Lord what is man, poor feeble man..............178

MAJESTIC sweetness sits enthroned...........346
Mary to the Savior's tomb...................348
Mighty God while angels bless thee.............355
'Mid scenes of confusion and creature com.....228
My dearest friends in bonds of love.............291
My drowsy powers why sleep ye so..............330
My God the spring of all my joys..................224
My God thy boundless love we praise...........157
My God consider my distress....................127
My hope, my all, my Savior thou............... 31
My lovely Jesus while on earth.................169
My Savior and my King......................... 10
My Savior thou thy love to me...................111
My Savior, my Almigthy Friend..................221
My soul be on thy guard.......................117
My soul with joy attend......................158

NOW gracious Lord thine arm reveal.......... 65
Now in the heat of youthful blood..........326
Now is the accepted time...................... 25
Now is the time, th' accepted hour.............. 39
Now the shades of night are gone.................169

INDEX OF FIRST LINES.

O ALL ye nations praise the Lord.....PAGE...327
  Oh all that pass by to Jesus draw near.....135
O could I find some peaceful bower...............235
Of all the joys we mortals know..................159
Often I seek my Lord by night.....................238
Oh for a sweet inspiring ray......................208
Oh for a closer walk with God.....................104
Oh how happy are they.............................209
Oh happy day when saints shall meet...........296
O happy is the man who bears..................... 36
O happy day that fixed my choice................359
Oh how I love thy holy law........................311
O if my soul was formed for woe.................. 92
O land of rest for thee I sigh........................227
On Jordan's stormy banks I stand................204
On the mountain's top appearing................. 42
On Judah's plains, as shepherds sat.............. 54
Once more we come before our God.............. 12
Once more my soul the rising day................166
Once more before we part.......................... 51
Oppress'd with fear, oppress'd with grief.......152
O tell me no more of this world's vain store...161
O thou to whose all-searching sight..............102
O thou in whose presence my soul takes del...216
O that I had a bosom friend.......................222
O that the Lord would guide my ways..........244
O thou God of my salvation......................303
O thou that hear'st when sinners pray.......... 93
Our life is ever on the wing....................... 67
Our God, our help in ages past...................178
O what amazing words of grace..................141
O what shall I do my Savior to praise..........250
O where shall rest be found.......................360
O Zion afflicted with wave upon wave..........363
PRAY'R is the soul's sincere desire..............120
  Praise ye the Lord who reigns above........249

INDEX OF FIRST LINES.

Prince of Peace, be ever near us..........PAGE...	52
RELIGION 'tis a glorious treasure...............	310
Religion is the chief concern.....................	235
Rejoice in Jesus' birth...............................	56
Remember, Lord, our mortal state................	191
Restless thy spirit, poor wandering sinner.....	138
Rise, my soul, and stretch thy wings............	230
SAFELY through another week...................	49
Salvation! O the joyful sound....................	50
Savior, visit thy plantation.........................	300
Savior, I do feel thy merit...........................	302
Saw ye my Savior, saw ye my Savior............	76
Say now ye lovely social band.....................	257
See the Lord of glory dying........................	75
See from Zion's sacred mountain..................	213
See the fountain opened wide......................	131
Seek my soul the narrow gate.....................	343
Shall wisdom cry aloud...............................	331
Shepherd divine our wants relieve...............	357
Show pity Lord, O Lord forgive...................	105
Sing to the Lord ye heavenly hosts...............	194
Sing the great Jehovah's praise...................	65
Since Jesus freely did appear......................	276
Sinner, art thou still secure........................	263
Sinners, hear the Savior's call.....................	353
Sinners, take the friendly warning...............	195
Sinners turn, why will you die....................	14
Sinners, the voice of God regard..................	143
So let our lives and lips express...................	159
Softly now the light of day.........................	177
Stop poor sinner stop and think...................	267
Sweet is the work my God, my King............	165
Sweet the moments rich in blessing..............	339
TEACH me the measure of my days............	179
Tell me, Savior from above........................	221

INDEX OF FIRST LINES.

That awful day will surely come.........Page..265
That doleful night before his death............ 283
Thee we adore, Eternal Name......................190
The day is past and gone..........................172
The God Jehovah reigns............................328
To thy pastures fair and large.....................252
The heavens declare thy glory, Lord............347
The Lord of earth and sky.......................... 66
The Lord's disciples when they spread......... 99
The morning light is breaking....................362
The name of the Lord is a fountain of life...... 97
The night on which Christ was betrayed.......289
The Savior calls, let every ear.....................141
The Savior, O what endless charms..............245
The Son of man they did betray................... 79
The swift declining day.............................. 52
The time is short—sinners beware................265
The wondering world inquires to know.........320
The voice of my beloved sounds...................144
There is a house not made with hands..........202
There is a voice of sovereign grace................243
There is a land of pure delight.....................239
These glorious minds how bright they..........214
This is the day the Lord hath made.............. 84
Thou art a God, a Spirit pure................ 242
Thou Shepherd of Israel and mine................234
Thou whom my soul admires above..............237
'Tis midnight and on Olive's brow...............281
To-day if you will hear his voice...................139
To God the Great the ever-blessed................. 13
To God in whom I trust..............................261
To show how humble Christians ought..........288
To thy pastures fair and large......................342
Through every age, eternal God...................191
'Twas on that dark, that doleful night.. 71

INDEX OF FIRST LINES.

'Twas the commission of our Lord........Page..	96
Thy life I read my dearest Lord.....................	184
Thy mercy, my God, is the theme of.............	164
Thy presence, gracious God, afford...............	35
UP to the fields where angels lie..................	236
VAIN delusive world, adieu........................	305
Vain man, thy fond pursuits forbear..........	335
WELCOME, delightful morn.....................	352
We sing the glories of thy love...............	42
We've no abiding city here...........................	41
Welcome, sweet day of rest...........................	34
What glory gilds the sacred page...................	91
What poor despised company........................	314
What various hindrances we meet................	121
When blooming youth is snatched.................	193
When gathering clouds around I view..........	254
When I survey the wondrous cross...............	69
When I can read my title clear.....................	219
When Jesus Christ was here below...............	290
When Jesus Christ, the Virgin's son..............	98
When Jesus did from heaven descend...........	46
When Joseph his brethren beheld.................	298
When languor and disease invade................	311
When on Sinai's top I see.............................	332
When rising from the bed of death...............	329
When sinners awake and perceive................	100
When we with welcome slumber...................	170
Where two or three with sweet accord..........	21
While with ceaseless course the sun..............	356
Who is this that comes from far...................	351
With grateful hearts and tuneful lays...........	276
With cheerful voices rise and sing...............	277
With humble heart and tongue.....................	119

With my whole heart I've sought thy..PAGE..128
With rev'rence let thy saints appear............. 12
With sacred joys we lift our eyes................... 33
While I keep silent and conceal.....................255
While life prolongs its precious light............142
While shepherds watch'd their flocks............ 59
Whilst thee I seek Protecting Power............112
Who is this fair one in distress....................160
Would Jesus have the sinner die..................152
Why do we mourn departing friends............184
Why doth the man of riches grow.................200
Why should we start and fear to die.............189
Why sleep ye my brethren come...................136
YE humble souls that seek the Lord............ 85
Ye nations all, on you I call..................... 56
Ye nations round the earth rejoice................250
Ye mourning saints whose streaming............344
Ye sinners, fear the Lord...........................150
Yes, the Redeemer rose...............................361
Ye that pass by behold the man...................277
Ye thirsty for God to Jesus give ear.............137
Ye weary heavy laden souls........................315
Ye wretched hungry starving poor...............149
Young people, all attention give................... 26

Anhang

einiger

Deutschen Lieder,

erbaulich zu singen in

Oeffentlichen Versammlungen

oder bei

Privat=Uebungen.

Anhang.

Nach eigener Melodie.

1 Liebster Jesu, wir sind hier,
 Dich und dein Wort anzuhören;
Lenke Sinnen und Begier
 Auf die süßen Himmelslehren,
Laß die Herzen von der Erden
Ganz zu dir gezogen werden.

2 Unser Wissen und Verstand
 Ist mit Finsterniß umhüllet,
Wo nicht deines Geistes Glanz
 Uns mit hellem Licht erfüllet:
Gutes denken, Gutes dichten,
Mußt du selbst in uns verrichten.

3 O du Glanz der Herrlichkeit,
 Licht vom Licht aus Gott geboren!
Mach' uns allezeit bereit,
 Oeffne Herzen, Mund und Ohren:
Unser Bitten, Fleh'n und Singen
Laß Herr Jesu, wohl gelingen.

Anhang.

METRE 25.
Gott des Himmels.

Hamburg.

1 Theures Wort aus Gottes Munde,
 Das mir lauter Honig trägt!
Dich allein hab ich zum Grunde
 Meiner Seligkeit gelegt;
In dir treff' ich Alles an,
Was zu Gott mich führen kann.

2 Will ich einen Vorschmack haben,
 Welcher nach dem Himmel schmeckt;
Gott! du kannst mich herrlich laben,
 Weil im Wort ein Tisch gedeckt,
Der mir lauter Manna schenkt,
Und mit Lebenswasser tränkt.

3 Komm, o Geist! und mich im Worte
 An die Lebensquelle leg',
Oeffne mir die Himmelspforte,
 Daß mein Geist hier recht erwäg',
Was für Schätze Gottes Hand
Durch sein Wort mir zugesandt.

4 Hilf, daß alle meine Wege
 Nur nach dieser Schnure geh'n;
Was ich hier zum Grunde lege,
 Müsse wie ein Felsen steh'n,
Daß mein Geist auch Rath und That
In den größten Nöthen hat.

5 Laß dein Wort mir einen Spiegel
   In der Folge Jesu seyn;
Drücke d'rauf ein Gnadensiegel,
   Schließ den Schatz im Herzen ein,
Laß ich fest im Glauben steh',
Bis ich dort zum Schauen geh'.

3   METRE 7.   *Dresden.*

1 Sieh' hier bin ich, Ehrenkönig!
   Lege mich vor deinen Thron:
Schwache Thränen, kindlich Sehnen
   Bring ich dir, du Menschensohn!
Laß dich finden, Laß dich finden,
   Von mir der ich Asch und Thon!

2 Sieh' doch auf mich, Herr ich bitt' dich,
   Lenke mich nach deinem Sinn;
Dich alleine ich nur meine,
   Dein erkaufter Erb' ich bin;
Laß dich finden, Laß dich finden,
   Gieb dich mir und nimm mich hin.

3 Ich begehre nichts, o Herre,
   Als nur deine freie Gnad',
Die du giebest, den du liebest,
   Und der dich liebt in der That:
Laß dich finden, Laß dich finden,
   Der hat Alles, wer dich hat.

4 Himmelssonne, Seelenwonne,
　　Unbeflecktes Gottes=Lamm!
In der Höhle meiner Seele,
　　Suchet dich, o Bräutigam;
Laß dich finden, Laß dich finden,
　　Starker Held aus David's Stamm.

5 Hör' wie kläglich, wie beweglich
　　Dir die treue Seele singt!
Wie demüthig und wehmüthig
　　Deines Kindes Stimme klingt!
Laß dich finden, Laß dich finden,
　　Denn zu dir mein Herze dringt.

6 Dieser Zeiten Eitelkeiten,
　　Reichthum, Wollust, Ehr' und Freud'
Sind nur Schmerzen meinem Herzen,
　　Welches sucht die Ewigkeit:
Laß dich finden, Laß dich finden,
　　Großer Gott! mach mich bereit.

4　　　Nach eigener Melodie.

1 Mir nach spricht Christus unser Held,
　　Mir nach ihr Christen alle,
Verleugnet euch, verlaßt die Welt,
　　Folgt meinem Ruf und Schalle;
Nehmt euer Kreuz und Ungemach
　　Auf euch, folgt meinem Wandel nach.

2 Ich bin das Licht, ich leucht' euch für
　　Mit heil'gem Tugendleben;

Anhang.

Wer zu mir kommt, und folget mir,
  Darf nicht im Finstern schweben;
Ich bin der Weg, ich weiß es wohl,
Wie man wahrhaftig wandeln soll.

3 Mein Herz ist voll Demüthigkeit,
  Voll Liebe meine Seele,
Mein Mund der fließt zu jeder Zeit
  Vom süßen Sanftmuthsöle;
Mein Geist, Gemüthe, Kraft und Sinn
Ist Gott ergeben, schau't auf ihn.

4 Ich zeig' euch das, was schädlich ist,
  Zu fliehen und zu meiden,
Und euer Herz von arger List
  Zu rein'gen und zu scheiden;
Ich bin der Seelen Fels und Hort,
Und führ euch zu der Himmelspfort.

5 Fällt's euch zu schwer, ich geh' voran,
  Ich steh' euch an der Seite,
Ich kämpfe selbst, ich brech' die Bahn,
  Bin Alles in dem Streite;
Ein böser Knecht, der still darf steh'n,
Wenn er den Feldherrn sieht angeh'n.

6 Wer seine Seel' zu finden meint,
  Wird sie ohn' mich verlieren,
Wer sie hier zu verlieren scheint,
  Wird sie in Gott einführen;
Wer nicht sein Kreuz nimmt und folgt mir,
Ist mein nicht werth und meiner Zier.

7 So laßt uns denn dem lieben Herrn
  Mit Leib und Seel nachgehen,
Und wohlgemuth, getrost und gern
  Bei ihm im Leiden stehen;
Denn wer nicht kämpft, trägt auch die Kron'
Des ew'gen Lebens nicht davon.

5 Mel. Mir nach spricht Christus.

1 Nun lobet Alle Gottes Sohn,
  Der die Erlösung funden;
Beugt eure Knie vor seinem Thron,
  Sein Blut hat überwunden;
Preis, Lob, Ehr, Dank, Kraft, Weisheit, Macht,
Sei dem erwürgten Lamm gebracht.

2 Es war uns Gottes Licht und Gnad'
  Und Leben hart verriegelt;
Sein tiefer Sinn sein' Wunderrath
  Wohl siebenfach versiegelt,
Kein Mensch, kein Engel öffnen kann;
Das Lämmlein thuts, drum lobe man.

3 Die Patriarchen erster Zeit,
  Den lang Verheiß'nen grüßen;
Und die Propheten sind erfreut,
  Daß sie's nun mitgenießen;
Auch die Apostel singen dir
Hos'anna mit den Kindern hier.

4 Der Märt'rer Kron von Golde glänzt,
  Sie bringen dir die Palmen;

Anhang.

Die Jungfrau'n weiß, und schön gekränzt,
  Die singen Hochzeitspsalmen;
Sie rufen wie aus einem Mund;
Das hat des Lammes Blut gekonnt.

5 Nun dein erkauftes Volk allhie,
  Spricht Hallelujah! Amen!
Wir beugen jetzt schon unsere Knie,
  In deinem Blut und Namen;
Biß du uns bringst zusammen dort,
Aus allem Volk, Geschlecht und Ort.

6 Was wird das seyn! wie werden wir
  Von ew'ger Gnade sagen!
Wie uns dein Wunderführer hier
  Gesucht, erlößt, getragen;
Da jeder seine Harfe bringt,
Und sein besonders Loblied singt.

6.
METRE 68.
Mel. Allein Gott in der Höh'.

1 Sey Lob und Ehr dem höchsten Gut,
  Dem Vater aller Güte,
Dem Gott der alle Wunder thut,
  Dem Gott, der mein Gemüthe
Mit seinem reichen Trost erfüll't,
Dem Gott, der allen Jammer stillt!
  Gebt unserm Gott die Ehre!

2 Es danken dir die Himmelsheer,
  O Herrscher aller Thronen!

Und die auf Erden, Luft und Meer,
  In deinem Schatten wohnen,
Die preisen deines Schöpfers Macht,
Die alles also wohl bedacht,
  Gebt unserm Gott die Ehre!

3 Was unser Gott geschaffen hat,
  Das will er auch erhalten,
Darüber will er früh und spat,
  Mit seiner Güte walten:
In seinem ganzen Königreich
Ist Alles recht und Alles gleich,
  Gebt unserm Gott die Ehre!

4 Ich rief dem Herrn in meiner Noth:
  Ach Gott, vernimm mein Schreien!
Da half mein Helfer mir vom Tod,
  Und ließ mir Trost gedeihen,
D'rum dank ich Gott! drum dank ich dir,
Ach danket, danket Gott mit mir!
  Gebt unserm Gott die Ehre!

5 Der Herr ist noch und nimmer nicht
  Von seinem Volk geschieden;
Er bleibet ihre Zuversicht,
  Ihr Segen, Heil und Frieden;
Mit Mutterhänden leitet er
Die Seinen stetig hin und her;
  Gebt unserm Gott die Ehre!

Anhang.

6 Ich will dich all mein Lebenlang,
   O Gott! von nun an ehren;
Man soll, o Gott! den Lobgesang
   An allen Orten hören,
Mein ganzes Herz ermunt're sich,
Mein Geist und Leib erfreue dich,
   Gebt unserm Gott die Ehre!

7   C. M.   *Primrose.*

1 Auf Seele, auf, und säume nicht,
   Es bricht das Licht herfür;
Der Wunderstern gibt dir Bericht,
   Der Held sey vor der Thür.

2 Geh weg aus deinem Vaterland,
   Zu suchen solchen Herrn;
Laß deine Augen sein gewandt,
   Auf diesen Morgenstern.

3 Gib acht auf diesen hellen Schein,
   Der dir auf'gangen ist;
Er führet dich zum Kindelein,
   Das heißet Jesus Christ.

4 Er ist der Held aus David's Stamm,
   Die theure Sarons Blum;
Das rechte ächte Gottes-Lamm,
   Israel's Preis und Ruhm.

Anhang.

5 D'rum höre, merke, sey bereit,
   Verlaß des Vaters Haus,
Die Freundschaft, deine Eigenheit,
   Geh von dir selbsten aus.

6 Und mache dich behende auf,
   Befreit von aller Last,
Ja laß nicht ab von deinem Lauf,
   Bis du dies Kindlein hast.

7 Du, du bist selbst das Bethlehem,
   Die rechte David's Stadt;
Wenn du dein Herze machst bequem
   Zu solcher großen Gnad.

8 Da findest du das Lebensbrod
   Das dich erlaben kann,
Für deiner Seelen Hungersnoth
   Der allerbeste Mann.

8   METRE 5.   *Sovereign Grace.*

1 Gott sey Dank in aller Welt,
   Der sein Wort beständig hält,
Und der Sünder Trost und Rath
Zu uns her gesendet hat.

2 Was der alten Väter Schaar,
Höchster Wunsch und Sehnen war,
Und was sie geprophezeiht,
Ist erfüllt nach Herrlichkeit.

3 Zion' Hülf und Abraham's Lohn,
   Jacob's Heil, der Jungfrau'n Sohn,
   Der wohl zweigestammte Held
   Hat sich treulich eingestellt.

4 Sey willkommen, o mein Heil,
   Dir Hos'anna! o mein Theil;
   Richte du auch eine Bahn,
   Dir in meinem Herzen an.

5 Zieh, du Ehrenkönig ein,
   Es gehöret dir allein;
   Mach es, wie du gerne thust,
   Rein von aller Sündenwust.

6 Herr wie deine Zukunft ist
   Und du selbst sanftmüthig bist;
   So wohn' in mir jederzeit,
   Sanftmuth und Gelassenheit.

7 Hülf, wenn du mein Lebensfürst,
   Prächtig wieder kommen wirst,
   Daß ich dir entgegen geh'
   Und vor dir gerecht besteh'.

9)   C. M.   *Balerma—Marlow.*

1 Mein Gott das Herz ich bringe dir,
      Zur Gabe und Geschenk;
   Du forderst dieses ja von mir,
      Deß bin ich eingedenk.

2 Gib mir, mein Kind! dein Herz, sprichst du,
    Das ist mir lieb und werth,
Du findest anders doch nicht Ruh
    Im Himmel und auf Erd'.

3 Nun du, mein Vater! nimm es an,
    Mein Herz, veracht es nicht,
Ich geb's so gut ich's geben kann,
    Kehr zu mir dein Gesicht.

4 Zwar ist es voller Sündenwust
    Und voller Eitelkeit,
Des Guten aber unbewußt,
    Der wahren Frömmigkeit.

5 Doch aber steht es nun in Reu',
    Erkennt sein Uebelstand,
Und träget jetzund vor dem Scheu,
    Daran's zuvor Lust fand.

6 Hier fällt und lieg't es dir zu Fuß
    Und schrey't: nur schlage zu;
Zerknirsch, o Vater! daß ich Buß
    Rechtschaffen vor dir thu';

7 Zermalm mir meine Härtigkeit,
    Mach mürbe meinen Sinn,
Daß ich in Seufzen, Reu und Leid
    Und Thränen ganz zerrinn.

Anhang.

8 Sodann nimm mich, mein Jesu Christ,
   Tauf mich mit deinem Blut,
Ich glaub, daß du gekreuzigt bist
   Der Welt und mir zu gut.

9 Hilf daß ich sey von Herzen treu
   Im Glauben meinem Gott,
Daß mich im Guten nicht macht scheu
   Der Welt List, Macht und Spott.

10 Weg Welt, weg Sünd! dir geb' ich nicht
   Mein Herz: nur Jesu, dir
Ist dies Geschenke zugericht,
   Behalt es für und für.

10   Nach eigner Melodie.

1 Herr Jesu, Gnadensonne,
   Wahrhaftes Lebenslicht!
Laß Leben, Licht und Wonne
   Mein blödes Angesicht
Nach deiner Gnad erfreuen,
Und meinen Geist erneuen,
   Mein Gott versag mir's nicht.

2 Vergib mir meine Sünden,
   Und wirf sie hinter dich,
Laß allen Zorn verschwinden,
   Und hilf gnädiglich:

Laß deine Friedensgaben
Mein armes Herze laben,
Ach! Herr, erhöre mich.

3 Vertreib aus meiner Seele
Den alten Adamssinn,
Und laß mich dich erwählen,
Auf daß ich mich forthin
Zu deinem Dienst ergebe,
Und dir zu Ehren lebe,
Weil ich erlöset bin.

4 Beförd're dein Erkenntniß
In mir, mein Seelen Hort!
Und öffne mein Verständniß
Durch dein heiliges Wort:
Damit ich an dich glaube,
Und in der Wahrheit bleibe,
Zum Trotz der Höllenpfort.

5 Tränk mich an deinen Brüsten,
Und kreuz'ge mein Begier,
Sammt allen bösen Lüsten,
Auf daß ich für und für,
Der Sündenwelt absterbe,
Und nach dem Fleisch verderbe,
Hingegen leb ich dir.

6 Ach zünde deine Liebe
In meiner Seele an,

Daß ich aus reinem Triebe
Dich ewig lieben kann,
Und dir zum Wohlgefallen
Beständig möge wallen
  Auf rechter Lebensbahn.

11   METRE 7.   *Dresden.*

1 Ich will lieben und mich üben,
  Daß ich meinem Bräutigam
Nun in Allem mag gefallen,
Welcher an des Kreuzes Stamm
Hat sein Leben für mich geben
Ganz geduldig als ein Lamm.

2 Ich will lieben und mich üben,
Im Gebet zu Tag und Nacht,
Daß nun balde alles Alte
In mir werd' zum Grab gebracht;
Und hingegen allerwegen,
Alles werde neu gemacht.

3 Ich will lieben und mich üben,
Daß ich rein und heilig werd,
Und mein leben führe eben,
Wie es Gott von mir begehrt,
Ja mein Wandel, Thun und Handel
Sei unsträflich auf der Erd.

Anhang.

4 Ich will lieben und mich üben
Meine ganze Lebenszeit,
Mich zu schicken und zu schmücken
Mit dem reinen Hochzeitskleid,
Zu erscheinen mit den Reinen
Auf des Lammes Hochzeitsfreud.

12   Metre 7.   Dresden.—Judgment.

1 Setze dich mein Geist ein wenig,
  Und beschau dies Wunder groß,
Wie dein Gott und Ehrenkönig,
Hängt am Kreuze nack't und bloß!
Schau die Liebe, die ihn triebe,
Zu dir aus des Vaters Schooß.

2 Ob dich Jesus liebt von Herzen,
Kannst du da am Kreuze seh'n:
Schau wie alle Höllenschmerzen,
Ihm bis an die Seele geh'n;
Fluch und Schrecken ihn bedecken,
Höre doch sein Klaggestöhn.

3 Seine Seel' von Gott verlassen,
Ist betrübt bis in den Tod;
Und sein Leib hängt gleichermaßen
Voller Wunden, Blut und Koth;
Alle Kräfte, alle Säfte,
Sind erschöpft in höchster Noth.

4 Dies sind meiner Sünden Früchte,
 Die, mein Heiland, ängst'gen dich;
 Dieser Leiden schwer Gewichte
 Sollt' zum Abgrund drücken mich;
 Diese Nöthen, die dich tödten,
 Sollt ich fühlen ewiglich.

5 Doch du hast für mich besieget
 Sünde, Tod und Höllenmacht;
 Du hast Gottes Recht vergnüget,
 Seinen Willen ganz vollbracht;
 Und mir eben zu dem Leben,
 Durch dein Sterben, Bahn gemacht.

6 Dir will ich, durch deine Gnade,
 Bleiben bis in Tod getreu;
 Alle Leiden, Schand und Schade
 Sollen mich nicht machen scheu;
 Deinen Willen zu erfüllen,
 Meiner Seele Speise sei.

13 METRE 6S. *Sounding Trumpet.*
Es ist gewißlich an der Zeit.

1 Wo soll ich hin? wer hilfet mir?
  Wer führet mich zum Leben?
 Zu Niemand, Herr, als nur zu dir,
  Will ich mich frei begeben,
 Du bist's, der das Verlor'ne sucht;
 Du segnest das, so war verflucht:
  Hilf Jesu, dem Elenden!

Anhang.

2 Herr meine Sünden ängst'gen mich,
  Der Todesleib mich plaget;
O Lebensgott, erbarme dich,
  Vergieb mir was mich naget!
Du weißt es wohl, was mir gebricht;
Ich weiß es auch, doch völlig nicht:
  Hilf Jesu dem Betrübten!

3 Du sprichst zu mir: verzage nicht!
  Du rufst: ich bin das Leben!
D'rum ist mein Herz auf dich gericht't,
  Du kannst mir Alles geben;
Im Tode kannst du bei mir steh'n;
In Noth als Herzog vor mir geh'n:
  Hilf Jesu, dem Zerknirschten!

4 Bist du der Hirt, der Schwache trägt!
  Auf dich will ich mich legen,
Bist du der Arzt, der Kranke pflegt;
  Erquicke mich mit Segen!
Ich bin gefährlich krank und schwach;
Heil' und verbind', hör' an die Klag':
  Hilf, Jesu, dem Zerschlag'nen!

5 Ich thue nicht, Herr, was ich soll:
  Wie kann ich doch bestehen?
Dies ängstet mich, das weißt du wohl,
  Ach wenn wird's noch geschehen,
Daß ich Elender endlich frei
Vom Leib' des Todes, bei dir sei!
  Ich danke Gott durch Christum.

Anhang.

14   Mel.: Nun ruhen alle Wälder.

1 Durch viele große Plagen
Hat mich der Herr getragen,
Von meiner Jugend auf;
Ich sah' auf meinen Wegen
Des Höchsten Hand und Segen;
Er lenkte meinen Lebenslauf.

2 Sein Weg war oft verborgen;
Doch wie der helle Morgen
Aus dunklen Nächten bricht;
So hab ich stets gespüret,
Der Weg, den Gott mich führet
Bringt mich durch's finst're Thal zum Licht.

3 War Menschenhülf vergebens,
So kam der Herr des Lebens,
Und half und machte Bahn;
Wußt ich mir nicht zu rathen:
So that Gott große Thaten,
Und nahm sich mächtig meiner an.

4 Bis in des Alters Tagen
Will er mich heben, tragen,
Und mein Erretter sein;
Dies hat mir Gott versprochen,
Der nie sein Wort gebrochen;
Ich werde sein mich ewig freu'n.

5 Er wird mir schwachen Alten,
Was er versprochen, halten,
 Denn er ist fromm und treu;
Bin ich gleich matt und müde,
Er gibt mir Trost und Friede,
 Und steht mit Muth und Kraft mir bei.

6 Nach wenig bangen Stunden
Hab ich ganz überwunden;
 Ich bin vom Ziel nicht weit.
Triumph! o welche Freuden!
Sind nach dem langen Leiden,
 Vor Gottes Thron für mich bereit.

15 Mel: Nun ruhen alle Wälder.

1 Gott hab ich mich ergeben
 In diesem Pilgerleben,
 Im Unglück und im Glück
In Schmerzen und in Freuden,
Und bis an's Ziel der Leiden,
 In meinem letzten Augenblick.

2 Gott war's, der für mich wachte
Noch eh' ich war und dachte;
 Des Ew'gen treue Hand
Hat gnädig mich geleitet,
Mir jedes Glück bereitet,
 Das ich so oft im Unglück fand.

Anhang.

3 Was helfen meine Sorgen?
Mein Glück ist mir verborgen,
　Mein Unglück kenn' ich nicht,
Dem Hüter meiner Seelen,
Dem will ich mich befehlen:
　Er weiß allein was mir gebricht.

4 Warum ich heute flehe,
Wird, wenn es gleich geschehe,
　Schon Morgen mich gereu'n;
Nur einen Wunsch von allen
Laß Herr, dir wohlgefallen,
　Den Wunsch, bald, bald bei dir zu sein.

5 Sich groß und kindlich zeigen,
Heißt tief im Staube schweigen,
　Und nehmen was Gott giebt.
Er kann uns nicht verlassen,
Die im Vertrau'n nicht hassen,
　Er schläget uns wenn er uns liebt.

6 Nicht das, warum ich flehe,
Dein Wille nur geschehe,
　Und was mir selig ist.
Herr deine Bahn ist eben,
Leit mich in diesem Leben,
　Und wenn mei Aug' im Tod sich schließt.

16　　Mel.: Wer nur den lieben Gott.
1 Nach einer Prüfung kurzer Tage
　Erwartet mich die Ewigkeit.

Dort, dort verwandelt sich die Klage
    In göttliche Zufriedenheit,
Hier übt die Tugend ihren Fleiß;
Und jene Welt reicht ihr den Preis.

2 Wahr ist's, der Fromme schmeckt auf Erden
    Schon manchen sel'gen Augenblick;
Doch alle Freuden, die ihm werden,
    Sind ihm ein unvollkommenes Glück.
Er bleibt ein Mensch, und seine Ruh'
Nimmt in der Seele ab und zu.

3 Bald stören ihn des Körpers Schmerzen,
    Bald das Geräusche dieser Welt,
Bald kämpft in seinem eig'nen Herzen
    Ein Feind, der oft den Sieg erhält;
Bald sinkt er durch des Nächsten Schuld
In Kummer und in Ungeduld.

4 Hier, wo die Tugend öfters leidet,
    Das Laster öfters glücklich ist,
Wo man den Glücklichen beneidet,
    Und des Verkümmerten vergißt;
Hier kann der Mensch nie frei von Pein,
Nie frei von eig'ner Schwachheit sein.

5 Hier such ich's nur, dort werd ich's finden:
    Dort werd ich heilig und verklärt,
Der Tugend ganzen Werth empfinden,
    Den unaussprechlich großen Werth;
Den Gott der Liebe werd' ich seh'n.
Ihn lieben, ewig ihn erhöh'n.

6 Da werd' ich das im Licht erkennen,
　　Was ich auf Erden dunkel sah!
Das wunderbar und heilig nennen,
　　Was unerforschlich hier geschah;
Da denkt mein Geist mit Preis und Dank,
Die Schickung im Zusammenhang.

7 Da werd' ich zu dem Throne bringen,
　　Wo Gott mein Heil sich offenbar't;
Ein Heilig, Heilig, Heilig! singen
　　Dem Lamme, das erwürget ward:
Und Cherubim und Seraphim
Und alle Himmel jauchzen ihm.

8 Was seid ihr, Leiden dieser Erden,
　　Doch gegen jene Herrlichkeit,
Die offenbart an uns soll werden,
　　Von Ewigkeit zu Ewigkeit!
Wie nichts, wie gar nichts gegen sie,
Ist doch ein Augenblick voll Müh!

17　　　METRE 25.　　　*Hamburg.*
　　Nach eigener Melodie.

1 Gott des Himmels und der Erden,
　　Vater, Sohn und Heil'ger Geist,
Der du Tag und Nacht läßt werden,
　　Sonn' und Mond uns scheinen heißt,
Dessen starke Hand die Welt,
Und was drinnen ist, erhält.

2 Gott! ich danke dir von Herzen,
    Daß du mich in dieser Nacht,
Vor Gefahr, Angst, Noth und Schmerzen,
    Hast behütet und bewacht,
Daß des bösen Feindes List
Mein nicht mächtig worden ist.

3 Laß die Nacht auch meiner Sünden
    Jetzt mit dieser Nacht vergeh'n,
O Herr Jesu! laß mich finden
    Deine Wunden offen steh'n,
Da alleine Hülf und Rath
Ist für meine Missethat.

4 Hilf daß ich mit diesem Morgen
    Geistlich auferstehen mag,
Und für meine Seele sorgen,
    Daß wenn nun dein jüngster Tag
Uns erschein, und dein Gericht,
Ich dafür erschrecke nicht.

5 Führe mich, o Herr und leite
    Meinen Gang nach deinem Wort,
Sei und bleibe du auch heute
    Mein Beschützer und mein Hort:
Nirgends als bei dir allein
Kann ich recht bewahret sein.

Anhang.

18   L. M.   *Rockbridge.*

1 Ihr junge Helden, aufgewacht!
   Die ganze Welt muß sein veracht,
D'rum eilt, daß ihr in kurzer Zeit,
Macht' eure Seelen wohl bereit.

2 Was ist die Welt mit allem Thun?
Den Bund gemacht mit Gottes Sohn,
Das bleibt der Seel' in Ewigkeit
Ein' zuckersüße Lust und Freud'.

3 Ja nimmermehr geliebt die Welt,
Vielmehr sich Jesu zugesellt,
So überkommt man Glaubenskraft,
Daß man auch bald ihr Thun bestraft.

4 Nun weg hiemit, du Eitelkeit,
Es ist mir nun zu lieb die Zeit,
Daß ich sie nicht mehr so anwend',
Daß ich den Namen Gottes schänd'.

5 Ich hab es nun bei mir bedacht,
Und diesen Schluß gar fest gemacht,
Daß es mir nun soll Jesu sein,
Und wollt' mein Fleisch nicht gern darein.

6 Zur falschen Welt und ihrem Trug,
Spricht meine Seel', es ist genug:
Zu lang hab ich die Welt geliebt,
Und damit meinen Gott betrübt.

7 Ich eil' nun fort zu meinem Gott,
Der mich erkauft von Fluch und Tod:
Darum ich auch nun als ein Reb'
Hinführo fest an Jesu kleb.

19   Mel.: Wer nur den lieben Gott.

1 Der Tag ist hin mit seinem Lichte,
  Die Nacht ist da mit Dunkelheit,
D'rum richte ich jetzt mein Gesichte
  Zur Sonne der Gerechtigkeit,
Die mir mit ihrem Glanz und Licht
Kann stets erleuchten mein Gesicht.

2 O Jesus, meines Herzens Freude,
  Dich lobe ich mit meinem Lied,
Und danke dir, daß du mich heute
  Vor allem Uebel hast behüt't,
Und mir von deiner milden Hand
So große Gaben zugesandt.

3 Auch wollest du, mein liebstes Leben!
  Mir heute eine sanfte Ruh,
In deinen Liebesarmen geben,
  Und mich mit Gnaden decken zu.
Daß mir der Feind in dieser Nacht
Nicht schaden kann mit List und Macht.

Anhang.

4 Du wollest über mir stets wachen,
　　Mit deinem lieben Engelsheer,
Und schicken alle meine Sachen,
　　Zu deines Namens Lob und Ehr.
Ich wache oder schlafe ein,
So laß mich immer bei dir sein.

5 Laß mir dein Licht stets helle leuchten
　　In meiner Seele und Gemüth,
Laß deinen Himmelsthau befeuchten
　　Mein Herze, daß es grün't und blüh't,
Und Früchte bringt zu deinem Preis,
Gleich einem schönen Paradeis.

20　　　METRE 68. *Harmonia Sacra.*
　　Mel.: Es ist gewißlich an der Zeit.

1 Die Glocke schläg't, und zeigt damit,
　　Die Zeit hat abgenommen,
Ich bin nun wieder einen Schritt
　　Dem Grabe näher kommen.
Mein Jesus, schlag' an meine Brust,
Weil mir die Stunde nicht bewußt,
　　Die meine Zeit beschließet.

2 Soll diese nun die letzte sein
　　Von meinen Lebensstunden,
So schließ ich mich durch den Glauben ein
　　In deine theure Wunden.
Doch gibst du mir noch eine Frist,
So schaffe, daß ich als ein Christ
　　Dir leb' und selig sterbe.

Anhang.

21 METRE 68. *Harmonia Sacra.*
Nach eigener Melodie.

1 Es ist gewißlich an der Zeit,
  Daß Gottes Sohn wird kommen,
In seiner großen Herrlichkeit,
  Zu richten Bös' und Frommen;
Dann wird das Lachen werden theu'r,
Wenn Alles wird vergehn im Feu'r;
  Wie Petrus davon schreibet.

2 Posaunen wird man hören geh'n
  An aller Welt ihr Ende,
Darauf bald werden aufersteh'n
  All' Todten gar behende:
Die aber nach des Lebens ha'n,
Die wird der Herr von Stunden an
  Verwandeln und verneuen.

3 Darnach wird man ablesen bald
  Ein Buch, darin geschrieben,
Was alle Menschen, jung und alt,
  Auf Erden hab'n getrieben;
Da dann gewiß ein jeder Mann
Wird hören was er hat gethan
  In seinem ganzen Leben.

4 O weh demselben, welcher hat
  Des Herrn Wort verachtet,

Und nur auf Erden früh und spat
   Nach großem Gut getrachtet,
Der wird fürwahr gar kahl besteh'n,
Und mit dem Satan müssen geh'n
   Von Christo in die Hölle.

5 O Jesu, hilf zur selben Zeit
   Von wegen deinen Wunden,
Daß ich im Buch der Seligkeit
   Werd eingezeichnet funden:
Daran ich denn auch zweifle nicht,
Denn du hast ja den Feind gericht't,
   Und meine Schuld bezahlet.

22
Nach eigener Melodie.

1 Alle Menschen müssen sterben!
   Alles Fleisch vergeht wie Heu,
Was da lebet muß verderben,
   Soll es anders werden neu;
Dieser Leib muß erst verwesen;
Wenn er anders soll genesen
   Zu der großen Herrlichkeit,
   Die den Frommen ist bereit.

2 D'rum so will ich dieses Leben,
   Weil es meinem Gott beliebt,
Auch ganz willig von mir geben,
   Bin darüber nicht betrübt:

Denn in meines Jesu Wunden
Hab' ich nun Erlösung funden,
Und mein Trost in Todesnoth
Ist des Herren Jesu Tod.

3 Christus ist für mich gestorben,
    Und sein Tod ist mein Gewinn;
Er hat mir das Heil erworben,
    D'rum fahr' ich mit Freud' dahin,
Hier aus diesem Weltgetümmel,
In den schönen Gotteshimmel,
Da ich werde allezeit
Schauen die Dreieinigkeit.

4 Da wird sein das Freudenleben,
    Da viel Tausend Seelen schon
Sind mit Himmelsglanz umgeben,
    Stehen da vor Gottesthron;
Da die Seraphinen prangen,
Und das hohe Lied anfangen:
Heilig, heilig, heilig heißt
Gott der Vater, Sohn und Geist.

5 O Jerusalem du Schöne!
    Ach wie helle glänzest du!
Ach wie lieblich Lobgetöne
    Hört man da in stolzer Ruh!
O der großen Freud' und Wonne!
Jetzund gehet auf die Sonne,
Jetzund gehet an der Tag,
Der kein Ende nehmen mag.

Anhang.

23 Mel.: Wer nur den lieben Gott.

1 Wer weiß wie nahe mir mein Ende?
   Hingeht die Zeit, her kommt der Tod:
Ach! wie geschwinde und behende
   Kann kommen meine Todesnoth!
Mein Gott, ich bitt durch Christi Blut,
Mach's nur mit meinem Ende gut.

2 Es kann vor Nacht gleich anders werden,
   Als es am frühen Morgen war;
Dieweil ich leb auf dieser Erden
   Leb ich in steter Tod'sgefahr:
Mein Gott, ich bitt durch Christi Blut,
Mach's nur mit meinem Ende gut.

3 Laß mich bey Zeit mein Haus bestellen,
   Daß ich bereit bin für und für;
Und sage frisch in allen Fällen:
   Herr, wie du willst so schick's mit mir:
Mein Gott, ich bitt durch Christi Blut,
Mach's nur mit meinem Ende gut.

4 Mach mir stets zuckersüß den Himmel,
   Und gallenbitter diese Welt,
Gieb daß mir in dem Weltgetümmel
   Die Ewigkeit sey vorgestellt.
Mein Gott, ich bitt durch Christi Blut,
Mach's nur mit meinem Ende gut.

Anhang.

5 Ach Vater, deck all' meine Sünden
    Mit dem Verdienste Jesu zu,
Darin ich mich fest gläubig winde,
    Das gibt mir recht erwünschte Ruh.
Mein Gott, ich bitt durch Christi Blut,
Mach's nur mit meinem Ende gut.

24   METRE 40.   *Sweet Repose.*

1 Freunde stellt das Weinen ein,
    Wischt die Thränen von den Wangen,
Was soll doch das Klagen seyn,
    Daß ich von euch weggegangen?
Trauret nicht um meinen Tod,
Ich bin frei von aller Noth.

2 Da mein Leib darnieder fiel,
    Fiel auch mit mein Feind darnieder,
Meiner Seele höchstem Ziel
    War je meinem Fleisch zuwider;
Weil mein Leib nun weggerafft,
Ist mir süße Ruh geschafft.

3 Sagt, was dieses Leben sey?
    Ist es nicht ein Weg zu nennen,
Der von Dornen niemals frey?
    Alle müsset ihr bekennen,
Daß mein schwerer Gang vollbracht,
Da ich gebe gute Nacht.

Anhang.

6 Ferner hat mein Jesu mir
   Dort die Seligkeit erworben,
Geh' ich ein zur Grabesthür,
   Ich bin dennoch unverdorben:
Durch des Herren Aufersteh'n
Werd' ich in den Himmel geh'n.

7 Stirbt ein Christ, so stirbt sein Leid,
   Auch sein Tod stirbt mit dem Sterben;
Ich erwarte nun die Freud',
   Die ich ewig soll ererben;
Zeitlichkeit fahr immer hin,
Weil ich jetzt verewigt bin.

25   L. M. *Magdeburg—Rockbridge.*

1 Begrabt den Leib in seine Gruft,
   Bis ihn des Richters Stimme ruft,
Wir säen ihn: einst blüh't er auf,
Und steigt verklärt zu Gott hinauf.

2 Aus Staube schuf ihn einst der Herr;
Er war schon Staub, und wird nunmehr,
Er liegt, er schläft, verwest, erwacht,
Dereinst aus dieser Todesnacht.

3 Des Frommen Seele lebt bei Gott,
Der sie aus aller ihrer Noth,
Von aller ihrer Missethat
Durch seinen Sohn erlöset hat.

Anhang.

1 Hier hat ihn Trübsal oft gedrückt,
Nun wird er, Gott von dir erquickt,
Hier wandelt' er im finstern Thal,
Nun ist er frei von Schmerz und Quaal.

5 Gott blieb er treu bis an sein Grab,
Nun wisch't Gott seine Thränen ab:
Was sind die Leiden dieser Zeit,
Gott, gegen jene Herrlichkeit!

6 Nun, du Erlöster, schlaf in Ruh,
Wir geh'n nach unsern Hütten zu;
Und machen zu der Ewigkeit
Mit Freud' und Zittern uns bereit.

26   L. M.   *Hebron — Windham.*

1 So grabet mich nun immer hin,
  Da ich so lang verwahret bin,
Bis Gott, mein treuer Seelenhirt,
Mich wieder auferwecken wird.

2 Ja freilich werd' ich durch den Tod
Zu Asche, Erde, Staub und Koth;
Doch wird das schwache Fleisch und Bein
Von meinem Gott bewahret sein.

3 Mein Leib wird hier der Würmer Spott,
Die Seele ist bei ihrem Gott,
Der durch sein's Sohn's Blut's Bitterkeit
Sie hat erlöst zur Seligkeit.

Anhang.

1 So laßt mich nun in sanfter Ruh,
Und geht nach eu'rer Wohnung zu,
Ein Jeder denke Nacht und Tag,
Wie er auch selig sterben mag.

27 METRE 25. *Hamburg.*

1 Wer sind die vor Gottes Throne,
　　Jene unzählbare Schaar?
Jeder träget eine Krone,
　　Jeder stellt dem Lamm sich dar;
Jeden ziert ein weiß Gewand,
Mit den Palmen in der Hand.

2 Laut erschallen ihre Lieder;
　　Heil sei dem der auf dem Thron
Sitzt, und auf uns blickt hernieder;
　　Heil dem großen Menschensohn;
Alle Engel stehen da,
Alles singt, Hallelujah.

3 Es sind diese, welche kamen
　　Aus dem tiefen Trübsalsmeer,
Die ihr Kreuz gern auf sich nahmen,
　　Die von eig'ner Würde leer:
Bey dem Lamme das geschlacht't,
Fanden sie die Kleiderpracht.

Anhang.

1 Der für sie das Heil erworben,
   Da er als das rechte Lamm,
Für die ganze Welt gestorben
   An dem hohen Kreuzesstamm,
Weidet sie, ja will allein
Selbst die süße Weide sein.

5 Er bringt sie zu Wasserquellen
   Wo das ewige Leben quillt;
Nichts kann ihre Lust vergällen:
   Hier wird nun ihr Durst gestillt;
Gott selbst, der ihr Heil und Licht,
Wischt die Thränen vom Gesicht.

6 Hilf, daß ich dir willig diene
   Als ein Priester Gottes hier,
Daß ich mich im Fleh'n erkühne,
   Dich zu nennen meine Zier:
Deine Hütte decke mich
Vor dem heißen Sonnenstich.

7 Wann willst du mein Fleh'n erfüllen,
   Komm mein Heil, daß ich dich schau!
Eile meinen Durst zu stillen;
   Führe mich auf Zion's Au';
Wische meine Thränen ab:
Wohl mir, wenn ich dich nur hab'.

Anhang.

28   METRE 4.   Penitence.

1 Ringe recht, wenn Gottes Gnade
   Dich nun ziehet und bekehret,
Daß dein Geist sich recht entlade
Von der Last, die ihn beschwert.

2 Ringe, denn die Pfort' ist enge,
Und der Lebensweg ist schmal;
Hier bleibt Alles im Gedränge,
Was nicht zielt zum Himmelssaal.

3 Kämpfe bis auf's Blut und Leben,
Dring hinein in Gottes Reich:
Will der Satan widerstreben,
Werde weder matt noch weich.

4 Ringe mit Gebet und Schreien,
Halte damit feurig an;
Laß dich keine Zeit gereuen,
Wär's auch Tag und Nacht gethan.

5 Hast du nun die Perl errungen,
Denke ja nicht, daß du nun
Alles Böse hast bezwungen,
Das uns Schaden pflegt zu thun.

6 Wahre Treu führt mit der Sünde
Bis in's Grab beständig Krieg,
Richtet sich nach keinem Winde,
Sucht in jedem Kampf den Sieg.

7 Wahre Treu kommt dem Getümmel
Dieser Welt niemals zu nah':
Ist ihr Schatz doch in dem Himmel
D'rum ist auch ihr Herz allda.

8 Liegt nicht alle Welt im Bösen?
Steht nicht Sodom in der Gluth?
Seele, wer soll dich erlösen?
Eilen, eilen ist hier gut.

9 Eile, zähle Tag und Stunden,
Bis dein Bräut'gam hüpft und springt,
Und wenn du nun überwunden,
Dich zum Schauen Gottes bringt.

10 Eile, lauf' ihm doch entgegen,
Sprich: mein Licht, ich bin bereit
Meine Hütte abzulegen,
Mich dürst' nach der Ewigkeit.

29   METRE 68.   *Harmonia Sacra.*
    Mel.: Es ist gewißlich an der Zeit.

1 O Seele, schaue Jesum an!
Hier kannst du recht erkennen,
Was wahre Demuth heißen kann,
Und was wir Sanftmuth nennen,
Er stellt sich dir zum Muster dar:
Wie Jesus Christ gesinnet war,
So sei auch du gesinnet!

Anhang. 41

2 Er war der große Gottessohn,
   Ihn ehrten Cherubinen;
   Doch ließ er seinen Himmelsthron,
   Und kam, um uns zu dienen.
   Er selbst, der Herr der Herrlichkeit,
   War Menschen Wohl zu thun bereit,
   So sei auch du gesinnet!

3 Er sah die ganze Lebenszeit
   Auf seines Vaters Willen,
   Durch Thun und Leiden stets bereit,
   Ihn treulich zu erfüllen.
   In Allem, was er dacht' und that,
   Verehrt' er seines Vaters Rath,
   So sei du auch gesinnet!

4 Das Böse sucht' er alsobald
   Mit Gutem zu vergelten:
   Man hörte, wann die Welt ihn schalt,
   Ihn niemals wieder schelten,
   Man hört' ihn nicht um Rache schrei'n,
   Er übergab es Gott allein;
   So sei du auch gesinnet!

5 Wenn Stolz und Eigenliebe sich,
   O Seele, bei dir reget,
   So stärke Jesu Beispiel dich;
   Dann wirst du nicht beweget,
   Ach nimm doch dessen Wort in Acht,
   Und denke, wie er's hat gemacht,
   So sei du auch gesinnet!

Anhang.

30 Mel.: Jesu meine Zuversicht.

1 Folgt mir, wollt ihr Christen sein,
  Ruft der Herr in seinem Worte;
Auf dem Kreuzweg geh't herein,
Und ring't nach der engen Pforte;
Laßt euch keinen eiteln Blick
Oder Weltbrauch zieh'n zurück.

2 Unverdrossen schickt euch nun,
Jesu Joch auf euch zu nehmen,
Seinen Willen gern zu thun,
Euren aber zu bezähmen:
Christen wissen anders nicht
Auszuüben diese Pflicht.

3 Tief erniedrig't sei der Sinn,
Hochmuth aber ausgetrieben;
Arm am Geistsein bringt Gewinn,
Reich genug sind, die Gott lieben,
Und sie fürchten keinen Feind;
Denn der Höchste ist ihr Freund.

4 Aller Kummer, der euch nagt,
Sei verbannt auf heut' und morgen;
Christus hat ihn untersagt,
Heget also keine Sorgen;
Weil er selber sorgen will,
Ach so seid getrost und still.

5 Eure Gottgelassenheit
Bleibe fest gegründ't im Glauben,
Eh' euch der Genuß erfreu't.
Laßt euch nicht die Hoffnung rauben;
In vergnügter Herzensruh'
Nehme sie beständig zu.

31   Metre 33.   *Germany.*

1 Jesu deine tiefen Wunden,
Deine Quaal und bitt'rer Tod;
Geben mir zu allen Stunden,
Trost in Leib's= und Seelennoth:
Fällt mir etwas Arges ein,
Denk ich bald an deine Pein,
Die erlaubet meinem Herzen,
Mit den Sünden nicht zu scherzen.

2 Will sich denn in Wollust weiden,
Mein verderbtes Fleisch und Blut,
So gedenk ich an dein Leiden,
Bald wird Alles wieder gut;
Kommt der Satan und setzt mir
Heftig zu, halt ich ihm für,
Deine Gnad' und Gnadenzeichen,
Bald muß er von dannen weichen.

3 Will die Welt mein Herze führen,
Auf die breite Wollustbahn,

Da nichts ist als Jubiliren,
Alsdann schau ich emsig an
Deine marterschwere Last,
Die du ausgestanden hast;
So kann ich in Andacht bleiben,
Alle böse Lust vertreiben.

4 Ja, für Alles, was mich kränket,
Geben deine Wunden Kraft;
Wenn mein Herz hinein sich senket,
Hab ich neuen Lebenssaft;
Deines Trostes Süßigkeit,
Wend't in mir das bitt're Leid,
Der du mir das Heil erworben,
Da du für mich bist gestorben.

5 Auf dich setz' ich mein Vertrauen,
Du bist meine Zuversicht;
Dein Tod hat den Tod gehauen,
Daß er mich kann tödten nicht:
Bringet mir Trost, Schutz und Heil:
Daß ich an dir habe Theil,
Deine Gnade wird mir geben
Auferstehung, Licht und Leben.

32   Es ist gewißlich an der Zeit.

1 Nach meiner Seelen Seligkeit
   Laß, Herr, mich eifrig ringen.

Anhang.

Sollt' ich die kurze Gnadenzeit
In Sicherheit verbringen?
Wie würd' ich einst vor dir besteh'n?
Wer in dein Reich wünscht einzugeh'n,
Muß reines Herzens werden.

2 Erst an dem Schluß der Lebensbahn
Auf deine Sünden sehen,
Und wenn man nicht mehr sünd'gen kann,
Gott um Erbarmung flehen:
Das ist der Weg zum Leben nicht,
Denn uns, o Gott, dein Unterricht
In deinem Wort bezeichnet.

3 Du rufst uns hier zur Heiligung;
D'rum laß auch hier auf Erden
Des Herzens wahre Besserung
Mein Hauptgeschäfte werden.
Herr, dazu gib mir Kraft und Trieb;
Nichts in der Welt sei mir so lieb,
Als diese deine Gnade.

4 Gewönn' ich auch die ganze Welt
Mit allen ihren Freuden,
Und sollte das, was dir gefällt,
O Gott, darüber meiden:
Was hülfe mir's? nie kann die Welt
Mit Allem, was sie in sich hält
Mir deine Gnad' ersetzen.

Anhang.

5 Was führ't mich zur Zufriedenheit
Schon hier in diesem Leben?
Was kann mir Trost und Freudigkeit
In Noth, im Tode geben?
Nicht Menschengunst, nicht irdisch Glück,
Nur Gottes Gnad' und dann ein Blick
Auf jenes Lebens Freude.

6 Nach diesem Kleinod, Herr laß mich
Vor allen Dingen trachten,
Und Alles, was mir hinderlich,
Mit edlem Muth verachten:
Daß ich auf deinen Wegen geh',
Und im Gericht dereinst besteh',
Sei meine größte Sorge.

:3:3   METRE 33.   *Germany.*
Mel.: Wie nach einer Wasserquelle.

1 Prange Welt mit deinem Wissen,
  Das du jetzt so hoch gebracht!
Ich kann deine Weisheit missen,
Die der weise Gott veracht:
Meines Jesu Kreuz und Pein,
Soll mein liebstes Wissen sein:
Weiß ich das im wahren Glauben,
Wer will mir den Himmel rauben?

Anhang.

2 And're mögen Weisheit nennen,
   Was hier in die Augen fällt,
   Ob sie schon Den nicht erkennen
   Dessen Weisheit Alles hält;
   Mir soll meines Jesu Pein
   Meine Kunst und Weisheit sein:
   Das Geheimniß seiner Liebe
   Ist die Schul', da ich mich übe.

3 And're mögen ihre Sinnen
   Schärfen durch Verschlagenheit,
   Daß sie Lob und Ruhm gewinnen
   Bei den Großen dieser Zeit:
   Ich will meines Heilands Schmach
   Ganz alleine denken nach;
   Christen will es nicht geziemen,
   Daß sie sich des Eiteln rühmen.

4 Ander'n kann und mag's gelingen,
   Wenn sie schleunig und geschickt
   Großes gut zusammen bringen,
   Und wenn ihnen Alles glückt:
   O! mein Reichthum, Glück und Theil,
   Ist der armen Sünder Heil:
   Dieses weiß mein Herz zu finden,
   Und die Welt zu überwinden.

5 Ei! so komm, mein wahres Leben,
   Komm und unterweise mich;

Anhang.

Dir will ich mein Herz ergeben,
Daß es wisse nichts als dich.
Allerliebste Wissenschaft!
Ach! beweise deine Kraft,
Daß ich einzig an dir hange,
Und nichts außer dir verlange.

6 Weiß ich keinen Trost auf Erden,
Klagt mich mein Gewissen an,
Will mir angst und bange werden,
Ist nichts, das mir helfen kann;
Drückt mich des Gesetzes Joch:
So laß mich bedenken doch,
Daß du hast mit deinem Blute
Gnad' erlanget, mir zu gute.

7 Ach mein Jesu! pflanze weiter
Dieses Wissen in mein Herz:
Sei mein treuer Freund und Leiter,
Und laß deines Todes Schmerz,
Deine schwere Kreuzespein
Mir stets in Gedanken sein;
Du hast dich mir wollen schenken,
Daran laß mich ewig denken.

8 Endlich wenn des Todes Grauen
Alles Wissen von mir treibt,

Anhang.

So laß meine Augen schauen
Diesen Trost der ewig bleibt:
Jesu Leiden, Kreuz und Pein
Soll mein letztes Wissen seyn,
Jesu hilf mir Das vollbringen;
So will ich dir ewig singen.

34 Mel. Alle Menschen müssen sterben.

1 Ach wann werd' ich von der Sünde,
　Gott mein Vater völlig frei,
Daß ich ganz sie überwinde,
Ganz dir wohlgefällig sey?
Noch nicht, ich gesteh's mit Thränen,
Kann ich mich von ihr entwöhnen!
Noch zu oft, noch regt sie sich,
Und versucht zum Bösen mich.

2 In der Andacht sel'gen Stunden,
Wo mein Geist die Wahrheit hört,
Hab' ich oft das Glück empfunden,
Das die Frömmigkeit gewährt;
Habe nichts so sehr hienieden
Mir gewünscht, als innern Frieden,
Als ein Herz, dir ganz geweiht,
Ganz der Tugend Seligkeit.

3 Voll von heiligen Entschlüssen
'Schloß ich dann dir treu zu seyn,

Und mit wachtsamen Gewissen
Meiner Unschuld mich zu freu'n;
Willig woll't ich da mein Leben
Dir mein Gott, zum Dienst ergeben,
Aller Sünde widersteh'n,
Standhaft deine Wege geh'n.

4 Aber ach! zu schnell empöret
Sich der Leidenschaften Macht,
Die verdunkelt, schwächt und störet,
Was ich sonst so gut bedacht:
Plötzliche Versuchungszeiten,
Beispiel, Reiz der Eitelkeiten,
Deren Schwarm mich stets umringt,
Das ist was zum Fall mich bringt.

5 O ich Armer, dem zur Treue
Feste Seelenkraft noch fehl't,
Den so oft die tiefste Reue,
Und so oft doch fruchtlos quält!
Ach wer wird mich ganz vom Bösen,
Von des Todes Leib erlösen?
Ich Elender, wer befreit
Ganz mich von der Sündlichkeit?

6 Du verzeihst mir die Gebrechen
Meiner sündlichen Natur,
Nicht die Schwachheit willst du rächen;
Bösen Vorsatz strafst du nur:

Hätt' ich nicht den Trost, ich würde
Unter meiner Fehlerbürde
Ganz erliegen, und mich dein,
Höchstes Gut, nie können freu'n.

7 Stellet mir denn hier auf Erden
Lebenslang die Sünde nach;
Kann ich nicht vollkommen werden,
Bin und bleib ich immer schwach;
O so segne mein Bestreben,
So gerecht ich kann zu leben,
Daß ich doch von Heuchelei
Und von Bosheit ferne sey.

8 Wenn ich falle laß mich's merken;
Laß mich streben aufzusteh'n;
Eile mich, dein Kind, zu stärken!
Lehre selbst mich fester geh'n;
Warne mich, sey mein Begleiter,
Täglich führe, Gott, mich weiter,
Bis mich einst die Ewigkeit
Bringet zur Vollkommenheit.

METRE 8. *Day Star.* Har. Sac.

35 Mel. Wer nur den lieben Gott —

1 Ich habe nun den Grund gefunden,
Der meinen Anker ewig hält,

Wo anders als in Jesu Wunden?
Da lag er vor der Zeit der Welt:
Den Grund der unbeweglich steht,
Wann Erd und Himmel untergeht.

2 Es ist das ewige Erbarmen,
Das alles Denken übersteigt;
Es sind die offne Liebesarmen
Deß, der sich zu dem Sünder neigt;
Dem gegen uns das Herze bricht,
Daß wir nicht kommen ins Gericht.

3 Wir sollen nicht verloren werden,
Gott will, uns soll geholfen seyn;
Deswegen kam der Sohn auf Erden,
Und nahm hernach den Himmel ein,
Deswegen klopft er für und für
So stark an unser's Herzensthür.

4 O Abgrund! welcher uns're Sünden
Durch Christi Tod verschlungen hat:
Das heißt die Wunden recht verbinden,
Da findet kein Verdammen statt,
Weil Christi Blut beständig schreyt:
Barmherzigkeit! Barmherzigkeit.

5 Darein will ich mich gläubig senken,
Dem will ich mich getrost vertrau'n;
Und wenn mich meine Sünde kränken,

Anhang.

Nur bald nach Gottes Herze schau'n,
Da findet sich zu aller Zeit
Unendliche Barmherzigkeit.

6 Wird alles and're weggerissen,
Was Seel und Leib erquicken kann;
Darf ich von keinem Troste wissen,
Und scheine völlig ausgethan:
Ist die Errettung noch so weit,
Mir bleibet doch Barmherzigkeit.

7 Muß ich an meinen besten Werken,
Darinnen ich gewandelt bin,
Viel Unvollkommenheit bemerken,
Und fällt wohl alles Rühmen hin;
So ist mir doch der Trost bereit:
Ich hoffe auf Barmherzigkeit.

8 Es gehe nur nach dessen Willen,
Bey dem so viel Erbarmen ist;
Er wolle selbst mein Herze stillen,
Damit es das nur nicht vergißt:
So stehet es in Lieb und Leid,
In, durch, und auf Barmherzigkeit.

9 Bey diesem Grunde will ich bleiben,
So lange mich die Erde trägt;
Das will ich denken, thun und treiben,

So lange sich ein Glied bewegt:
So sing ich einsten höchst erfreu't:
O Abgrund der Barmherzigkeit!

36 METRE 25. *Hamburg. Har. Sac.*
Mel. Gott des Himmels und —

1 Komm, o komm du Geist des Lebens,
  Wahrer Gott von Ewigkeit!
Deine Kraft sey nicht vergebens,
Sie erfüll' uns jederzeit;
So wird Geist und Licht und Schein
In den dunkeln Herzen seyn.

2 Gieb in unser Herz und Sinnen
Weisheit, Rath, Verstand und Zucht;
Daß wir anders nichts beginnen.
Denn was nur dein Wille sucht;
Dein Erkenntniß werde groß,
Und mach mich von Sünden los.

3 Zeige, Herr, die Wohlfahrtsstege;
Das, was hinter uns gethan,
Räume ferner aus dem Wege,
Schlecht und Recht sey um uns an:
Wirke Reu' an Sünden statt,
Wenn der Fuß gestrauchelt hat.

4 Laß uns stets dein Zeugniß fühlen,
Daß wir Gottes Kinder sind,

Anhang.

Die auf ihn alleine zielen,
Wenn sich Noth und Drangsal find't:
Denn des Vaters Liebesruth
Ist uns allewege gut.

5 Reiz' uns, daß wir zu ihm treten
Frei mit aller Freudigkeit
Seufz' auch in uns wenn wir beten,
Und vertritt uns allezeit:
So wird uns're Bitt' erhör't,
Und die Zuversicht gemehr't.

6 Wird uns auch nach Troste bange,
Daß das Herz oft rufen muß;
Ach! mein Gott, mein Gott wie lange?
Ei so mache den Beschluß;
Sprich der Seele tröstlich zu,
Und gib Muth, Geduld und Ruh'.

7 O du Geist der Kraft und Stärke,
Du gewisser neuer Geist,
Förd're in uns deine Werke,
Sey von uns stets hoch gepreißt,
Schenk uns Waffen in dem Krieg,
Durch dich werde uns der Sieg.

8 Herr bewahr auch unsern Glauben,
Daß kein Teufel, Tod noch Spott
Uns denselben möge rauben;

Anhang.

Du bist unser Schutz und Gott;
Sag't das Fleisch gleich immer nein
Laß dein Wort gewisser seyn.

9 Wenn wir endlich sollen sterben,
So versich're uns je mehr,
Als des Himmelreiches Erben
Jener Herrlichkeit und Ehr,
Die uns unser Gott erläßt
Und nicht auszusprechen ist.

37 METRE 33. *Harmonia Sacra.*
Mel. Zion klagt mir Angst und.

1 Herr es ist von meinem Leben
Abermals ein Tag dahin,
Lehre mich nun Achtung geben,
Ob ich frömmer worden bin;
Zeige mir auch ferner an,
So ich was nicht recht gethan,
Und hilf du in allen Sachen
Guten Feyerabend machen.

2 Freilich wirst du Manches finden,
Das dir nicht gefallen hat;
Denn ich bin noch voller Sünden
In Gedanken, Wort und That,
Und von morgen bis jetzund
Pfleget Herze, Hand und Mund
So geschwind und oft zu fehlen,
Daß ich's nimmermehr kann zählen.

Anhang.

Aber, du Gott der Gnaden!
Habe noch mit mir Geduld:
Ich bin freylich schwer beladen,
Doch vergib mir meine Schuld
Rechne nicht die Missethat,
Sondern zeig mir deine Gnad
So will ich auch deinen Willen
Künftig mehr als heut erfüllen.

4 Herr! dein Auge geh't nicht unter
Wenn es bei uns Abend wird
Denn du bleibest ewig munter,
Und bist wie ein guter Hirt,
Der auch in der finstern Nacht
Ueber seine Heerde wacht,
Also gib uns, deinen Schafen,
Daß wir alle sicher schlafen.

5 Laß mich dann gesund erwachen
Wenn es rechte Zeit wird seyn,
Daß ich ferner meine Sachen
Richte dir zu Ehren ein:
Oder hast du, lieber Gott!
Heute mir bestimmt den Tod,
So befehl ich dir am Ende
Leib und Seel in deine Hände.

Register der deutschen Lieder.

                                                                Seite.
Ach wann werd' ich von der Sünde 49
Alle Menschen müssen sterben 31
Auf Seele auf und säume nicht 11
Begrabt den Leib in seine Gruft 35
Der Tag ist hin mit seinem Lichte 28
Die Glocke schlägt und zeigt damit 29
Durch viele große Plagen. 21
Es ist gewißlich an der Zeit 30
Freunde stellt das Weinen ein 34
Folg't mir wollt ihr Christen seyn 42
Gott des Himmels und der Erden 25
Gott hab' ich mich ergeben 22
Gott sey dank in aller Welt 12
Herr Jesu Gnadensonne 15
Herr es ist von meinem Leben 56
Ich habe nun den Grund gefunden 51
Ich will lieben und mich üben 17
Ihr junge Helden aufgewacht 27
Jesu deine tiefe Wunden 43

Register.

                                                              Seite.
Komm, o komm du Geist des Lebens 54
Liebster Jesu wir sind hier 3
Mein Gott das Herz ich bringe dir 13
Mir nach spricht Christus unser Held 6
Nach einer Prüfung kurzer Tage 23
Nach meiner Seelen Seligkeit 44
Nun lobet alle Gottes Sohn 8
O Seele schaue Jesum an 40
Prange Welt mit deinem Wissen 46
Ringe recht wenn Gottes Gnade 39
Setze dich mein Geist ein wenig 18
Sey Lob und Ehr dem höchsten Gut 9
Sieh' hier bin ich Ehrenkönig 5
So grabet mich nun immer hin 36
Theures Wort aus Gottes Munde 4
Wer sind die vor Gottes Throne 37
Wer weiß wie nahe mir mein Ende 33
Wo soll ich hin, wer hilfet mir 19

www.ingramcontent.com/pod-product-compliance
Lightning Source LLC
Chambersburg PA
CBHW032130010526
44111CB00034B/575